W9-CND-935

JUMPED IN

JUMPED IN

What Gangs Taught Me about Violence,
Drugs, Love, and Redemption

Jorja Leap

BEACON PRESS
BOSTON

Beacon Press
25 Beacon Street
Boston, Massachusetts 02108-2892
www.beacon.org

Beacon Press books
are published under the auspices of
the Unitarian Universalist Association of Congregations.

15 14 13 12   8 7 6 5 4 3 2 1

This book is printed on acid-free paper that meets the uncoated paper
ANSI/NISO specifications for permanence as revised in 1992.

Text design by Wilsted & Taylor Publishing Services

The lyrics in the epigraph for chapter 12 are used with permission
of the writer, Quentin Moore.

Many names and distinguishing characteristics of people mentioned
in this work have been changed to protect their identities.

Library of Congress Cataloging-in-Publication Data
Leap, Jorja
Jumped in : what gangs taught me about violence, drugs, love, and
redemption / Jorja Leap.
p. cm.
ISBN 978-0-8070-4456-8 (hardcover : alk. paper)
1. Gangs.—California.—Los Angeles. 2. Gang members.—California.
—Los Angeles.—Biography. I. Title.
HV6439.U7L773 2012
364.106'6092—dc23
[B]

*This book is for Mark
and for Shannon.*

To live outside the law,
you must be honest.
BOB DYLAN

CONTENTS

Napalm

Don't go believin' anything unless you see it.
And even then, don' be too sure.

—Big T.

I cannot say exactly when I saw my first dead body. Probably my earliest experience with one was when I was around eleven years old and my grandmother was diagnosed with brain cancer. My mother's reaction was that I should go, as soon as possible, to a funeral, any funeral. There was a crazy kind of logic to this. Open caskets were de rigueur at Greek Orthodox funerals. My mother wanted to protect me from being surprised or upset when I eventually gazed upon the body of my soon-to-be-dead grandmother, who was terminally ill with brain cancer.

She also decreed that I wear navy blue, because I was far too young for basic black. Consequently, my attendance at this first funeral was preceded by a shopping expedition. From then on, death and new outfits would be inextricably linked in my mind. And so, wearing a navy blue dress with white piping and matching jacket, I saw my first dead body. The body itself belonged to a distant and elderly relative and resembled nothing so much as a mannequin in a dress shop for "mature" women. I felt curiously detached. I had the same feeling eight months later when my grandmother actually died. Somehow the body remained abstract, unreal.

Since then, I've been to many funerals and have seen a lot of bodies. These ceremonies involved godparents, aunts, uncles, and extended family. What I looked at seemed more some sort of cosmetic marvel—carefully made up, well dressed and artificial—a stand-in for the person who had died. I finally saw the real deal—bodies without benefit of a mortician's makeover—when I was a young social worker at an LA

County hospital emergency room. The bodies there had, for the most part, met some grim ending. Dead of a gunshot wound or decapitated in an auto accident. They were so freshly dead, they often appeared to be twitching (and in some cases were). These were the bodies of the barely departed, yet they still failed to register within me, emotionally. Even more extreme experiences awaited me beyond the ER. Several years later, serving as a UN volunteer in post-war Kosovo, I saw bodies in varying states of decomposition, twice at mass burial sites. Still I looked upon them with detachment, an example of "man's inhumanity to man."

Until a summer night in August 2002.

I do not remember all the details of this particular night. All I know is that some switch got flipped for me—all my cells turned over—and nothing was the same.

It is after midnight, and I am standing inside the yellow police tape blocking off part of a neighborhood intersection in South Los Angeles. Small bungalows and ramshackle apartment buildings line both sides of the street, in an architectural style that can best be termed "urban depressed." Each one comes equipped with burglar bars and dark screen doors, and behind the mesh it is possible to make out the faces of people peering out the windows tentatively. The more brazen among them— old women and young men—mill around in groups outside their houses or on the sidewalk or in the street, their expressions registering hostility or suspicion.

Children play in the street, and even though it is summer and school is out, I keep wondering, *What are those kids doing up? They should be in bed; they should be asleep,* until I realize how idiotic this all sounds given the level of noise and confusion rising up from the street. I am struck by how strange it is that they are playing in the middle of all this, and I wonder if it's nothing out of the ordinary, just another summer night, just another crime scene. A police helicopter flies noisily overhead. Four black-and-white patrol cars are parked at varying angles in the middle of the street, their headlights outlining three teenage boys lined up against a chain-link fence with their hands cuffed. The three adolescents appear so young, it looks like they haven't even started shaving yet.

There is another boy. He resembles the other three children in every way except one. He is lying in a pool of blood and his body is being photographed and probed by members of the Los Angeles Police Department. He is nameless, unknown, and he is dead. I cannot stop staring at the body as the blood slowly spreads on the pavement. It is impossible to turn away. My heart is beating and I am thinking, *Whose baby is this? Whose brother? Whose grandson?* He is frozen, forever, dead. I am trying not to cry.

The three handcuffed youngsters deny having any idea who he may be. Whatever the question, they uniformly mumble, "I d'know." The police officers show varying signs of sadness, resignation, anger, and detachment, establishing a makeshift command post and dolefully noting that the shooting is "gang related." They are taking notes, making jokes, and gossiping. One woman wearing the LAPD uniform looks over at me and we exchange nods of recognition. I have a grudging respect for Sergeant Mitzi Grasso, a small, wiry force of nature. She has just finished a term as president of the Police Protective League—the officers union. She, for one, is not talking about gangs. Grasso is focused on a work-schedule issue and I hear her saying, "Look, the mayor is going to listen because he wants to be reelected." Meanwhile, the dead boy's body is being covered and prepared for transfer to the coroner's office. Several conversations are going on at once, and no one is speaking in hushed or respectful tones. Talk ricochets between a discussion of which gang sets are currently warring and a debate over who might be selected as the next chief of police for the LAPD. I hear snippets of gang names—the Grape Street Crips, the Rollin 60s, Florencia, MS-13—coupled with speculation over how Bill Bratton, the current favorite to become chief, will get along with Mayor Jim Hahn, given how frequently Bratton, as New York City commissioner, once clashed with Rudy Giuliani.

Police radios crackle. Even though everyone is tuned to the same frequency, the multiple radios set up an echo chamber—it's almost like the police operator is channeling a rap singer—and the new locations of police activity reverberate through the night. "Two-A-Fifty-One: handle a 211 in progress at Seventh and Alvarado, Code 3. Suspects are three male Hispanics armed with a gun attacking a transient at the bus bench."

"Two-A-Ninety-One: handle an unknown-trouble 911 open line at the Hamburger Stand, Seventeenth and Vermont, Code 3."

It's all static interrupted by voices interrupted by more static—until there is almost a rhythm to the cacophony of noise. The radio operator keeps announcing streets, intersections, locations, incidents. It is the city of Los Angeles as performance art, courtesy the LAPD.

The police helicopter continues to circle overhead and I can hear its blades cutting the air. The co-pilot directs a spotlight down on the organized chaos, which will endure for approximately an hour and then be restored to normal, with no traces left of "the crime scene." And inexplicably, over and over in my head, there is the antic voice of Robert Duvall in *Apocalypse Now*, declaring, "I love the smell of napalm in the morning." The noise and the people and the warmth of the night feel altogether unreal, as if I have stumbled upon the filming of some television cop show.

Instead, it is 2002, and the city of Los Angeles is experiencing one of the bloodiest outbursts of gang violence on record. And I am standing in the middle of it. I am one of the few non-uniformed individuals here. I am one of the few white people inside the yellow tape. I am one of the few women here, and I am definitely the only woman *not* wearing a police uniform. I do not fit in, and I cannot stop staring at the body of the young boy. His skin is light, coffee colored and unmarked. It is the skin of a child—there are no blemishes, no signs of a beard. This boy—not yet a man—looks impossibly young, on the edge of adulthood. He has no tattoos, and his hair rings his face in soft curls, partially covered by a sweatshirt hood. I keep looking at his skin, almost wanting to reach out and touch its softness.

I keep my head down until my tears drain out, then I look up past the boy's body at a beautiful, silent man wearing a beige T-shirt, black jeans, and a menacing expression. His black skin shines in the streetlight and his eyes are olives, angry and impenetrable. Khalid Washington, the silent man, looks back at me, but we do not acknowledge each other. We are not speaking—yet. We will call each other in a few hours and meet in the late morning at a small barbecue restaurant in South Los Angeles and talk quietly about what happened, dissecting who might be involved, who might retaliate, and what he has done in the early-morning hours. This is later.

Right now, I cannot acknowledge Khalid's presence in front of the LAPD and I am frightened by the rage that I see in his eyes. He is recently released from prison and is working as a gang-intervention "street worker." In the eyes of the LAPD he is just another knucklehead, just another gangbanger probably getting into trouble, connecting with his homies and trying to avoid arrest. He is an outsider here, muttering "Muthafuckas" under his breath as a uniformed officer approaches him and, ignoring me completely, asks, "Can I help you, sir? Did you know the deceased?"

"No, I did not know the deceased," Khalid enunciates with exaggerated formality.

The officer stares at him and masks a demand as a question. "May I ask what you are doing here?"

"I'm a street interventionist with the Unity Collaborative," he announces tersely. "I got a call from Bo Taylor, who heard about the shooting. We were called in to try to help stop any more shooting or retaliation." He produces a business card that the officer considers while grimacing.

The officer's eyes narrow. "Mind if I keep this?" he asks while pocketing the card. Khalid shrugs.

The exchange is brief but speaks volumes.

They hate each other.

The current law-enforcement ethos equates joining a gang with losing one's virginity. It's a permanent state, and you can never go back, no matter what you may claim about your purity. Khalid may or may not still be gang affiliated. I would bet he is. *But it really does not matter.* The only thing of which I am certain is that he is going to leave the scene soon to connect with individuals who belong to conflicting sets and gangs. He will try to negotiate a cease-fire of some sort, after the shooting, to prevent retaliation and further bloodshed. The agreement will be fragile, informal, and with luck will hold for a few days, weeks, or months. There is no way of knowing if it will work or if the violence will continue. And in the end, Khalid will never get credit for any lives saved.

I don't know if I trust Khalid. While I have spent time alone with him, I have never felt completely safe. Some of it is sexual tension; some of it is the impact of listening to his seemingly endless supply of stories about shooting people, the force of his telling me, "I've felt the fuckin' blood running through my hands." I don't know if he is lying, and I definitely don't want to ask. Still, I recognize his strengths. He is tough, angry, and articulate. He is also a natural-born leader. Of course, if I utter those words in front of the LAPD, they will fill out a field interview card on me and I will undoubtedly join Khalid on the federal crime database or the CalGang list.

So far I have been completely ignored by the cops. I don't feel particularly afraid in this situation, because my badass rebellious streak has kicked in. Just in case that isn't enough, there is one man nearby who would step in if any of these uniformed officers started to hassle me. He is wearing the lightweight, short-sleeved LAPD summer uniform and he is neat, pressed, and in complete control. He has one star on each lapel indicating that he is a commander—only one of seventeen—in the LAPD. He is standing quietly by, although everyone present is deferential and respectful toward him. No one knows we are seeing each other. "Dating" seems too idiotic a word to describe the texture of our relationship. No one knows that four hours earlier we left his home thirty miles northwest of Los Angeles and drove into the city together.

Mark Leap is nowhere near me, though; he is engaged on the far-opposite side of the incident—talking to several other uniformed officers about what has happened. Instead, David Gascon, an assistant chief, has hovered around me, practically on top of me, all night. He is blissfully unaware that I have arrived with Mark Leap. Instead, because he knows I am "working on the gang problem," he just assumes I have shown up after learning about the shooting. He probably even believes I have come to find him. With a kind of territoriality that I suspect is imprinted in the DNA of every sworn member of the LAPD, he takes for granted that I am there to stay with him, under his protection. He begins lecturing me on what has occurred at the crime scene.

Khalid Washington looks on with disgust as Gascon asserts, "We're never gonna know who did this. And it doesn't matter. They're gonna go on killing each other." His voice is authoritative. I smile involuntarily.

This is the same voice that officiated at *the* media event of 1994: the press conference during which Gascon had to admit that the LAPD had inadvertently "lost" murder suspect O.J. Simpson, adding that the football great was currently on the freeway in a white Ford Bronco driven by Al Cowlings. The intervening years have not been kind to Gascon. He has lost out in his bid to become the next chief of police. Gascon also possesses critics within the power structure of the LAPD and LA city government. Tonight he is an unwelcome reminder wearing a polo shirt, a symbol of the recent bad press that outgoing chief Bernard Parks and the LAPD have received.

Gascon is well into his lecture on how the gang problem should be solved. While there is confusion all around, he holds forth as if there is no noise, no helicopter cutting at the air above him. It's clear that he knows what he is talking about, but the trouble is *he is slightly off in his logic.* He is deriding the whole idea of gang interventionists—all within earshot of Khalid Washington. "Y'know, you got cops who think some of these interventionists are gonna help us. But they're nothing but double agents—gangsters who know how to talk to the powers that be." I am distinctly uncomfortable with this conversation. The gunshots I keep hearing do not appear to be the only threat to my safety in these early morning hours.

Why am I here in the dark, on this anonymous street in South Los Angeles, in the middle of the night? I should be at home in my cottage in Rustic Canyon, sitting on my patio, finishing a glass of wine. Instead all my nerve endings are on red alert as I watch and listen and try to stay still when I hear the popping sound of gunshots.

What am I doing here?

I suppose I could be glib and say I am here because of my personal and professional commitment. I have a reputation to uphold, after all. I was this tough little UCLA professor who studied violence, writing and lecturing on the "gang problem."

The gang problem consists of stories and police reports and rumor. There are accounts of young women being subjected to brutal gang rapes. And descriptions of suspected snitches getting their tongues cut out because they have shared information with the police. And if that's not enough, there's always the media. For the past few days a video has been making the rounds on the Internet, offering up a drive-by shooting filmed in the kind of bloody detail that only Quentin Tarantino fans could love.

The gang problem involves a world where tattoos are not merely decorative but threatening and sinister. I think of the adolescent who had LET'S FUCK tattooed on his eyelids, along with his friend, who had FUCK YOU on his cheek.

There is a multiple choice of personal motives for me. I am here because I am looking for a solution. Or to give kids hope. Or to help save lives.

I am here for all of the above but I am also here for the strange sort of electricity that's in the air. Along with all the danger and sadness, at every crime scene there is a pulsating high. This night, like other nights, I am feeling it again. And I find the excitement narcotic.

Standing between Dave Gascon and Khalid Washington, I hear a low series of pops—more gunfire—and the cocktail of terror and excitement drives up the adrenaline of everyone inside the yellow tape. One of the cops calls out, "There's a shooter!" and for a split second everyone freezes.

I am a walking, talking, multiple-personality disorder of fear. I am scared that Khalid will discover I am on a first-name basis with some of the LAPD; I am frightened that this familiarity will incite his mistrust or, worse still, his anger. But I am also scared of the LAPD and how many of these Boy Scouts on steroids have demonized every adolescent in the vicinity; I am frightened someone may shoot at them or that they may shoot at the wrong person. I am afraid of the random, rampant danger in the air. And there is no doubt in my mind that in an instant, someone could drive by and shoot into the crowd—campaigning to be immortalized as a cop killer.

More than anything, I am overwhelmed, knowing that at any moment, if something were to go wrong, someone could die—including me. And still there is the body of the young boy. Who was he?

As if listening to my internal monologue, one elderly woman, probably a grandmother, observes, "Just a baby, just a baby," shaking her head as she walks back to her white frame bungalow.

It is another forty minutes before things settle down. After the body is taken away and Khalid Washington disappears into the night and the cops drive off to their next radio call and people go back to hiding behind their locked doors, I linger at the scene. And I cannot stop thinking, despite the noise and the chaos and the resignation of so many involved, about him. That nameless boy, his body the first to reach me after so many funerals, so much death.

I am crying again. I keep thinking of H. Rap Brown's folk wisdom, "Violence is as American as apple pie." I keep thinking of the fifteen-year-old who told me he was "just trippin', just trippin'" after he shot the four-year-old son of a rival gang member. I keep thinking of Father Greg Boyle and his motto, "Nothing stops a bullet like a job."

I am standing on the street, thinking of the body and becoming aware of the noise of the freeway traffic a few blocks away. Its steady and persistent hum tells me that life in Los Angeles goes on, oblivious, despite this dead boy, despite the violence, and despite the "gang problem." I don't realize it yet but it is one of those very few moments in my life when, as the saying goes, a door opens and the future begins. Because of this night, I feel alive and determined to understand.

Chameleon

No one wants to tell the truth—that gangs have been
here as long as there's been the City of the Angels.
We are some of those angels. Or devils.

—Agustin Lizama

A few months later, at the end of 2002, the National Youth Gang Center reports that there are 731,500 known gang members in the United States. Of these, Los Angeles County counted 80,000 active gang members, making up 1,200 different gangs. This means that roughly one out of every eight active gang members in America was living in Los Angeles. I keep thinking about this after meeting with Lee Baca, the sheriff of Los Angeles County, who has just given me that week's "official" list with the names of every gang set and clique in Los Angeles County. The list numbers somewhere around 6,000—with names as prosaic as "Fuck yo' mama" and "Playboys 30 Tre." It will be outdated in one week.

Trying to decipher the gang family tree from all of this is a fool's errand. The genealogy of gangs and their history is neither linear nor chronological—it is impossible to understand in Western terms. I am lucky I am an anthropologist. And, after being far from the neighborhoods of Los Angeles for almost ten years, I am lucky to be back.

I had worked with gangs before—as a neophyte social worker operating out of Martin Luther King Hospital in South Los Angeles in the 1970s and 1980s. Now it was almost twenty years later and here I was, talking to people from the neighborhoods. I had a PhD, a faculty appointment at UCLA, and a half dozen years' experience in violent environments internationally. I had once thought I would spend the remainder of my career working in foreign settings. But things had changed, and I wanted to figure out what to do about violence that was occurring close to home.

With the support of UCLA, I was hired to evaluate gang-prevention and -intervention programs. This gave me a reason to walk the streets, to interview people, to ask questions about the neighborhoods. My work was no different than that of an anthropologist who sets out to understand the caste system of India or the problems of youth in Japan. I begin by explaining that I am studying gangs and want to know how to end gang violence. I ask people for their life histories and their opinions. Most of all, I listen. Along with the black and brown "neighborhoods," people in community agencies, government offices, and public schools have found that I am willing to go anywhere and talk to anyone to learn about gangs. This forms the substance of my writing and research. Most of the research is not published. Instead it finds its way into evaluation reports and curriculum guides about what is needed to keep kids out of gangs or what works effectively with former gang members. But I know that I am doing something beyond conventional research.

I want to understand the truth about gang members and the reality of their lives. I do not devise formal questionnaires. Instead, I depend on people in the streets. This includes law enforcement officers, priests, politicians, poets, and gang members—active and former. This is why, two days after meeting with the sheriff, I am in South LA talking to Kenny Green. Kenny is a former gang member who rarely speaks of his street associations. He is no longer active and works as an interventionist and case manager. I settle in for the long haul. Any discussion with a gang member or a former gang member is always a long-term commitment; whenever I sit down with Kenny, I budget a minimum of two hours. I will not leave his office until the sun has gone down. An account of any event—even the smallest street altercation—becomes an occasion for a history lesson and a recitation of gang genealogy.

There are no historians like former gang members. They remember everything—every incident, every fight, every event—and they are ready to serve it up in real time. It is a dream come true for me and for any student of the streets. There is no need for a carefully designed questionnaire or follow-up probes. What is needed is trust. It has taken me over a year to gain Kenny's trust. He knows I will not betray his confidence. But there are other challenges.

When talking with any gang member, there are invariably things that are "off the record." They are left this way for two reasons. First, gang members—active or former—exaggerate. There is no way of knowing if they are telling the truth. It is often unclear if an incident actually happened to them or if they believed it happened to them. Second—and here's where things get murky—some gang members will confide their involvement in past crimes for which they were never caught. I am careful to warn the men and women who sit down with me, "Do *not* tell me names." At all times, trust is fundamental, and it is earned once you are viewed as *someone who does not talk*.

I ask Kenny to explain the gangs of Los Angeles to me as simply as possible. He thinks carefully, then says, "To understand gangs in LA you gotta remember it's the blacks and the browns. And the neighborhoods are different, really different. You can ask anyone."

Kenny's words are crucial to understanding the gang family tree. They are also at a far remove from media sensibilities and conventional wisdom. That is because the popularly accepted face of Los Angeles gangs is invariably black. Most people believe there are two major gangs—the Crips and the Bloods—who are viewed as the Hatfields and McCoys of the street. But this simplification is the first lie in all the information about gangs both in Los Angeles and in general. The Bloods and the Crips are to LA gang life what the cell phone text is to the Rosetta stone. This shorthand robs a message of all meaning but the immediate. And it bears no relation to reality.

What is true is that the Crips and the Bloods, the gangs that compose two main branches of the African American gang family tree, were born in Los Angeles. There is a mythology that these gangs—or neighborhoods—had their origins in the death rattle of the Black Panther political organization. The story goes that as the Black Panthers and other affiliated radical civil rights organizations splintered and fell apart, political activism gave way to gang violence. None of this is true.

What is true is that the Crips were founded as an exclusively black gang in 1971 in Los Angeles by two enterprising fifteen-year-olds: Raymond Lee Washington, leader of the East Side Crips, and Stanley "Tookie" Williams, leader of the West Side Crips. After several bloody confrontations, they set up a street merger to consolidate their power and territory. This "deal," brokered in a high school cafeteria, created what would eventually grow to be a loosely connected network of individual sets that engaged in "warfare" with rival gangs—which included murders, robberies, drug dealing, and other criminal pursuits.

Raymond Lee Washington and Tookie Williams are now both dead. But the gang they created lives on and has gone global, with branches in exotic locales like the Australian outback, Edinburgh, Scotland, and the foreign and domestic bases of the US military. The Crips remain one of the largest and most violent associations of street gangs in the United States, with an estimated thirty thousand to thirty-five thousand members in Los Angeles County. Long known for wearing the color blue, their monochromatic haberdashery is no longer as evident, due to police crackdowns and growing sophistication. "It's old school," a Crips Original Gangster (OG) tells me. "The only thing that don't change— we still fightin' the Blood cliques."

In gang culture, legends and acronyms abound. "Bloods" is often said to be an acronym for "Brotherly Love Overcoming Our Depression," just as "Crips" stands for "Community Revolution in Process" or, alternately, "Continuous Revolution in Process." And deciphering the organization of the Bloods and the Crips is like reading hieroglyphics: they are broken into "sets" that have subtle variations in their colors and are as strife-ridden as the Middle East. "If the Bloods aren't fighting the Crips, they are fighting each other," T. Rodgers has told me.

T. Rodgers and Lawrence Chin organized the Bloods to break the street monopoly of the Crips in Los Angeles. In 1972 the Pirus, a Crips set who took their name from the Swahili word for "blood," severed their ties with the Crips during an internal gang war. Together with other loose, unaffiliated smaller gangs, they bonded to "found" the gang that would ultimately be the Bloods. Originally the gang focused on extortion and robbery. With the rise of crack cocaine in the 1980s, the gang's business shifted to drug production and distribution. Bloods sets operate independently of each other, are currently located in almost every state in the Union, internationally, and—just like the Crips—in the US military.

Yet it is the ultimate irony that street gang "culture" has become so strongly identified with African American gangs like the Bloods, the Crips, and their offshoots, when the largest, most well-established gangs, with the longest history, are not black. The oldest branches of the Los Angeles gang family tree are actually composed of the Sureños (Spanish for "southerners"), or Hispanic gangs, which invariably account for over six hundred of the twelve hundred gangs in Los Angeles County. It's old school to think that Hispanic gangs are exclusive to East Los Angeles. In truth, their geographic reach extends throughout Los Angeles, across the Midwest and the Sunbelt, and on to the East Coast of the United States. In addition to African American and Hispanic gangs are the lesser-known but equally criminal Asian-Pacific gangs, whose LA membership hovers at around twenty thousand.

While the Sureños trace their roots to the barrios of East Los Angeles, over the past decade a powerful trinity of gangs has dominated media coverage and seriously challenged law enforcement. Florencia-13, 18th Street, and MS-13 are the new kids on the block in the evolution of Hispanic gangs—and they bear little resemblance to their small, neighborhood forerunners who fought over control of a few blocks in the housing projects. The gang known simply as 18th Street is a fifteen-thousand-member violence collaborative composed of twenty independently operating neighborhoods located everywhere from the eastern San Gabriel Valley to the southeast pocket of Los Angeles County. Each gang faction—or set—typically has a membership of anywhere from fifty to one hundred, but their origins can be traced to the area of Los Angeles known as Pico-Union.

The establishment of 18th Street represented a shift in the gang endeavor from the more parochial, small gangs of East Los Angeles that included The Mob Crew (TMC), Cuatro Flats, Clarence Street Locos, Big Hazard, White Fence, and El Sereno. In 1959 members of the Clanton 14 neighborhood organized a new clique that offended their parent gang. Clanton 14 core members insisted that the new clique—Clanton 18—either obey the leadership or break off and start their own gang. In the end, Clanton eventually lost their territory and dominance to the "disobedient" former clique, now known as 18th Street. In the end 18th Street also learned an important lesson from the overcontrol of Clanton 14: discipline should be minimal. In addition, any and all new members should be accepted. Leaving the neighborhood is another matter, however, and 18th Street is unforgiving. "If anyone tries to leave," Kenny tells me, "18th Street will really try to stop them. Other neighborhoods might think about lettin' you go. Not 18th Street. If you try to leave, they'll frame you for a crime or beat you up."

Gang dominance in Los Angeles is linked to geography: territory is power. As a result, the urban sprawl of Southern California is echoed in the territorial spread of successful gangs. While 18th Street may be depicted as the predominant Hispanic gang in terms of membership numbers, the largest Hispanic gang covering the most territory is actually one of 18th Street's main rivals, Florencia-13. Their turf stretches from Central to South Los Angeles, and their businesses reach beyond state borders. Florencia tags with a little flower—an innocent icon for such a lethal entity. And they are as unforgiving as 18th Street. "The only way you can leave Florencia," Kenny tells me, "is feet first. Stay away from them."

I already know that the world of Florencia and 18th Street is a scary one. They are two neighborhoods I rarely have contact with during these first months of interviewing gang members. Instead, a few days after seeing Kenny Green, on a rainy night, I sit in a deputy sheriff's patrol car driving through Florencia territory and listen to a radio call reporting a gang rape involving a fourteen-year-old female victim. When I hear the disembodied voice of the police dispatcher describing the crime, I know Florencia is different.

While I embrace alternative approaches to working with gangs, like prevention and intervention, on this night I did not want to be traveling alongside a gang worker; I wanted to be riding with a uniformed officer carrying multiple firearms. There were choices I had to make and this was one—Florencia was not a group I wanted to associate with, nor was 18th Street. "They are the most violent," Mark has warned me. "I don't want you to go out seeing them on your own." I had argued frequently with Mark that he was overreacting or buying in to the hysteria of his colleagues in law enforcement. "You are too rigid," I'd argue. "You are too much a cop." But that night, I agreed. It was one of the few times I would listen to him.

I feel differently about the third gang in this urban trinity—MS-13. Perhaps because I have grown close to a former gang member, Alex Sanchez, who has helped me to navigate the transnational gang panic.

"I keep thinking about the police and the media and the FBI. They created us, they demonized us, but they don't understand us," Alex tells me. "I was MS-13 and yes, there were some dangerous characters there. But that is not the whole story. People have come to us because they want to belong somewhere, because people felt safe, because the system itself didn't provide the structure that immigrants needed."

The demonization of MS-13 stems from the public belief that it originated in Central America and oozed over the border like something out of a monster movie. The truth is that MS-13—Mara Salvatrucha—was established by Salvadoran immigrants in the Pico-Union neighborhood of Central Los Angeles to provide local residents with protection from other Hispanic gangs, most notably 18th Street. Despite its rather matter-of-fact beginnings, there is a mystique to MS-13. Part of this derives from the name—"Mara" is said to come from La Mara, a Salvadoran street gang, while "Salvatrucha" is shorthand for the guerilla fighters of El Salvador's Farabundo Martí National Liberation Front, who many claim form the backbone of the MS-13 *veteranos*. The 13 indicates their affinity with the Mexican Mafia, a US prison gang also known as La Eme.

The gang is distinct from the predominantly Mexican gangs of Los Angeles: its membership is composed of Guatemalans, Hondurans, Nicaraguans, and Salvadorans. But like other gangs, MS-13 is a confederation of loosely associated cliques or sets with some ten thousand members in Los Angeles and fifty thousand members nationwide—expanding as far north as Washington state and east to Virginia, Maryland, and Washington, DC. While membership varies, MS-13 engages in typical criminal activities—dealing in guns, drugs, and contract killing. There are also reports of human trafficking along with prostitution. But any member of MS-13 will explain—as I have been told—that their ultimate goal is to become the most powerful gang in the world. And ironically, their goal has been aided and abetted by the US government.

Many active members of MS-13 are undocumented or criminal offenders or both—rendering them ripe for deportation to their countries of birth. The deportations usually last long enough for individual MS-13 members to recruit new members and then return back to the States. As a result, the largest mechanism for Hispanic gangs spreading beyond borders is deportation—it's government-sponsored gang recruitment. Left to their own devices, the gang members I know are about as organized as the Keystone Cops—territorial, petty, and far too focused on local violence to ever form an international crime syndicate. I witnessed this firsthand talking to a tagger who was arrested for vandalism in a small Los Angeles suburb and threatened with deportation.

"You don't understand," he told me. Although I was growing tired of hearing that I did not understand, I still listened closely. "If they send me back to El Salvador I will not be safe. I will be told to get new members or they will send someone to kill me. So I will get new members for the neighborhood. Then I will come back here. Then I will get caught again, probably. Then I will go back there. It will not end until I die. And I want it all to stop. I would rather be in prison here than go back there."

I have grown tired of hearing "We cannot arrest our way out of the gang problem," "We cannot deport our way out of the gang problem." But one thing my rather embryonic understanding of the gang family tree has convinced me of is that the problem is a lot more complicated than who claims what territory and who throws which gang sign. Ironically, no one knows more than the people who are never consulted. There are real experts. They do not write reports or make public policy. They are the ones who understand "the gang problem" and its causes better than any talking head with an advanced degree. The experts are the people who have been or continue to be active gang members. Their voices are rarely heard. And I am determined to bear witness to their truth.

I have learned that if I come with an open mind and I am honest—if I explain who I really am—an anthropologist, a UCLA researcher, a crisis interventionist, a sister, a teacher, all of the above—sooner or later everyone in the gang world finds something in me they can relate to. I am a chameleon of the neighborhoods. I will fit in where I need to when I need to.

It doesn't always work; there are people who will not speak to me—mainly because I am female or because I am white or because of the combination of the two. "I don't bang with any woman," a member of the Bounty Hunter Bloods snarled when I tried to interview him. But he didn't scare me—he was loaded on heroin and kept going on the nod.

There are others around whom I am more careful. T. Rodgers, the self-proclaimed founding father of the Bloods, alternately hugs me and looks as if he is sixty seconds away from killing me. "You don't call me, ever, you little bitch," he had complained once with barely contained rage because, in fact, I had failed to return his voice-mail messages. Although I joked around and said, "I'm just no good," I felt anxious and have worked hard to stay on his good side ever since that brief but threatening confrontation.

How did I get people to trust me? I have been trained as a clinician and as a researcher. I also relied on any connection that I had—UCLA, the sheriff, the mayor, Father Greg Boyle or Alex Sanchez or Kenny Green—to vouch for my credibility. It was all of those factors but it was something more. And it was something I failed to realize for a long time. I identify with the gang members. I identify with their outsider status, with their self-sabotage, with their rebellion. I even identify with their murderous rage. And I am willing to go almost anywhere at any time to spend time with a gang member who wants to talk with me.

Of course, there is fallout for all of this. There are people on the streets who do not trust me. Some members of the LAPD welcome my presence; some want me gone. My two brothers repeatedly tell me that they are worried about my safety. These are not my biggest problems. The biggest problem is my husband. Mark.

THREE

Mi Vida Loca

Why don't you just face it? Everyone's relationships are
fuckin' crazy. What are we gonna do? La vida loca.
—Joanna Carillo

It was not only the world of gangs I was reentering. I was also in the
midst of slowly—and quite unsteadily—reentering the world of marriage. Not an easy task under the best of circumstances.

And my circumstances were less than "optimal." They included a
previous marriage and several romantic but wildly inappropriate relationships. My first husband was smart and successful. He wore custom-
made suits, donated to liberal causes, and for eighteen years provided
me with all the comforts money could buy. Unfortunately, he was more
intimately involved with his computers than our marriage. He neglected
our love life, our sex life, and our social life. In the meantime, I had a
personal shopper at Neiman Marcus, a house featured in the *New York
Times*, a closet full of Armani, and a Mercedes in the garage. And I was
miserable. I kept going to therapy—trying to figure out what to do. I
had two serious love affairs in rapid succession, one of which my husband discovered. When the dust settled and the papers were signed, the
marriage was over and I was divorced.

I wanted to get married again, and I did not want to make the same
mistake twice. So I fell in love with someone who was physically gorgeous, sexy, and incredibly attentive. He was the wet dream of middle-
aged dating—a widower with a charming eight-year-old daughter.
Unfortunately, he wore a uniform, carried a gun, and thought the death
penalty was enlightened public policy. Mark Leap was a commander—
soon to be a deputy chief—in the Los Angeles Police Department. In all
fairness, Mark rarely donned LAPD attire, usually opting for a suit and

tie. He cooked elaborate gourmet meals and collected fine wines. His other car was a Mercedes. As a birthday gift to me, he changed his voter registration from "Independent" to "Democrat."

I never imagined I would date a member of the LAPD. They were Rodney King and Rampart—police brutality and the abrogation of civil rights—all rolled into one. I criticized the LAPD in forums on "The Future of Los Angeles" and marched in protest against them. In short, I had spent most of my anti-authority life acting out against law enforcement. My bias was so strong that when UCLA offered me the plum assignment of helping design and teach a series of classes on "Leadership for the 21st Century" to the command staff of the LAPD, I balked. Then I remembered the post-divorce credit card debt I was rapidly accumulating and backpedaled, agreeing to work on the project for one year. It turned out to be a great success, and I actually developed friendships with several of the captains, commanders, and deputy chiefs, including Mark. After one class, he invited me to visit him at Parker Center, LAPD headquarters. A few weeks later we met for lunch. Back at UCLA, one of my closest friends and colleagues, Shelly Brooks, asked, "So, how was lunch with the LAPD?"

"He's the one," I told her.

"What?"

"I'm gonna marry him."

"You're gonna marry him? Just how much did you have to drink at lunch?" Shelly burst out laughing.

"He's not like a cop. I've never met anyone like him. Believe me." Shelly just shook her head. "You're crazy. Here we go again. This will be over in a month."

"No, this is it. He's different."

A year and a half later, we were married.

I wanted to believe it would be different. I wanted to believe *he* was different. But despite everything Mark told me when we were dating— that he was not a typical cop, that he did not own a speed boat, that he did not read, eat, or breathe law enforcement. Despite every bottle in his fifteen-hundred-bottle wine cellar—despite all of this, I soon came to realize, I had married the LAPD. And try as I might, I couldn't fit in.

I was the LAPD's worst nightmare. I had experimented with Marxism and controlled substances. I was a card-carrying member of the ACLU. And I believed that those three little words, "rule of law," made up one of the most dangerous phrases in the English language. I was not good "cop wife" material. But—in a thoroughly misguided way—I believed love would conquer all. Instead, no sooner was the ring on my finger than the fight was on. My identity was at stake, and defending it felt like a full-time job. If I managed to forget the cold, hard reality of what my husband did for a living, the truth would march up and bite me in the ass.

Before we married, I was no stranger to war and violence. Alternately terrified and fascinated, I voluntarily worked in both Bosnia and Kosovo. In Pristina, I was attached to a UN mission that continued to function throughout bombardment. The next stop after that was New York City in the aftermath of 9/11 to work at Ground Zero, feeding and counseling the workers who were clearing the rubble and dealing with loss on a daily basis. Now I was running around some of the most dangerous streets in Los Angeles. Before we were married, Mark had insisted that he didn't want me to change. Ever.

But this was all forgotten once we returned from our honeymoon and settled into domestic bliss. If there was a major gang bust involving the FBI, or the Counterterrorism kindergarten color wheel of elevated threat suddenly turned, I would be treated to a display of male macho that would send me running to check the expiration date on my NOW card. No gangbangers for me. I was to stay at home and watch the little girl who was now "our" daughter, Shannon, while Mark drove off into the big world.

Along with maintaining a division of labor straight out of *Leave It to Beaver*, it also gradually became clear that Mark and I approached life very differently. The operating principal of my existence continued to be organized chaos. I would be working on a research grant, going to court to help some baby mama trying to get her children back from DCFS (the Department of Children and Family Services), and due at a meeting of the Watts Gang Task Force in South LA—all in the same day. And I was never happier than when I was juggling three catastrophes at the same time. Not my darling husband. There might be cancer, tragedy, infidelity, illness—or all of the seven deadly sins simultaneously being committed—but he always possessed a plan. The two most frequent phrases I would hear in the early days of our marriage were "I love you" and "Here's what we're going to do."

The problem is, I was beginning to experience my life as filled with plans, plans, and more plans—there was lots of control but very little drama. By the time I met Mark, I had grown accustomed to having a breakdown if someone frowned at me. I dwelled in the land of emotional extremes; if I was happy, I was delirious, and if I was angry, I was furious. Mark's idea of an emotional outburst was admitting, "I'm a little frustrated." The gap between my Mediterranean hysteria and his WASP stoicism widened by the day. But wait, there was more.

In yet another way, Mark was pure LAPD. Although he spent most of his waking hours working "to protect and serve" Los Angeles, he—along with most of his colleagues—believed that Los Angeles was not a good place to live. The inconsistency of this failed to strike any of them—or me. I was madly in love, and so I moved into Mark's house. I quickly abandoned bohemian Rustic Canyon, rented out the funky cottage I owned, and suddenly discovered myself living smack-dab in the middle of Stepford.

Mark, like most of his blue brethren, lived behind gates in a planned community. This one, thankfully, was not in Santa Clarita or the Simi Valley. Instead, every morning I was waking up in an area described as "the city in the country," Westlake Village. This was neither the city nor the country—it was the petrified forest.

Of course, our neighborhood had a name—every neighborhood had a name—no doubt dreamed up by an Anglophile on crack. Kensington Park consisted of a series of pristine, neatly manicured townhouses. If you came home drunk, you would definitely not know which house was yours. And there was a chance you might not care.

Upon retirement, there would surely be more of this. I grew anxious that a time-share in Coeur D'Alene, Idaho, loomed large in my future. But Mark reassured me he did not want to move to Idaho or own a time-share. This was a relief. But remember, this was the LAPD. There was a plan. Mark wanted to spend one year onboard a small sailboat, navigating the seven seas. There was just one problem: I did not swim.

None of this was good. My idea of a relaxing evening was to sit on my patio and smoke pot. Mark's recreational activities focused on working out at the gym. The fact that we got together was probably due to a combination of sexual attraction, intellectual openness, and—how do I say this?—true love. The fact that we stayed together was nothing short of a miracle. We began shopping for a new house, preferably not behind gates, in Westlake. I tried to restrict my activity in the streets. Just when I thought things were settling down, however, the real trouble began.

Mark and I were out for a walk, talking about—what else?—the LAPD. Chief Bill Bratton, newly arrived and claiming his own territory, was bent on reshuffling the entire command staff. Mark carefully explained he would be working longer hours, probably six days a week, along with call-outs in the middle of the night. There would be trips to Washington, DC, law enforcement conventions, and top-secret counter-terrorism meetings that he would be required to attend. He wrapped up this itinerary by announcing, "I will be depending on you to take care of Shannon. And you should probably sell your house in Rustic Canyon."

It was one of those rare times in my life when shock rendered me inarticulate. He was marching off to fight crime and leaving me with the child. This did not square with my self-image. I never had been the one to keep the home fires burning. In all my relationships up to this point, I had always been the girl who left, packing my bag to fly off somewhere full of danger, poverty, disaster—or all three. But now I was supposed to stay home in the suburbs and mind Shannon? While I struggled to recover the ability to create sentence structure, Mark took my silence for agreement and moved on to outline the summer vacation he had planned, sharing a houseboat at Lake Powell with two other LAPD families. "Remember, honey," he said, smiling, "it's not going to be work all the time." I suspect he thought this glorious possibility would render maternal responsibilities well worth the effort: *Surrender your life. In return you will experience amazing sex and an annual tour of America's National Parks.* For a woman who loved to brag that her passport required extra pages, this was beginning to sound like the seventh circle of hell.

I was not sure how this was going to work out. I tried to put blue heaven out of my mind. I began to spend more time in the streets. This was a bad idea at a bad time. Crime in general and gang crime in particular was starting to climb. We would have to make other arrangements for Shannon. What those were, I wasn't quite sure. There was only one thing that was certain. I wasn't about to stay put in Westlake Village.

FOUR

Living with the LAPD

It is the mission of the Los Angeles Police Department to
safeguard the lives and property of the people we serve, to
reduce the incidence and fear of crime, and to enhance public
safety while working with the diverse communities to improve
their quality of life. Our mandate is to do so with honor and
integrity, while at all times conducting ourselves with the
highest ethical standards to maintain public confidence.

—LAPD Mission Statement

Fuck the cops.

—Khalid Washington

My first year of domestic "adjustment" is under way—with mixed results. To justify the time I am spending away from home, I throw myself
into multiple gang-related projects. These include a needs assessment
for the Los Angeles Unified School District to figure out how to prevent gang violence from spreading throughout its 730 schools. I quickly
decide that the best experts to consult for this project are the gang
members who once attended these same schools.

Mark is apprehensive about my research plan; his fear is being fed
by the latest crime statistics and his years in the LAPD. His response is
to attempt to command and control . . . me. I am trying to stay one step
ahead of him so I can interview as many homies and homegirls as I can
(while he's not looking). From late 2003 and into 2004 in the city of Los
Angeles, there is an average of two gang-related homicides a day. Peter
Jennings and ABC News arrive to tape a special on LAPD's Southeast
Division one evening while I am hanging out with Bo Taylor, a gang

interventionist, and talking with three gang members about middle-school gang recruitment. All five of us notice the camera crew.

"The blood is gonna flow if that foo' stays here with a camera," one homie predicts, and Bo quietly tells the camera crew to move on. It's a good recommendation. Southeast Division has ten square miles, 140,000 people, five housing projects, and the most gang-infested middle and high schools in the city of Los Angeles. The area averages somewhere between seventy and eighty murders a year. When I report all this to him the next morning, Mark does not blow up. Instead, he offers me what I start to think of as alternative employment.

"It's time for you to understand this all from the cops' perspective," he tells me. "What if I can get you complete access to the LAPD Gang Unit? Will you stop running around on your own?"

I readily agree, knowing I will never have to make good on this promise. I laugh, thinking, *In your dreams*.

I should have known better. It's a complicated task, but Mark finds a way to cross it off his to-do list. He pulls a few strings so I can "conduct research on the department's response to gangs." The good news is that I have access to the LAPD that no other "non-sworn" person is ever going to have. The bad news is that I now have a bodyguard, Deputy Chief Mike Hillmann.

It's a gray fall morning when I first meet Mike Hillmann. He is wearing a long-sleeved LAPD dress uniform and jackboots. Hillmann is more enthused about the practice bomb blast he witnessed the day before at Edwards Air Force Base than the LAPD Anti-Gang Initiative. This is fine with me, as I am trying very hard to avoid any discussion of my research. More to the point, I don't want to have to talk about what I've seen various gang members doing that may fall slightly outside the law. It's nothing major, nothing violent, but it is also nothing that is legal. Instead, I ask Hillmann his plans for dealing with "the gang problem."

"Let me tell you," he says, and then points to a full-color photo on his wall offering a view over the shoulder of a pilot in the cockpit of what looks to be a fighter jet.

"That's me," he says, and I find myself wondering if he is actually flying the plane. But I stifle my confusion and Hillmann continues.

"I'm always the observer. Even at the LAPD. They tell me what to do about gangs. And then I go out and do it. I drop those bombs. Someone has got to lock up those knuckleheads once and for all."

So this is the newly enlightened LAPD policy? And this is the guy Mark has selected to show me the law enforcement side of the story? Good luck.

It turns out to be exactly the right choice. Bill Bratton has leapfrogged Hillmann up two promotional levels from captain to deputy chief, and ordered him to solve the gang "crisis," a chronic problem that Bratton has redefined. Despite the big promotion, Hillmann is not easily domesticated. While I never find out just exactly who was pictured in the fighter-jet cockpit, it quickly becomes obvious that Hillmann feels much more at home inside a helicopter—where he immediately takes me—than behind his desk at LAPD headquarters. His conversation is riddled with malapropisms that would make Yogi Berra blush. "Jorja is one of those sociologicals," he explains to the helicopter pilot flying us to South Los Angeles. "And we need our aca-dames. They can really help us."

My profession has begun to sound like it is starring in a 1940s comedy. But despite the fact that Hillmann is a cross between Ronald Reagan and Captain Marvel, I like him. There is something perversely dignified about him. And then there is the charisma. The full head of silver hair, the watery blue eyes, the strong jaw, the chiseled features; he is central casting for the role of LAPD Deputy Chief. And he presents me with an unexpected gift—a letter of introduction and a list of LAPD gang lieutenants that he asks me to interview. Along with this, he invites me to every meeting and every conference, large or small, involving gangs and their suppression. I have even been sworn in as an LAPD Specialist Reserve Officer. I find myself gripping my ACLU card to remember who I am.

"I want you there riding right next to me," he tells me. "You can learn all you ever want to know. Really. I promised Mark I would do everything I could for you and I am going to."

"You really don't have to," I begin, and he cuts me off.

"Mark is a good man. He was my boss for four years. He helped me—that's why I still call him boss. And you—you're very special."

I laugh. I am expecting to hear about my status as a UCLA professor, my slowly growing reputation as a gang expert, my credentials as an "aca-dame." I have forgotten that up here on the sixth floor of LAPD headquarters, it is 1950.

"You married Mark and you're taking care of that little girl of his. There must be a special place in heaven reserved for you."

I know that Mike Hillmann means every word that he is saying. And I am trying desperately not to burst out laughing. There is a special place reserved for me, I think. But probably not in heaven. I'm feeling a little bit anxious, a little bit like the cheating wife I once was.

After hanging out with gangbangers, I am now consorting with the enemy. That night, I look at my interview notes from the week before. "You just can't trust the cops, any of them," one homie told me angrily. Another insisted, "It's not just that cocksucker Pérez at Rampart—they're all like that—all of them. They lie, lie, lie, all the time. And the next thing you know, you're locked up. I wish those Rampart guys were locked up. But we is the ones who's gonna get locked up."

Even interventionist Bo Taylor, a favorite of LAPD captain Charlie Beck, counseled, "You can only trust a few of them. The rest are no good."

I had good reason for not announcing I was living with one. And now I would be spending time with them. But the offer was too irresistible to refuse. I could go out at night. I could visit crime scenes. And I could get Mark off my back—temporarily. Maybe once I did this, I reasoned, he would feel more comfortable with me spending time with the interventionists and the homies I was meeting.

I spend several months under the watchful eye of Mike Hillmann. I fly in helicopters at night and see gang members spotlighted from above as the LAPD moves in to arrest them. It is as if some avenging light is shining through the night air to assist the cops on the ground. "Those gangbangers," a pilot grunts during one flight. "They're on the freight elevator to hell." I watch while suspects are interviewed. Mark and I go together to gang call-outs and I see more dead bodies than I can count. After spending two months with Mike Hillmann, I thank Mark profusely for setting this up. In turn, Mark laughingly relates what occurred at a senior staff meeting that afternoon. "Hillmann loves you." Mark adds, "He went on and on about how smart you were. Bratton finally had to cut him off."

Things grow peaceful at home. I am surprised—and confused—by some of the things I discover during the interviews Hillman has requested I conduct. In the past, law enforcement in Los Angeles practiced a kind of zero-tolerance response to gangs. If you were suspected of being a gang member, you were pretty much guilty until proven innocent. All the violence and mistrust festered into one enormous sore that erupted with the Rampart scandal of 1999—when it was discovered that something happened to the notion of the cops as the thin blue line between good and evil. Instead, that thin blue line got stretched so far in certain places, it snapped. Cops were planting evidence, shooting suspects, and had taken up permanent residence on the other side of the law.

These are not the cops I am spending time with in early 2004. Rampart, indeed all of the LAPD, is in the midst of being reformed, operating under a federal consent decree. But as I nose around, holding up Mike Hillmann's letter as my paper shield, I find the LAPD is not "all better." Instead, it appears to be suffering from multiple personality disorder. Some cops are paramilitary zealots, some are social workers with guns, but the majority are caught somewhere between the two. It is an organization in transition—and not a pretty sight. Probably the most striking example of all this could be found at Devonshire Division, deep in the San Fernando Valley.

When I meet Captain Joe Curreri, despite the turquoise bracelets wrapped around his wrists and his effort to appear supportive of community policing, I know our discussion is dead in the water. For one thing, Captain Curreri does not meet with me alone. Instead he has his sergeant, Vic Masi, sit in on the meeting. He controls the entire interaction—which turns into a forty-five-minute monologue featuring a sleep-inducing combination of war stories and crime statistics. When Curreri finally pauses to ask if I want coffee, I decide I will bring up the work of gang interventionists. I figure things can't get any worse. But the minute I hear the clipped tone of Curreri's response, I see that there is still room for deterioration.

"There are people in the LAPD who think those gang interventionists like Blinky Rodriguez and Bobby Arias walk on water, but the fact is all the interventionists have gang connections. You should stay away from those guys, Mrs. Leap, they're no good." I listen, speechless. When I don't respond, Curreri continues.

"Lemme tell you—with gang connections, it's serious. I am almost sure Blinky is connected to the Mexican Mafia. In fact, most of them have ties to Eme, not just Blinky."

This is the default position of certain folk in the LAPD. I am sure it appears in their unofficial handbook: *Here's a helpful hint: whenever someone mentions an interventionist in the world of Latino gangs—link them to the Mexican Mafia.* Blinky Rodriguez was about as closely tied to the Mexican Mafia as I was.

"Well, thank you so much for your time," I say sweetly, hoping this will end the discussion. But Curreri suddenly looks hopeful.

"We do some gang prevention that's good for our kids. That's the Explorer Program."

I try hard to hide my disbelief and it looks like I succeed, because he goes on with his spiel.

"This is such a great program. Do you know, forty in our Explorer classes have gone on to law enforcement careers?"

I find myself wondering what drug I was on—here was an LAPD captain insisting that their police internship program was a worthy antidote to gang involvement. While there were exceptions, this was a program for wannabe cops, not at-risk kids. With a belief system like that, I knew that Joe Curreri was going to need more than turquoise bracelets to save him.

By this time, I am beginning to worry. Despite riding around in helicopters and interviewing cops, I still cannot quite figure out exactly what the LAPD anti-gang strategy is—beyond "hook 'em and book 'em." When I confess this, Mike Hillmann quickly reassures me, "Don't worry; go see Ron Bergmann." I hear the name and my heart sinks. I have already been introduced to Deputy Chief Bergmann and I don't particularly like him. He is old-school LAPD. A week later, sitting outside his office in the San Fernando Valley, I tell myself, *I will spend thirty minutes with him and then I'm out of here.*

But something happens.

Ron Bergmann starts to talk and I wonder if I have been loboto-mized: I am agreeing with every word he is uttering, my head bobbing up and down as he speaks. *What the fuck is the matter with me?* I keep thinking. The trouble is, the more he talks, the more I nod; it gets so bad that I start planning how to speed dial an exorcist—for him! My thoughts seem to be coming out of Bergmann's mouth as he describes work-ing with the community and collaborating with gang interventionists.

"Blinky has my home phone number and I have his—we call each other anytime, day or night, whenever there is a problem. We need the street interventionists out there talking to gang members, helping to stop the shooting. The cops can't do it alone. We need partners. We need the interventionists, we need social workers, and we need small businesses—all working together to stop the violence. But that is not enough. We have to help these youngsters go back to school. And we have to help them find jobs. The problem is never going to be solved by law enforcement. We've had decades to get the job done—and it hasn't worked."

After this initial meeting, I drive out to the Valley several times to have lunch with Ron Bergmann and talk about gangs. He is an unlikely ally. He looks like a basset hound—with doleful eyes and a cynical view of human behavior. But gangs are his passion, and I cannot fail to rec-ognize the kindness in his face. He is as gentle as he is controlling; he reminds me of Mark. He is a mixture, like everyone, but I genuinely like and respect him. In the meantime, I am making a serious mistake and it's happening so gradually, I don't realize it. I am slowly, inexorably drinking the LAPD Kool-Aid. However, reality intrudes two weeks later during lunch. Ron and I are eating Chinese food when I mention Joe Curreri and his denouncement of the interventionists.

"Too bad," Bergmann tells me. "I decided, and they're gonna have to do it. I don't care. I'm the chief, I'm in charge. The cops are gonna listen. The community is not the problem—but some of these cops are. But I think their attitudes are gonna change when they see all the posi-tive things Blinky and Bobby do for the community. And y'know—Joe Curreri is gonna have to listen. I'm calling the shots."

Later, driving home to Mark and Shannon, I am struck by his unin-tentional pun. I nearly rear-end the car in front of me when I realize it's still LAPD *über alles*. Here is the truth no one wants to face, least of all me. In the rock-paper-scissors world of power plays, the guys with the guns trump all. I am furious—at the LAPD, at Mark, at myself.

"I love Ron," I tell Mark later, "but he *is* a cop."

"And your point is?"

"My point is—he thinks he should be in control."

"I agree with him."

"What?" I ask, half-hoping Mark is joking.

"Look, the LAPD ultimately should be out in front of any community effort—you know that—it's common sense."

Once again, I feel as if I am having a stroke and have lost the power of speech. But it is momentary.

"What are you talking about?" I finally ask.

"I'm saying that we are probably the most well-equipped to bring together different groups in a consensus."

"You all have the same mentality—and even if you work with the community, you still think you're first among equals. He still wants Blinky and Bobby reporting to *him*. Charlie Beck—out in South LA— he still wants Bo Taylor reporting to *him*. And you still want me reporting to you."

"I'm not talking to you anymore," Mark says quietly. "I have to make dinner." He takes a pizza out of the freezer. "Then I am going to cigar night."

I am so angry, I can feel the blood pounding in my veins. What is happening here? It's the domestic bad dream, Part 4. I will babysit while Mark sits around smoking cigars with his cronies from the LAPD, talking politics. *No way.*

"You'll have to take Shannon, because I'm leaving," I announce.

Mark continues looking inside the oven as if his gaze will cause the frozen pizza to heat up more quickly.

"That's fine," he finally says.

"You know, I don't know what is going on with us, but our relationship is really in trouble. I want to talk to you and you don't respond. I tell you I am leaving and you don't care. You. Don't. Care. *I can't take you anymore!*" I stop screaming abruptly when I see Shannon out of the corner of my eye.

"Are you leaving us?" she asks tearfully.

"Just for tonight."

"Don't go. Please."

I can't take her pleading, and look at Mark.

"We'll all go to cigar night together," he announces. I am still enraged but I can feel Shannon's anxiety so I compromise.

"You go ahead, I'll come in an hour. I need to calm down."

Things do not get better when I join them later. Two hours into cigar night, Mark points at his watch and tells me, "You need to get Shannon home." He is taking full advantage of the fact that we have driven separate cars. I am being punished for being a very bad LAPD wife.

After a sleepless night, I get up early the next morning. In a miracle of bad timing, I am scheduled to attend a "Gang Summit" organized by Bill Bratton. What is billed as a two-day executive session on gangs is actually a forty-eight-hour showcase for the chief of police. Bratton does an excellent job—he is smart, innovative, and a masterful self-promoter. Chief Mike Hillmann has no place at the table—literally. An elite group of law enforcement executives sit in a square-shaped arrangement of tables and chairs. Meanwhile, Hillmann sits with me in the "observers' section." We know where we are—it's the bleachers—but Hillmann is a good soldier, dutifully accepting his status. Later in the morning he one-ups Bratton with newly minted statistics regarding the location and prevalence of gang crime in Los Angeles and I wonder if this is as innocent as he is playing it. "Dumb like a fox," my grandmother used to say, and I am once again impressed with Hillmann. On the other hand, I try to figure out what the fuck I am doing with this roomful of national experts who have not been anywhere near the streets in Los Angeles.

The second day of the summit, I'm still not talking to Mark and overjoyed to have a reason to leave the house early. Later, while I am adjusting to another day of sleeping with my eyes open, the conference is crashed by three interventionists who stand against the wall, clad in black, wearing sunglasses, looking very gangsta. I immediately recognize one of them. It is Khalid Washington, who acknowledges me by raising his chin in the direction of where I am sitting on the opposite side of the room. While the street threesome remains silent throughout the morning, everyone at the summit has noted their presence and is trying to figure out what the hell to do with them. Except Hillmann, who has other plans. He abruptly leaves the executive session before lunch is served. He doesn't really belong, and more importantly he doesn't want to be here. Instead, he goes off to address the LAPD mechanics at Air Support Division. *Off to the cockpit again*, I grimly think while he prepares to abandon me.

The session wears on into the afternoon. I can't control myself and raise my hand. I talk about the need for community outreach and the chief nods. Later on, when Bratton refers to something I said, he forgets my name and refers to me as "the young woman from UCLA. I think we should discuss what she is talking about—"

In the middle of this valedictory, Khalid starts laughing and interrupts Bratton. "You're talking about Dr. Leap, sir," he shouts. "You should use her name. And you should know that she is out there in the community, spending time with gang members, not sitting around some table, talking." There is a small buzz as the seminar participants try to figure out who he is. Bratton listens attentively and then says, "I think it's time for a break."

We all know what this means. It's a convenient excuse to get Khalid and the two other interventionists out of the room. I follow and we stand outside the USC meeting center, where the executive session is now grinding on without us. Khalid tells me to follow him down to South Central. "There's someone I wantcha to meet." I immediately start trotting off to my car.

"Jorja!" Khalid yells. I feel a frisson of excitement and terror.

"Yeah?"

"Homegirl—doncha want to know where we're going? You just gonna follow me into hell?" Khalid is laughing.

"Okay, what are we doing?" I ask, not really caring about the answer.

"You gotta meet Big Mike."

FIVE

Big Mike

I love these children. Every last one of them. The badder
they are, the more I love them. I was one of them.
                                        —Reverend Mike Cummings

Mike Cummings is about six feet tall and, I am sure, easily tips the scales
at three hundred pounds. His skin is so black it shimmers violet, and his
neck is huge, muscular. I keep glancing over at his neck and arms while
I ride shotgun, holding on for dear life in a white Chevy Suburban with
We Care Outreach Ministry stenciled in gold calligraphy on either side.
Big Mike is at the wheel, and it is safe to say he completely lives up to his
gang moniker. Grinning, with a mega-watt smile to match his girth, he
pilots this enormous SUV through the streets of South LA while talking, occasionally taking his hands off the wheel to emphasize a point. It's
been two weeks since Khalid took me to meet him, and I'm spending
the day in the hood with Big Mike.

"I'm just here tryin' to save the children, trying to keep them out of
the life I lived. We're using our love and Scripture to do the job." He
resembles an NFL blocker—huge, strong, and running for daylight. "I
am at it 24/7, workin' with these children. Praise the Lord." Big Mike
is part preacher without portfolio, part tow truck driver, and part savvy
businessman. "I don't need much," he tells me, "just enough to buy gas,
and every once in a while I gotta go buy my wife some Louis [Vuitton]
or Gucci." We both laugh—he's a reformed gangbanger on a first-name
basis with several European designers. But even with his grin and bon-
homie, I still wouldn't want to meet him in a dark alley. I feel both
thrilled and reassured to be under his protection.

Back in the day—the late 1980s and early '90s—Mike Cummings
was notorious in Watts. Before both the Lord and three years in county

jail saved him, Big Mike was one of the scariest, baddest gangsters in South Los Angeles. On the street he is recognized as the real deal— an OG—Original Gangster. "I'm gonna school you in the neighborhoods," he tells me. "It's time for you to understand what's goin' on here. Because y'know, things are bad, really, really bad. We got innocent youngsters dyin' every day."

I ask him how things have gotten this bad. He doesn't hesitate before answering, and he is very clear.

"The biggest problem is guns, guns, guns."

National statistics back him up. A child or teenager is killed by gunfire almost every three hours—nearly eight times a day. Homicide is the prime cause of death among African American males between the ages of fifteen and thirty-four. On top of this, black males between the ages of fifteen and nineteen are almost four times as likely as their white counterparts to die from a gun-inflicted injury; they are six times as likely to be homicide victims. While I am contemplating the problem of guns and gangs, Big Mike has stopped at a gas station.

"You gotta understand that it's like the Pentagon out there," he tells me while he fills the tank. "Only they got more guns than the Pentagon. They got more guns than the military. They kill more people than the military. This is where the war is, in our streets. You got kids, they got guns, pistols, automatic weapons, Uzis—you name it, they got it." Big Mike doesn't know how right he is. At the end of this year—2004— 2,825 children and teenagers will die as a result of being shot by firearms, more than the number of American combat deaths in Iraq and Afghanistan that will eventually be recorded through the end of 2006.

There are three men sitting on plastic chairs outside the gas station mini-mart. The smell of marijuana, or bud, is in the air. One of them calls me over and tells me I am standing on hallowed ground.

"You know where you standing—they filmed a scene for that movie starrin' the brother—whazzit called, whaz dat movie?"

"Yo, *Training Day*."

"*Training Day*, starring my man Denzel."

"They wanted it to be, what's that word, realism . . ."

"No foo', *authentic*—"

"Yo muthafucka, aks me, they wanted real, you feel me—"

While the young men with pants slipping down their hips and black do-rags crowning their heads are playing the hood version of 365 Days to a Stronger Vocabulary, a small homie who couldn't be more than ten years old quietly walks up, a purple bandana covering his face from the eyes down. The color of his makeshift mask indicates that this little boy, who should be at school studying fractions, is associated with the Grape Street Crips. He is carrying an AK-47. The gun looks like it weighs more than he does. Big Mike is immediately on alert. "You gotta put that away, my little homie," he intones. "We have a lady here." What my sex or gentility has to do with this automatic weapon escapes me, but I am intrigued. Mike senses my curiosity. He puts his hand on my shoulder.

"Come on, these foo's playin' around a little too much for me. You there—take care of this little man," Mike commands, and the three stoned homies snap to order and take the weapon from the youngster. "Come on, Jorja Leap, you can talk with the homies another day. Let's go." *Where?* I wonder.

As if he can hear my question, he explains, "I need to drive you around so you can see what's goin' on in the neighborhoods. You been here at night. Now you gotta see what goes on in the daylight."

I agree with his plan wholeheartedly. One thing that has eluded me so far is the whole geography of black and brown gangs in Los Angeles. Aquil Basheer, the LA City firefighter, community activist, and leader who is a constant in my life, tells me, "Black gangs are based on territory and economics." This is all too accurate an assessment. Black gangs are rooted in a street-by-street mentality. Along with this, their gang activity occurs where they live, where they deal drugs, where they shoot one another, where they bring up their children. I knew that to truly understand black gangs in LA, it is essential to possess a street-level view. Latino gangs are different.

"The Latino gangs have changed. They used to operate out of the projects. But now they are commuter gangs," Father Greg Boyle, the beloved Jesuit priest who runs Homeboy Industries, a gang-intervention and reentry program, has explained. "They live out in Bell or Montebello or Hawaiian Gardens and drive in to commit their crimes." Not so the black gangs.

We climb back into the *We Care Outreach Ministry* mobile, with the air-conditioning blasting. It is 1:00 in the afternoon, with a blazing sun and temperatures in Watts approaching 90 degrees. Homies are hanging out on the street, just kicking it. Mike is in his element. He wags his left index finger at every mad-dogging gangster we pass.

"I am gonna take you where you can see just how many guns there are out there. Just how many of our young men are gettin' ready to die."

"Where are we going?"

"We're goin' to the projects," Big Mike tells me. "Nickerson Gardens. Imperial Courts. Jordan Downs. You know what they say in City Hall. They call them the housing developments. This ain't no developments, these here are the projects."

Despite the doublespeak of every city politician and bureaucrat who rarely ventures out of their office, the cops and people who live here know better. "We are from the projects, don't go changin' that up," Saint, who claims the Bounty Hunter Bloods as his "hood," or gang, has told me. "We all wanna get out, nobody wants to live here. But y'know, we all grew up here. We proud of the projects inna strange way."

The projects officially fall under the auspices of the Housing Authority of the City of Los Angeles. But for the past two decades, HACLA has barely controlled the hundreds of two-story family "units" with one to five bedrooms sprawling throughout this pocket of South LA. It is the architecture of despair, suburban cellblock—white buildings with black trim, every other window boarded up and no glass replacements. The sides of buildings have numbers instead of names. The "townhouses"— built facing courtyards and strips of grass—appear indistinguishable from one another. However, each of these public-housing projects possesses a personality all its own.

Despite its bucolic name, with its thousand-plus townhouses Nickerson Gardens is about as far from Mister Rogers' Neighborhood as you can get. Since the Aliso Village housing projects of East Los Angeles were torn down in 2000, it has the twin distinction of being the largest public housing project west of the Mississippi and the birthplace of the Bounty Hunter Bloods. Opened in 1955, it is a hot spot for the gangs of South Los Angeles, anchored at the corner of Central Avenue and Imperial Highway, then spreading north and east, encompassing Watts and

Compton. Only a few blocks away is Imperial Courts. Built in 1944, the Imperial Courts development is older and—with nearly five hundred townhouses—half the size of Nickerson Gardens. It is also headquarters for one of the Bloods' major enemies—the P Jay Crips. Farther east and off by itself, Jordan Downs is actually the oldest of the three projects. It was originally built in the 1940s as housing for World War II workers, but as these tenants moved on, buying their own homes, residents who were poor and predominantly black replaced them. In 1955 Jordan Downs was officially converted to public housing, and by the 1960s it had become a synonym for violence—Big Mike's territory—the birthplace of the Grape Street Crips. Ironically, the Crips and Bloods ultimately participated in a peace truce that marked the period from 1992 to 2002 as relatively stable. But this was no longer true. There is now an ever-shifting group of sets that change alliances on a weekly basis.

"They been at it again for the past year—bad. We can go through the projects and you can see what happens to the kids," Mike explained. "Some kids cannot go to after-school programs because they cannot cross gang territory."

As he drives, Mike points out a house for sale. "I would love to buy that and start an after-school program," he offers.

We are in the middle of a housing slump and I am curious. "How much do they want for it?" I ask.

"$350,000," Mike laughs.

"*What??*" The house looks like it could be airdropped into post-war Kosovo and fit right in. It cannot be worth more than $20,000.

"I bet I could take it off the bank's hands for $200K." Mike winks. "It's a fixer-upper, y'know.

"Okay, now we're gonna go into Grape Street Crips South Side territory," my three-hundred-pound tour guide intones. Big Mike is the favorite son returning home, merrily waving to everyone he sees. We drive through streets with tiny shotgun houses. He points out one abandoned house. "I grew up there with my grandma."

We turn into Jordan Downs, which is now completely controlled by the Grape Street Crips. Something is really wrong with this picture. It's a hot summer day and there is no one out. I turn to Mike in confusion and he starts laughing when I ask, "Where *is* everyone?"

"I'll show you where they are—they're in the cut." He shows me where to look—at the small grassy areas in between cinder block buildings. Sure enough, there are clusters of young black men—late teens, early twenties, sitting on webbed lawn furniture. There is no one out—only them. They wait.

"They are in the cut, sitting on the grass, hidin'," he explains. "Out on the front stoop—there's the lookout. They know everyone who is in the projects. They see my car comin' in here. They are on their cell phones, using this little device." He demonstrates while driving, holding the cell phone a few inches from his mouth and speaking into it as if it is a microphone.

"Everyone in Jordan Downs knows everyone who's comin' in here. They know who belongs and who doesn't."

"So," I ask, "if I rolled up in my Prius they would know I was here."

He nods. "They would know you was here and where you was at every single minute until you're outta their territory."

I am beginning to wonder if this kind of intelligence system might have prevented 9/11. Mike points out two elderly, wizened men.

"They're on lookout," he says, and on cue, they look up. He waves and they wave back. He points out parking lots where dope is dealt and where it is possible to find heroin or meth any time of the day or night. It's strange to see how openly drugs are sold—unimpeded—in the daylight. As long as there is no violence, dealers freely ply their trade. Just another neighborhood business. Trouble starts if a rival dealer tries to interfere with someone's corner.

"You can't move in on someone's drug territory—it's business. Corners belong to different neighborhoods," Mike explained. "You can't move in on a neighborhood's corner. Then it's war."

This is fine with the cops—several officers have told me that the projects are a "self-cleaning oven." That's one take on community policing.

"Who is here buying? How on earth do these people afford heroin or cocaine or crack?" I don't even bother to hide my surprise.

"Well y'know, some of them comin' from your community, all the way from the Westside, Pacific Palisades, Hancock Park, Beverly Hills." Mike winks at me again. "We got lawyers and doctors, they comin' by at night, probably on their way home from work. But they're not the only ones. The people here are good customers, too. They boost stuff all the time. Then they pawn it and buy what they need."

We leave Jordan Downs, and Mike waves to several young men sitting on front stoops. All with nothing to do but hang out and wait for the shots to be called—or to call them. But then, as we cross the border into Nickerson Gardens, Big Mike grows solemn.

"These are the Bloods, we are in Bloods territory—and there are times I am not safe here. Right now it's okay. See them?" He points out five young men sitting in the cut. "They're all cool—that's 'cuz they got an automatic weapon with them—an AK 47." There is street after street cutting through this housing project—it is a gated community on crack. There is not one single police car in the entire area. In fact, during this little tour of Mr. Cummings's Neighborhood, we never see the LAPD. The only police car in sight belongs to the understaffed Los Angeles School Police Department. And the LASPD officer doesn't get out of his car. The Bloods are everywhere, and they are easy to see. They wear some form of red—nothing blatant.

"Sometimes they got something small—a pen with a little red pen cap." Mike Cummings is a walking, talking encyclopedia of gang semiotics. *He will forget more than I ever know*, I think, as he explains the Bloods' tactics, and all of gang imperialism, to me.

"All the neighborhoods do the same thing. First they settle into the projects. Then they start takin' over all the houses and the apartment buildings surroundin' the projects. One by one. They control everything and anything."

The neighborhoods' power goes unchallenged. The cops will not come here—there is no one controlling these streets but the gangs and a handful of former gangbangers who are self-labeled street interventionists. I was just learning about the whole religion of the interventionists and their faith in the sanctity of the "license to operate"—the permission gang leaders granted interventionists to work in their territory. I wasn't sure how effective the interventionists were, but right now I wasn't asking questions.

Big Mike had long belonged to this loosely organized group of former gang members who practice "gang intervention" or "street peace outreach." Just what the definition of "gang intervention" was depended on who you were talking to. Everyone from Father Greg Boyle to Mike Cummings was involved in gang intervention, with varying degrees of credibility and success.

The former gang members who worked in the streets trying to stop retaliation and control rumors insisted that they practiced the "hardcore gang intervention." Then there were those individuals—like Greg Boyle—who believed gang intervention began when an individual decided he—or she—was finished with the gang.

Big Mike positioned himself somewhere in the middle of street outreach and long-term intervention. I begin to ask him about this when his cell phone rings.

"I gotta go tow someone. I gotta make some money. Come back," he tells me by way of good-bye. "We gonna talk some more."

I lean over and kiss Big Mike. "I will."

"Promise?"

"Promise!"

Two weeks later I make good on my word. I am driving to see Big Mike, who has promised to introduce me to more people working on intervention and "street peace." It is a Chamber of Commerce morning— bright and sun-washed; tall palm trees loom glossy and green against an azure sky. The street I am driving on is quiet. But the night before it had been the scene of three shootings and one death. I am deep into gang territory; the Watts Towers spindle up a few blocks away. I think of how beautiful South Los Angeles is—and at the same time unfair. The people here who work hard and believe in "family values" are forced to deal with violence on a daily basis.

My reverie is interrupted by the sight of Big Mike standing on the curb, the ever-present grin plastered on his face while he guards a parking space in front of the agency where he rents space and computer access.

"So, so glad you are here," Mike says as he ushers me back into a classroom where, smiling just as broadly, sits an African American man immaculately groomed in a polo shirt and crisply pressed khakis: Luther Keith. Luther runs group homes for youth just released from probation

halls and camps. The word "camp" is far too innocent, suggesting a holi-
day away from home, a brief sojourn to help a child in their struggles.
In reality, some of the Los Angeles County Department of Probation
camps function more as a holding facility for kids who just don't fit in
anywhere and whose primary task seems to be developing a permanent
criminal record. Once inside the worst of these camps, there is a prison-
like atmosphere and underground certification in gangbanging.

"They call them camp-bangers," Carol Biondi, a tireless advocate
for children and youth in the system, had told me. "They come into the
camps maybe slightly involved with gangs and come out full-fledged
gangbangers." I know the rest. At some point many will wind up in
graduate school—the California prison system. Here, in overcrowded
and racially tense quarters, these young gangbangers will all learn
new and better techniques for committing crimes and intimidating others. But while they are locked up—our streets will be safe.

"We gotta save these children comin' out of these camps," Luther
tells me. "We gotta keep them from joining gangs. These children are
our future."

Luther has never been in a gang. "I was saved by sports," he tells me,
but as I start talking with him I also learn that Luther comes from an
intact family. I ask Luther what he does and he tells me, "I patrol around
the whole city." He also works at Washington High School, and as he
elaborates, the names of the gangs come thick and fast.

As usual I am thinking five things at once. I am trying to keep track
of the sets he is listing. I am trying to figure out if they are Crips or
Bloods. I am also wondering, *Where the fuck do they get these names?* Luther tells me he is trying to put peace treaties into place. He is earnest
and wholesome and represents one extreme of African American gang
intervention in South Los Angeles.

The other extreme, which arrives about fifteen minutes later, is
Marlo "Bow Wow" Jones. Marlo looks rough around the edges and I can
barely understand what he is saying. His words are mumbled as though
he is speaking with a mouth full of oatmeal. He starts talking about the
gangs he is working with and I am even more confused. There are sets
he is naming that I have never heard of, but I sit quietly. Something tells
me I should not ask questions.

Mike ends the session at noon and says, "We all gotta go watch over the kids while they get outta school." This is the centerpiece of Big Mike's work in the community. His Safe Passages gang-intervention program is designed to work as advertised: former gang members function as bodyguards to make sure kids get safely home from school without being robbed, beaten, or raped.

We drive over and park in front of David Starr Jordan High School, positioned right next door to the Jordan Downs housing project. Jordan High is one of the ten-lowest-performing schools in the Los Angeles Unified School District—earning a 1 out of 10 on the Academic Performance Index. It's a favored recruiting ground for both the Bloods and the Crips.

I trot along beside Big Mike, and my heart is thumping while I think, *He will protect me, he will protect me.* It is the mantra I am using against my rising anxiety, which notches up when I see a knot of homies standing on Grape Street, throwing gang signs to three boys inside a car driving by with the windows rolled down and rap music playing. I feel naked, out in the open, and I stand as close as I can to Big Mike. The sun is beating down on us, and it seems like all of Watts is on the street. I am approached by an emaciated black woman who announces, "I know you—you were on TV the other night, I just loooooooove you!" I freeze, but Big Mike starts laughing and pushes her away saying, "Move on, mama."

"She did too much PCP in the '80s and she never been the same since," he explains. I decide I won't tell him that I *had* been on TV, two days earlier.

"You know what PCP did to this neighborhood, in these projects, in the 1980s?" Mike asks. I explain that I worked then at the emergency room of Martin Luther King General Hospital, which filled nightly with people who'd OD'd on PCP. "One guy was so high he threw me up against the wall," I say.

"I feel that. I used to take it. PCP could give you the strength of a monster, a real monster," Mike adds. "But the worst was crack."

I nod. The PCP epidemic was bad, but it was nothing compared to the devastation that was to come with crack. While we talk, we walk toward the entrance to Jordan Downs. Mike points to the cluster of gang members I have already noticed.

"They just waitin' to go through the pockets of the children who are goin' into their houses. They're takin' anything they want out of those children's backpacks. We gotta stop them."

Big Mike whispers directions into his walkie-talkie. He and another interventionist are watching two boys on bicycles in front of the housing project. "If another kid on a bike shows up there are gonna be shots fired. Get ready to duck."

Mike scans the area and I hear what sounds like a car backfiring. I know what this is and I carefully drop down behind Big Mike. Someone is out there shooting; someone is trying to kill someone.

"It's okay, it's okay, nothin' is gonna happen to you," Big Mike says reassuringly. "They are gonna have to get through me to get to you." He has a death grip on my arm. The air is vibrating.

"Come on, kids, getta move on," Mike says calmly to a group of girls giggling and walking by him. A woman weaves in front of him and Mike gives her two dollars and tells her to get out of the way. She takes the money, asks him for more, and he rebuffs her, good-naturedly. She crosses the street and without looking at its destination, gets on a waiting bus. An LASPD patrol car drives by. We are still waiting for one more bicycle rider. A fight has broken out on the school campus.

"Looka that." Mike laughs while pointing at several kids who are fighting. "I know those two boys—they are gay, tryin' to beat up three little girls." It looks like the girls are fighting back. The walkie-talkies crackle.

But I am not paying attention. I hear someone calling my name. "Hey, Jorja, Jorja, Jorja."

"Hey Bo!" Big Mike cries out.

Bo Taylor parks his minivan and walks over to Big Mike and me.

"So what's goin' on here this fine mornin'?" Bo asks. Bo and Mike are laughing while I stand between them, slightly dazed. A former Crip and US Navy veteran, Bo Taylor also works on the front lines of gang intervention and heads up the Unity One gang-intervention agency.

I am not exactly sure what Bo does—everyone has a slightly different story. Bo negotiates peace treaties; Bo stops retaliation; Bo has the ultimate license to operate—he can talk to the OGs and the shot callers and get them to stop shooting. He has served as an unofficial bodyguard for University of Southern California football coach Pete Carroll and dignitaries from City Hall and Sacramento. Bo has the letters of transit into the community. He is the one who can get you in and out of Casablanca.

Despite the intermittent shots being fired, I also know that Mark shouldn't worry—I am never going to be as safe as I am right now, standing between Bo and Big Mike. Bo indiscriminately passes out cash to the children walking by. I know that he can travel into any housing project at any time of the day or night and people will talk with him, sit down with him—offer him something to drink, something to eat. He talks to young people, he urges them to stay in school, he tries to organize games, activities, tours, and trips to Disneyland. But he does not want to file the necessary papers to obtain the necessary grants; he just wants to believe the money will come. And it does. But what does Bo really do?

What Bo and Big Mike and Aquil Basheer, among others, are trying to do is raise all the fatherless, motherless children in the neighborhoods. Solving the gang problem is not about peace treaties and midnight call-outs. This is what no one seems to be getting—not the police, not the Mayor's Office, not the researchers drilling down into results. Someone needs to love these unlovable children.

"They need fathers," Big Mike offers.

And Bo quietly says, "All they see is prison or death. They need family."

SIX

Adopting New Ideas

What do I want for my baby girl? I don't want her to
belong to a neighborhood. I want her to be safe. I want
her to be strong. I don't want her to be like me.
—Cherilynn Jackson

I knew that Big Mike was right about the needs of the children. But at
this point in my life, I felt like a fraud. While I nodded and agreed and
talked about parental attachment, part of me was convinced that the
Department of Children and Family Services was about to show up at
my front door, investigating my credentials as a parent. And of course,
this wasn't exactly a sentiment I could share at the monthly meeting
of the Westlake wives. In the weeks that followed, while I turned in
my final report on the LAPD's anti-gang efforts to Mike Hillmann and
started spending time with Big Mike and Father Greg Boyle at Homeboy Industries, I thought about the rather well-intentioned but half-
assed wife and mother I was turning out to be. Was I really cut out for
domestic life? Over a year after I put on a red dress and marched down
the aisle to marry Mark in front of our assembled friends and families,
I still wasn't sure.

While I loved Mark and Shannon, there was clearly trouble on the
home front. My husband would plan romantic date nights out, then
insist I go golfing with the Dodsons, friends of his who thought that
George W. Bush might be too liberal. Shannon would cling to me, then
act remote, invite me to school activities, then ignore me in front of her
friends. And there I was, a rebel without a cause. A soldier without a
war. One restless little white woman with a PhD and a belly piercing, all
dressed in black, acting tough but feeling terrified. There were homies
who had me on speed dial and kept calling all hours of the night and day.

And right in the middle of all this, I had petitioned the courts to permit me to adopt Shannon. What was I doing?

Mark was of little comfort here. He had decided—even before we were married—that I would be the perfect new mother for Shannon. He had also managed to tell several people—including Shannon's grandparents—that this was his intention. But somewhere along the line, he had forgotten to discuss this with me. When he finally talked with me about adopting Shannon, I was frightened. I wasn't sure I was mother material. And I had a long history to back me up.

Up to that point, I had been quite contentedly childless. This was a choice, not a condition. I had never wanted children. All my adolescent role models were childless women. Margaret Bourke-White. Lillian Hellman. Oriana Fallaci. Thea Ernie. My aunt, or "thea," Ernie was my father's favorite sister, Ernestine. An executive with AT&T, she drove a vintage Thunderbird and had been married five times. I wanted to be her. I wanted to work. I wanted to travel. I wanted to drive a Thunderbird. And I didn't want to have children.

Of course, there was that rather perverse little idea of "the biological clock." I never could take this quite seriously—in fact, the whole concept reminded me of *Peter Pan* and the alligator that swallowed the clock. When the ticking grew louder, you knew danger was at hand. So I kept listening for the alligator or the clock or whatever I was supposed to hear to alert me it was time. When my friends got pregnant, I expected to hear it. When my beloved grandmother died, I expected to hear it. When I turned forty, I expected to hear it. Either I was hearing-impaired or I just didn't want to have children.

But still, everyone prevailed upon me to experience the joys of motherhood. My first husband, my therapist, my friends, my family—even my lovers. One lovesick boyfriend suggested we have a child and pass it off as my husband's. But I knew, in my bones, that I did not want children. And I knew this because I did not think I would be a good mother. I was moody, I was selfish, I was self-indulgent. And then, when my first marriage ended, I looked like a genius. Although the divorce was painful, no one suffered except my former husband and me. After the divorce was final, there was no shared custody, no arguments over visitation rights, no need to ever see the ex-spouse again. I was free.

Once I began dating, I realized that it was more than likely that my next relationship would include children. So I jumped right in the deep end. My first postmarital relationship involved a man with seven children. I wasn't quite sure I wanted to be around them. *He* didn't even want to be around them. When he accepted a UN posting in Afghanistan, I figured out he probably didn't want to be around anyone. The second man who came into my life had four children. Although separated, he put me in the ring with his Catholic guilt and I wasn't a contender. Exit ready-made-family number two. After that, I found someone with no ambivalence—a man whose wife had abandoned him and their two young daughters. I admired his devotion to his children and the way he played the twin roles of Daddy and Mr. Mom, until it dawned on me that he also used his daughters as a human shield against any serious involvement.

I was tired. It was three strikes and I was out. I announced I was taking a sabbatical from dating for a year, to spend time alone sitting on my patio, where I would read the classics and "consider my options." This was when I met Mark, the man I had waited for all my life. We fell madly in love. But there was a catch, and it was a big one. He had a child—an eight-year-old daughter, Shannon. After two months of dating, he assured me, "She'll love you." Of course she would. In the TV movie of my life, Shannon would immediately recognize me as the perfect combination of Mary Poppins and Lara Croft, bonding to me instantly. I prepared myself for Mark setting a land-speed record in his haste to propose. We'd all live happily ever after.

This was not a total and complete fantasy. In my professional life, I had served as a nationally recognized expert in "childhood attachment, separation, and loss." I trained clinicians and social workers; I testified on custody issues in court; people asked me for professional "therapeutic consultation." Even Mr. Mom's two daughters still called me surreptitiously. I was Dr. Jorja—as many kids called me—the queen of child welfare. And I'd know exactly how to handle Shannon once I met her.

Of course, I had no idea what I was in for. The first time Mark brought her to my house, a three-foot-tall little sprite with strawberry-blonde hair and freckles climbed out of his SUV, ignored my warm greeting, and looked me up and down. She then turned to Mark and said,

"She's very pretty." I, meanwhile, watched in complete awe. In those ten seconds, Shannon had assumed complete control of the situation.

I spent eight of the most exhausting hours of my life that day. Mark smiled and barely spoke while Shannon called the shots. She wanted a tour of my house, she wanted to go rollerblading, she wanted to eat ice cream. Mark had planned for the three of us to end the day with dinner at a local Mexican restaurant. No. Shannon decided we would eat at home—my home. Shutting the kitchen door on Mark, she announced, "This is girls only, Daddy." She was a chip off the old block—and it was making me anxious. I had the Mini-Me of control ruling my kitchen. But there was one thing Shannon could not direct—my seventy-year-old cottage. The oven mercifully exploded in the midst of our preparations. Mark quickly went to pick up Italian food while Shannon and I watched TV. When they finally departed after dinner, I fell asleep on top of my bed, fully clothed.

My audition was a success of sorts. Unfortunately I did not get the part I tried out for. Instead of playing wife and mother, Shannon decided I would be her girlfriend. Both Mark and I agreed that for a few weeks we'd follow her lead, "Just till she gets comfortable," we assured each other. Sleeping with my boyfriend was replaced by sleepovers with his daughter. Our plan was a partial success. Shannon granted Mark permission to date me. "However," she added, "you can't get married."

It's maddening to have an eight-year-old directing your courtship. I give Mark complete credit here. I was a disaster. I was in love, impatient, and, most importantly, I was still ambivalent about motherhood. But I loved this man and I was determined to build a relationship with this little girl. So I spent an enormous amount of time with Shannon, alone. She slept over at my house, hung out with me at UCLA, and turned out to be a very good girlfriend. And of course, we fought over the one thing that divides all girlfriends—a man. Still, Mark and I continued to keep the "seriousness" of our relationship from Shannon.

My friends all thought I was crazy. The women in the neighborhoods who knew me laughed. "Whatcha gonna do, Mama, wait for her to go to college?" They had a point. After six weeks of playing "weekend at Jorja's," Mark reached his breaking point and decided the time had come for Shannon to accept who I really was—Daddy's girlfriend.

Unfortunately, he had forgotten just who he was dealing with. Shannon brought out the big guns and cried, "I miss Mommy." I could neither deny the pain of her loss, nor accept her plan to keep me on the periphery. I also knew this problem was a whole lot bigger than me and all my expertise, and that it was time to see the man I called Papa. My therapist.

I have been in therapy intermittently my entire adult life. It helped me survive adolescence, college, graduate school, marriage, and divorce. Surely it could help me deal with Shannon. Therapy helped me with my rage and my fear. But that still left the problem of the girl who was going to be—for all intents and purposes—my daughter.

I picked the night Mark answered a SWAT call-out to sit Shannon down and tell her that I knew she hated me. She began a perfunctory protest until I told her to stop. I told her I thought she probably wanted me dead and her mother alive; that she hated seeing me sleeping on her mother's side of the bed. And I told her what I truly felt—that I wished both Shannon and Mark had never been forced to watch a young woman die. We both started to cry.

In the TV movie version of my life, this is the point where we are supposed to all walk into the sunset, holding hands. In reality, there continued to be difficult moments shot through with pain while we bonded and became a family. I knew, however, that Shannon's feelings had altered when I returned after a three-day work trip to New York. She had trouble sleeping while I was gone and told me, "I'm scared something is gonna happen to you." I took the opportunity to ask Shannon how she felt about me adopting her. She held her arms out to hug me and said, "I really want you to."

It was clear that neither Mark nor Shannon had any doubts. That left me. I was the uncertain one. It was the feeling that had washed over me when I spent time with Big Mike and he talked about children and their need for love. It was time to confront this. For over two years, I had floated around in domestic purgatory, feeling like a hip and sensitive cross between a legal guardian and a child therapist. That was about to end. This would be "for reals," as the homies often exclaimed. I knew that the love Shannon and I shared was also "for reals." That knowledge gave me the strength to go ahead, despite my fear. And I was scared out

of my mind. By adopting Shannon, I knew I was making the only irre-
vocable commitment of my entire life.

As for the actual adoption, I wasn't worried. After all, we were
dealing with Dr. Jorja, the queen of child welfare. I envisioned sailing
merrily through the adoption process. So many friends and family had
applauded my efforts that I started to believe my own publicity. I was
the Angelina Jolie of Westlake Village—bringing love and cheer to this
repressed WASP family.

But my adoption plan hit a snag. I discovered that the legal docu-
ments had to be filed in Ventura, not Los Angeles, County. In Ventura
County I was not the queen of child welfare. Instead, I was "Hmmm . . .
I don't know how to pronounce your first name. Is it Jorgé?" All my
behind-the-scenes machinations to shortcut the bureaucratic process
were met with polite dismissal, so one Monday night I settled down to
fill out the adoption application form with Mark.

It was horrendous. About the only piece of information not required
was the date of my last period. We had to submit detailed financial records and letters of recommendation. Once that was done, we could
look forward to background checks and, of course, the inevitable personal interviews. It was worse than Mark's application for a Top Secret
security clearance from the FBI. We moved through this process in fits
and starts. But after six months, the paperwork was complete and it was
time to be individually interviewed. Truth be told, the people at Ventura County could not have been kinder. Shannon and Mark were interviewed together and then Shannon was left alone with the social worker
while Mark came outside to sit with me in the waiting room. It was there
that he dropped a bomb.

"The social worker is very nice," he began calmly. "She asked me
if I wanted your name to appear on the birth certificate as Shannon's
mother. I told her yes, you *are* Shannon's mother."

The true meaning of those words did not hit me until the birth certificate arrived about six weeks later and there it was, my name, date and
time of Shannon's birth. It was so official that I had to check my body
for stretch marks. A few days after the birth certificate arrived, we received notification of the hearing for my adoption petition. We traveled
to court on the assigned date and signed the papers that officially made

Shannon my daughter. The pictures of that day are even more beautiful than our wedding photographs. In every frame, Mark looks jubilant while Shannon stands close to my side and smiles shyly. I look happy and confident. Unfortunately, I felt like I was about to jump off a cliff.

No one had ever successfully explained to me what it meant to be a mother. I knew I felt connected to Shannon in a way that was totally different from any other relationship I had experienced. It did not matter that I had not carried her to term; I felt like I had birthed her. Everything that I had encountered, learned, believed, or valued was poured into her. And I wanted to share my world with her. So a few months after the adoption, I arranged a family field trip.

It was time for Shannon to see the Watts Towers and South LA. As soon as I brought the idea up, she announced that she did not want to go into "the ghetto." Sighing, I prepared myself for the latest scene of the Coen Brothers movie I found myself starring in, *Raising Whitey*. The more Shannon struggled against my plan, the more obstinately I insisted we go. Mark smoothed the way, telling her we could go for a special treat—breakfast at Roscoe's House of Chicken 'n Waffles. He could barely make the suggestion before I energetically agreed.

"Dad is right. You will *love* Roscoe's."

It was good to have a partner in parental crime. A détente had been declared at home. I had insisted Mark go to therapy and he had agreed. In turn, I had promised to limit the time I would spend out with homies to twice a week. But I had also declared, "Shannon is going to learn about what I am doing and where I work."

"You'll like Roscoe's," Mark told Shannon, announcing, "We're going this Sunday."

Shannon settled for the bribe, happily anticipating breakfast and never dreaming it would be accompanied by a lesson in race relations. However, once we arrived at Roscoe's, there was no question that she was, indeed, the whitest person in the room, with skin so pale it would burn if she even thought about the sun. The only thing that saved her from total isolation in the sea of black faces at Roscoe's was Mark. "Ooooh, honey, she looks just like you, you can't deny her," the hostess told him as she showed us to our table. I, on the other hand, fit in perfectly. I knew this would happen. With the olive skin that came courtesy my Greek genetics, I could always pass. In dicey situations, I rarely corrected the impression that I was biracial or Latina depending on the color, ethnicity, and hostility of the homie I encountered. No one was paying much attention to me in Roscoe's—but all eyes were focused on Mark and Shannon. The setting did not affect Shannon's appetite but it did provide her with an opening for the latest round of attacks disguised as questions.

"Why is everyone looking at us? And why are you doing all this stuff with gangs? Why are you going into the ghetto? It's stupid."

At this point I lost it and demanded, "Just what do you think this fucking ghetto is like?"

An African American woman at the next table shushed me. "Now don't you go talking to that baby like that. Whatcha tryin' to do?" she admonished while I bit back my self-righteous retort: *Trying to raise her not to be a racist.*

Shannon's eleven-year-old view of the ghetto was nurtured more by DVDs than reality—she saw it composed of tall, dark buildings populated by gangs and rodents. But that day, after breakfast, Shannon learned that the Watts Towers were built by Simon Rodia, an Italian, who probably suffered with schizophrenia along with artistic passion. Rodia labored for forty years, taking broken pieces of pottery that he crafted into sculpture. I had arranged through the local museum for a tour guide: a gorgeous African American woman told us folk tales about the towers and recited a poem she had written in their honor. All the bits and pieces of dishes and brightly colored glass that composed the towers charmed Shannon. We literally walked through each tower and examined their construction carefully. I also told Shannon stories about people who lived in the area—adding that they weren't all gangsters, that most of them had children and families. Several residents who lived in small houses across the street from the towers walked outside of their houses to wave at us. One older man said, "Welcome to Watts, we hope you like the Towers." South Los Angeles appeared at its best that day— poor, benign, proud.

"I see why you like it here," Shannon admitted. "It's not the way I thought it would be."

I had negotiated a truce.

SEVEN

Nuns and Bitches

No one believes I'm in a gang. My mama don't believe I'm
in a gang. That's because I'm a woman. And I got a baby.
And that's supposed to make me different.

—Alicia Perez

Perhaps it is because I am now officially a mother, but I find myself increasingly drawn to the women in the neighborhoods. I want to understand more about their role in gangs. For months now, I have heard conflicting stories about how active women are. One thing was clear, however. Some women *were* full-fledged gang members, moving far beyond the more traditional status of baby mama. Kenny Green told me, "They're a part of it now—they are bad—they roll up and start shooting."

Various experts had as much trouble as I did trying to figure out just how active young women are. The National Gang Center highlighted a purposive study conducted in fifteen major cities revealing that 7.8 percent of females, compared with 8.8 percent of males, between the ages of eighteen and thirty self-reported that they were gang members. Law enforcement offered a different view—insisting there were far fewer female than male gang members. The only thing academics and practitioners agreed upon was that the actual number of female gang members was impossible to estimate.

In the past year, both Greg Boyle and Big Mike have insisted that probably less than 5 percent of "at-risk" young women became active gang members. The numbers weren't the only area where information was soft. Early on, the accounts of "girls in gangs" mirrored mainstream society: young women were the second sex, playing a supporting role. But from the mid-1980s and into the aptly named decade of death— when Los Angeles experienced up to one thousand gang-related homicides a year—homegirls proved to be much more than Dale Evans with tattoos. Women did not just carry guns—they shot them. They did not just hide drugs for their homeboys—they dealt them, taking care of the cash and the transactions.

All this female activity in gangs ultimately gave rise to reports of sexual violence. The streets buzzed with stories of girls getting "sexed in" to neighborhoods by being gang-raped. In one rumored initiation rite, aspiring homegirls were forced to have sex with a gang member who was HIV-positive. There were tales of bloody beatings using fists and clubs, with no exceptions for gender. But all of this was secondhand. When I start talking to women in the neighborhoods, joining the gang sounds almost organic—evolving alongside criminal activity.

"We partied together and then they invited me to go on a drive-by," Vanity "Dimples" Benton explains. "Next thing I knew, 'cuz I was the only one with a license, they told me to drive while one of my homies opened up shooting. After that I was in the neighborhood. When they caught us and locked me up—I still thought it was worth it, I wanted to gangbang and slang drugs and just hang out."

Despite all the information and titillation, it takes me a long time to catch on to what happens with women in the neighborhoods. Too long. I am late to the party because, up until now, I have never been particularly interested in women. Hanging out with the homegirls was just not my speed. In my mind, there were two kinds of women—nuns and bitches—and I placed myself firmly in the latter category. Growing up in a Greek extended family, I watched how "good girls" exhibited a version of female dependency I wanted desperately to avoid.

Because of this I had no use for the girlfriends of gang members. These girls—some of them only fourteen or fifteen—surrendered their lives. As they entered the bloom of adulthood, they had no plans other than giving birth to multiple children and ensnaring a man. Marriage did not exist; pregnancy was the closest they would come to long-term commitment, and infidelity was the aftermath.

The attitudes of men in the neighborhoods resembled something circa the 1950s. Women were good for one thing—sex; sex with a beautiful woman was even better and, for God's sake, domestic sex was bound to be supplemented. Of course, all this possession and infidelity caused unending problems between the neighborhoods. Kenny Green was my guide to the sexual politics in the gang world.

"Everyone thinks that gangbanging is about turf," he instructed. "No way. Most of it is about women—they make all the trouble. And now there are the women who want to be shooters and slang; they want to be part of the neighborhood."

These are the women who catch my interest. I am not interested in the nuns—the girls who behave as if they are tattooed with the word VICTIM. I stay as far away from them as possible. I want nothing of their silent suffering, their fortitude, or their devotion. Instead, deep down, I know I am just a tough little bitch with too much rage. I identify with the female gangbangers who are angry and "down for the neighborhood." But, despite my empathy, the women I meet are even more suspicious than the men of the neighborhoods.

"What do you want?" Dimples questions me after I ask her if we can hang out together. I am blunt; I tell her I want to know why she gang-bangs and deals drugs. I may be a chameleon, but I refuse to lie. Lying is dangerous; your street credibility—no matter who you are—depends on telling the truth. Gang members come equipped with a bullshit detector; they call you out for "fronting." Slowly, Dimples and other women I meet react to the honesty I express. Their stories spill out while I am at Homeboy Industries, gathering information for a research proposal I am writing.

"This is not about girls becoming like guys," Meda Chesney-Lind, a gang researcher at the University of Hawaii, tells me. "Although the themes are the same. The girls come from toxic, abusive families, and are re-victimized in the gang setting." I wonder how the women I am getting to know would feel about being seen as "re-victimized." They openly describe the trauma they have experienced, the abuse they have known. There are stepfathers who demand blowjobs or cousins who force them to have anal sex. But making the deliberate choice to become part of a neighborhood involves something beyond trauma. Sometimes the act of joining a gang is experienced as *empowerment*. It doesn't really matter if it's a male gang or a female gang—all that matters is the feeling of control, with the added attraction of rejecting both traditional female passivity and victimhood. Chesney-Lind sums it all up by saying, "Girls choose the gang for entirely understandable and even laudable goals, given the constraints that they experience in a society that is increasingly likely to police and pathologize girlhood." The women I know want to rewrite the rules. These are not the nuns—these are the bitches, the girls who want, somehow, to have control.

In the midst of my research, I start spending a lot of time with Dark Eyes, whose real name is Joanna Carillo. Joanna is a self-proclaimed third-generation gang member. She grew up watching her grandparents, parents, cousins, and uncles all caught up in the life of different cliques that eventually merged into Florencia-13. Her father was killed in a drive-by shooting a week after Joanna's thirteenth birthday. After he died, her mother supported the family by dealing drugs.

"Oh, she's still dealing," Joanna volunteers offhand, when we are discussing our relationships with our mothers and how we want to raise our daughters differently. "It's never been a problem. I've always told her, don't fuckin' do it around me. You can deal, but go away from the house, go somewhere else. *I've got values.*" But a few minutes later, Joanna tells me that she is more worried than usual about all this "business" because her mother is moving in with her.

"After all, she is my mother," she explains. "She can't take care of herself. But y'know, we've talked about my house rules. She can't do any business in front of the kids. There are enough bad influences around the kids without them seeing their grandmother dealing drugs."

"How old is your mother?" I ask Joanna.

"She is sixty-one—but she seems older, y'know? Her back is bad, her health isn't good, I need to get a daytime nurse for her. My ex-husband has said he would help out. He's moved into the apartment downstairs from mine." I calmly take in this tasting menu of insanity and then the stray thought enters: *Well, she seems closer to her mother than I am to mine. Who am I to judge?*

"I wanna meet your mother," I tell Joanna.

"Why? She's no damn good. She's left me so many times. She's never there when I need her. And she makes me feel like shit. I gotta take her in because no one else will take care of her. It doesn't mean I love her or she's part of my life."

Women and their mothers—is there any way to escape it?

So many of the women I kick it with feel both tied to and emotionally abandoned by their mothers. This is not something I expected to find. But the words are familiar.

I understand Joanna. She is my sister under the skin, seesawing between two identities: the attentive mother, hovering over her baby girl as she feeds her applesauce, and the enraged homegirl, threatening to split open the face of some bitch who has disrespected her. Men, love, freedom. Joanna's life runs along the same plot lines as mine—but it is much more complicated.

"It was always there—the neighborhood was always there," Joanna tells me. "Everyone in my family was part of it, gangbanging and slanging and getting locked up. And of course there was always domestic violence, my dad beating my mom. Everyone feared my dad—he was high up, a leader—he had a lot of power. I figured the only way I could deal with it was when I said to myself, I am gonna do what I gotta do to earn my respect in the neighborhood. I was only seven years old when I started out there in the street."

There are tattoos wreathing Joanna's neck and upper arms. She is wearing polka-dotted acrylic press-on nails and they curl out like claws. Her nose is pierced, and I can see barely discernable scars on her face.

"Maybe I understand a lot more now that I am older. But back in the day, it became like an obsession—I stopped being a kid—I lost my childhood. And the weirdest part of it is that my parents were proud—they would look at each other and laugh and say, 'Yeah, they're our kids'— y'know in that proud kinda voice—they fuckin' enjoyed what we were doing. No one ever said, 'What you guys are doing is wrong.' If my brothers got beat up or got arrested or got kicked out of school—they were proud of them. And when I started gettin' into trouble, they were all right with it. They thought that was good."

Adolescence brought on her first boyfriend, Flaco, and serial pregnancies—a son at fifteen, a daughter at eighteen. In between there were arrests, time spent in probation camps, and a trip to the California Youth Authority. But Joanna focused on being a mother.

"I'd dress my kids in gang clothes—I thought they were so cute. I thought I was so smart. I dropped out of school and there I was, a baby mama with two kids in Florencia-13 clothes."

Then—at nineteen—Joanna attracted a boyfriend who was "totally different. Roberto wasn't in a neighborhood; he had been raised in a convent school. I guess he was meant to come into my life . . . he was serious; he said we had to get married before we had kids. He was very Catholic and we got married in the Church."

But even in a religiously sanctioned marriage—a rare occurrence—she continued to gangbang and slang drugs, refusing to settle down—attracting and discarding men. She also had two more children—another boy and another girl. There was a decade of marriage and infidelity until her husband finally left her. Joanna took up with someone new. But Juan was the one boyfriend who was stronger and bigger than she is and abused her repeatedly.

"I let him take over," she tells me. "I don't know why. He made me feel like he was good, I was bad. He would tell me, 'Stop dealing drugs, stay home, take care of the kids, I will make the money.' I liked that for a while. But then he got crazy. He started beating me. He thought I was cheating on him. But it turned out he was cheating on me. One night he kept hitting me and said the next time he was gonna kill me. He got really drunk and then he crashed. When he was sleeping, I packed up the kids, started the car, and just when I was getting ready to go, I started to panic. I couldn't breathe. I didn't know if I could make it. But somehow, I calmed down and made myself drive. I finally got to a friend's house—someone Juan never met—and she let me and the kids spend the night. In the morning she took me to see Father Greg. He helped me." Joanna smiles. "He hired me. And he told me, 'I'll be here 'til the wheels fall off.'" Joanna started working at Homeboy Industries and promptly found a new boyfriend—Silent.

"It was the first time I really fell in love with someone," she tells me, "but then I found out—he was married. What a mess! I broke up with him, but I was so fuckin' angry. I got stress seizures. I was twenty-nine and I sick. I would act out rather than say how I was feeling—I would look to fight with somebody to take my frustration out. And I was looking for someone to love. And that was Luisa."

Joanna breaks down telling me this. I don't know it but I am listening to the most confusing part of Joanna's past. I have seen Luisa around Homeboy Industries, but she defies any of the categories I have constructed for gang members. With her shaved head and swagger, her multiple tattoos, she is channeling *Boys Don't Cry*, but no one is fooled. Everyone knows Luisa is fronting as a man—that she is actually a girl. Greg Boyle calls her Baby Girl.

"We embraced her," G—as the homies call Greg Boyle—remembers. "We surrounded Baby Girl with love." The homies think Luisa is strange or "mental," but they also pity her. She has no mother, no father, no family. She meets Joanna—who takes one look at her underfed, over-tattooed, androgynous frame—and announces she wants to adopt her. The model of multitasking, Joanna mothers Luisa while she is breaking up with Silent and hustling and seeing a therapist and trying to go straight. Things deteriorate. Despite Joanna's steadfast connection, Luisa will not stop her ninety-pound demolition derby of self-destruction. There is a long line of arrests and offenses—busted for murder, assault with a deadly weapon. And then she is gone.

Joanna is crying.

"It hit me harder than losing Silent."

I ask her why.

"I was trying to save Baby Girl. I think at that point it still didn't click—maybe I was trying to save my first son—he died when he was five."

Joanna stops. I wait, quietly.

"I need to think about this." She puts her head down on the table in front of me.

She doesn't elaborate; I don't probe. Maybe we will come to a point in our relationship when she'll explain what happened to her son. Maybe not. All I know is that we're not there yet. She raises her head and moves on.

"I had always pretended my son was still alive. Every once in a while, Flaco—his father—would call. I would make up stories about our son, what he liked to eat, how he was doing in school. I would say he was asleep or he was out playing, lying about why he couldn't come to the phone."

But after ten years hiding out in Mexico, Flaco returns to Los Angeles, wanting to see his son and daughter. Joanna is finally forced to tell him the truth. In the days that follow, Flaco grows increasingly upset that his son is dead and Joanna's other children, including her son and daughter with Roberto, are alive. Flaco reports Joanna to DCFS, saying she is gangbanging and slanging drugs. A children's social worker investigates, removes the children from Joanna's custody and places all the kids with Roberto.

"I don't know how I got through it, but I did." Joanna's voice is flat.

"When they took my kids away, I decided I was gonna concentrate on being a mother. I wanted my kids back, I was not gonna have another baby. I decided to get an IUD. The doctor told me this would guarantee I wouldn't get pregnant."

Joanna is decidedly not a nun. In a few weeks, she begins a relationship with Bullet, who belongs to a neighborhood that is one of her gang's rivals. After they break up, Joanna discovers she is pregnant.

"I had the IUD in, and I didn't know why I was throwing up and not getting my period. I couldn't believe I was pregnant. All the doctor said was, 'These things happen.' I kept thinking, *Why?* Then I thought maybe this was the baby I was getting back—because my son had died. So I couldn't get an abortion. I told Father Greg what had happened, and I asked him if he would help me. I'll always remember what he said: 'I'll be there till the wheels fall off the bus, kiddo.' And he meant it."

I can hear Greg's voice speaking those words. But there is more. The baby—a little boy—is born premature with underdeveloped lungs and one kidney instead of two. His first two years are punctuated by a series of medical emergencies. He cannot breathe on his own, requiring an oxygen tank. He is undersized and the doctors doubt he will ever walk. Then his kidney begins to fail. "Why did God give me another baby who isn't going to live?" Joanna cried.

"These women," Greg tells me, "their pain is so deep."

A week later, Joanna calls me and says she wants to talk. We meet, and she tells me about Bullet. They are back together, trying to take care of their son, whom they call Poco Marcos—Little Marcos. That morning, she found the bag of works—spoons and syringes—that he had hidden from her. Bullet loves to slam crystal meth between his fingers. He is a sad little bad boy who alternately lives with his mother and depends on Joanna. He will never take care of Joanna, which is the one thing she craves. Underneath her tattoos and her gold jewelry and her acrylics, all Joanna wants is to lay down her head. Instead, she is in charge of everyone.

"I don't wanna go on this way," Joanna tells me. "I don't know why, but when I had Marcos, that's when I decided I had to change."

I know why. Little Marcos represents a chance for Joanna to try again—to have a normal family with birthday parties and friends, a life unfettered by drugs hidden in diapers or Daddy hitting Mommy. But she is not there yet. I know this because I am always meeting Joanna in public—at Homeboy, at a restaurant. Unlike the other women who ask me to visit them at home, I am never invited to Joanna's house. I suspect it is crawling with Florencia-13.

"Joanna won't have anyone over," a homie tells me. "Her house is too crazy, trust me." I am not alone. No one is invited to kick it at Joanna's.

"What do you want to do about Bullet?"

"Fuck him. He's slamming again," Joanna spits out. I am worried about Joanna—how on earth is she making it financially? Is she dealing again? I don't want to ask, I don't want to know.

Two days later, a group of homies and their kids, including Joanna and Bullet, all go to Magic Mountain. Joanna calls to tell me there has been trouble with Bullet. She begins reading the X-ray of their relationship.

"I love Bullet," she tells me, "but I am not in love with him. Do you know what I mean?"

Sadly, I do. I loved my first husband deeply—the way I would a brother. But my second marriage is different; with Mark I am truly "in love." I try to explain.

"See, you did it right," Joanna says, sighing. "I was in love with Silent. I only love Bullet—not the 'in love' part. And we fight so much."

Joanna tells me that coming home from Magic Mountain, Bullet began to ridicule her. "I can kick your ass," he taunted. She tells me that they were fighting inside of their minivan with children in the car. She looks at me anxiously.

"You think I am a fool in the car, banging with Bullet in front of the kids," she starts.

"Not really. I am thinking that my husband and I bang too. Just like you and Bullet."

Joanna is looking at me skeptically.

"I don't hit him—but we bang—with words."

As of late, things had been tumultuous at home. A few days before, Mark had announced he was traveling to the FBI Hazardous Devices School in Huntsville, Alabama; he would be gone for a week. The whole plan made me furious—but I couldn't say anything. Intellectually, I knew I was being unreasonable. But emotionally, I did not want to stay home and be solely responsible for Shannon. I was worried about Joanna's stability and Big Mike's safety and my homies' illegal enterprises. I try to explain my rage, but I also tell Joanna that Mark and I have gone to therapy.

"I need to get Bullet to go with me. I really love therapy. I think it would help him to talk. He never tells me his feelings." Joanna is echoing what has been my mantra through two marriages and numerous relationships.

"Isn't he in the Building Positive Relationships class at Homeboy?" I ask her.

"I kicked him out. I didn't want him there. I think every woman should take that class alone. Without any men around. The men ruin it. They talk about themselves all the time. They should go away. We don't need the men there. We should be able to talk openly. Bullet can go to therapy with me, but I need a place just for women."

I remember the first consciousness-raising group I attended in the early 1970s and how men were banned from it. I tell Joanna I will call her the next day to see how she is doing, but when I call, her cell phone is disconnected. No one knows where she is.

A day later she calls. She is out in Chino, temporarily living at her aunt's house.

"Bullet came over to my apartment and we started fighting and he hit me," Joanna explains. "I can't take it anymore. I don't want him to know where I am. I told him I was going to Texas to visit some of my cousins. I just don't wanna see him."

Two months after this break, Joanna tells me that Little Marcos is sick. So sick that kidney surgery is scheduled for the first week in November. Joanna arranges for Marcos to be baptized at Dolores Mission Church, the tiny parish in East Los Angeles where Greg Boyle was once pastor. It is a heartbreaking ceremony. Her son looks so small and perishable, and Joanna is clearly terrified. It is the first and only time I have seen Joanna openly falling apart.

In my wildest dreams I could never imagine feeling close to someone like Joanna. But then again, there was a time when I could not imagine being a mother. Watching Joanna gently kiss the crown of her son's head, I think about how I would feel if Shannon were endangered. We are not bitches, we are mothers. My heart cracks open.

EIGHT

Poor Black Woman

According to a panel of experts at a forum at University
of California, Los Angeles, on Monday, America is just as
vulnerable to attack as it was on 9/11, with street gangs
funding terrorist groups and also draining resources from
law enforcement agencies working to head off future attacks.

—*New York Times*, May 23, 2007

Spending time with the homies and homegirls had brought a new dimension to my research. I was deeply involved in trying to figure out what interventions truly helped gang members. I was also invested in their lives. By early 2007 I had completed several evaluations and had been asked by noted civil rights activist and attorney Constance Rice to serve as one of a team of experts for the groundbreaking report she was writing on gangs in the city of Los Angeles. Connie keeps referring to me as a "gang anthropologist." And I want to be in the field—living with homies, learning more, filling the gaps in my knowledge. Because of this, I am in Nickerson Gardens with Saint, whose real name is Ronald, or Ronny, Dawson. Ronny grew up here, in a three-bedroom unit with twenty-nine other people.

"It was a lot of fun. My dad was gone and when I was four my mom got addicted to crack and my granny took custody of me. I don't know what happened with my granny—nine out of her ten kids were addicts—but she raised all the grandkids. I loved school and had great grades. I played every sport—football, basketball, swimming—up to Jordan High."

Ronny brags that he never missed a day of school because "I got a welfare lunch every day." The plastic tiles stamped "subsidized lunch" were all that stood between Ronny and starvation. "My granny was

poor. She never had enough money. Most times that lunch was my
only food."

Ronny tries to portray his childhood as one continuous house party.
But there is always deprivation. His life embodies the national statistic
showing that more than one-third of all African American children live
below the poverty line. When I ask if being poor bothered him, Ronny
thinks for a moment.

"It wasn't that I minded being poor; everyone was poor. I just hated
being poorer than anyone else in the neighborhood." But Ronny's family created a ready defense. They were the Marine Corps of the projects.
They took their liabilities—poverty and multiple children—and turned
them into strengths, organizing their own neighborhood, the Hillbilly
Bloods. But this also makes it impossible for Ronny to ever leave the
gang. I catch on immediately. They're not just his neighborhood—
they're his family. Literally. How is he going to leave that?

This sounds all too familiar. I was raised in a neighborhood that
was *My Big Fat Greek Wedding* cut with anxiety. Every action—real or
contemplated—was subjected to the litmus test of "What would the
Greek community say?" The infighting and rivalry and psychological
retaliation prepared me—in the most perverse way—for life with the
neighborhoods. This is in no way meant to minimize gang lethality—it
just means that underneath, we all get jumped into something that we're
not sure we can ever leave.

When I was young my family's propaganda maintained that there
was nothing better than being Greek. We went to church every Sunday,
not only for religion, but also for the sense of community. Our social
life was exclusive—we interacted with Greek American families. My
suburban neighborhood tract in Torrance, California, featured Greek
households on literally every block. On top of that, my father served on
the board of the directors and my mother sang in the choir of the Greek
Orthodox church conveniently located fifteen minutes away. We vaca-
tioned with Greek families—usually our cousins. My brothers and I even
went to Greek church camp. No aspect of our life remained Greek-free.
Our doctors, our dentists, our babysitters—everyone was Greek. And
the whole rationale for this existence was the expectation that we—my
brothers and I—would perpetuate this pattern into the next generation.
It was a gang. We had colors and a language and loyalty. And control.

It was all the same—whether you grow up in a neighborhood or in the Greek community. You would be secure and someone would have your back, but you would never know freedom or independence. You would never grow. Your wings were clipped in full view of the crowd.

I felt controlled from the moment I could walk. Of course, one of my childhood responses was to obey. But the other response was to run. I knew that I could not stay. I was going to suffocate. I was going to die. I had to get out of the gang.

I was good at escape. When I turned four years old, I was found on a street corner about a half mile from home, holding the hand of a friendly stranger, wearing a T-shirt that said I LOVE MY DADDY. I ran away from home, I ran away from Sunday school, I ran away from Greek school and the six-fingered, sadistic Greek instructor. But I always came back—first because I had to, then because I wanted to.

I grew up and out. But still, in unguarded moments, the cunning, indirect, and manipulative Greek girl would burst forth. I wanted my family and the Greek neighborhood. I wanted the warmth, the familiarity. I insisted on taking a family vacation with my brothers, their spouses, and their children, and I attempted to control everything, quietly, behind the scenes.

You just can't leave the gang.

As if listening in on my thoughts, Ronny declares, "We are not just Bloods, this *is* my blood. They are my family."

Ronny's family has also passed down a history of violence. He traces all of it to his father, who still checks in occasionally. "My daddy was never around all the time, he still isn't." In his family romance, Ronny's father juggled two wives and three sons, never living with one family full-time. But Ronny maintains, "My daddy loved my mama till she started doing crack. Then they fought. It's 'cuz she drove him crazy. He lost control and beat her. Then he left. He had his wife, my mama had crack, and I had my granny."

But his father's violence was not strictly domestic. There had been trouble in Louisiana, where his father killed a man and did time in prison. Ronny relates this story with nonchalance, adding that his father's other two sons—his half brothers—also murdered people during the Los Angeles gang wars of the mid-1980s.

"What happened to your brothers?" I ask.

"They're both dead," he says flatly. "I'm the only son my daddy has left."

"So you're the third generation of violence," I offer.

"Yeah, the cycle has gotta be broken." Ronny could truly go either way. He starts to talk about what went down two nights earlier, when the LAPD showed up at his auntie's house to arrest his cousin, Little Joey, for murder.

"What happened?" I ask.

"Little Joey went to West LA to see his girlfriend. He was in Crips territory and they cornered him. He had to shoot his way out. The cops got him."

"Does he have a lawyer?" I am already looking up numbers in my cell phone.

"Oh, he told them he did it."

"What?"

"Why are you surprised? He did it. So he told the cops. But I am thinkin' maybe he can get off on—whacha call it?—self-defense. He went there before to see that girl and some guys from the set told him, 'Don't come back or we gonna kill you.' I think he could say he did it because they were gonna kill him."

"One little problem," I snap. "He had a gun—that shows premeditation. And I'm sure he didn't buy the gun at Sears."

Ronny is unfazed by my sarcasm.

"You're right. Oh well. I guess he's gonna do time."

There is a resignation to Ronny that comes from years without. Without parents. Without money. Without anyone to take care of him. While I am thinking about this, we both see an eleven-year-old riding around on a bike and Ronny motions with his chin.

"That's me. You wanna know what I was like back in the day, look at this little homie, Darius."

Darius rides up to exchange greetings with Ronny, eyeing me suspiciously. Ronny responds with the same line he uses on everyone in the projects.

"That's Jorja, she's my godmother." Satisfied, Darius rides off and we walk over to a two-story unit and stand outside the security door— a heavy-duty screen made out of steel. The smell of marijuana comes wafting out. Ronny's cousins and friends are inside smoking a combination of bud and crack and God knows what else. When they see me through the grille they start joking, then invite us in.

"This yo' first time at Nickerson Gardens, little mama?"

"She's a cute little spinner, Saint. Mama, you been here before?" Ronny doesn't even have time to launch into introductions before I start talking and laughing with them. They offer me some of their spliff, but I decline.

"No, I was here before any of you were born. In the '70s and the '80s, I worked at Martin Luther King Hospital." I leave out the fact that most of the time I came to the projects I was there to pick up children for placement in the foster-care system.

"You was at Martin Luther King?" One homie is suddenly interested.

"Yeah. I loved it there."

"You saw me born! I came through there. I was the little baby with an Afro!" He is suddenly excited, high, and the air fills with laughter. He is choking on smoke, and Ronny and I walk him outside to breathe fresh air. As if on cue, a black-and-white pulls up and the police jump out of their car so rapidly they leave the doors open. They are running across the grass.

"It's the popo," I observe, and Ronny starts laughing.

"Yes it is. They gonna arrest someone," he adds. His prediction comes true while Darius rides by on his bike, watching carefully, collecting data. We all witness two men who look to be in their twenties being handcuffed and pushed into the back of the police car.

"They got Little Devon," Darius reports. "Little Devon is so stupid, he got hisself arrested by a rookie. What a dumbass."

The arresting officer looks up, walks over to where we are standing, and asks what we are doing. Darius's assessment is accurate; this is a rookie. I doubt the LAPD officer has even started shaving. He begins to give Darius and Ronny a hard time until he looks at me and pulls up short.

"Ma'am?" He is tentative.

"Yes?" I truly don't want to say a thing. I don't want to introduce myself. He is a rookie and this is South LA, but I don't want to take the one–in–a–million chance that he is going to recognize Mark's name. I am prepared to remarry my ex-husband on the spot and reclaim my old identity.

"May I ask what you are doing here?"

I want desperately to tell him, No you may not, this is wrong. But I tell him that I am a social worker meeting with my client. That suffices and he moves away. Ronny, meanwhile, starts complaining about the LAPD and their constant "fuckin' with everyone in the projects." This is not the friendly, easygoing Ronny—he morphs into angry-black-man mode. Destiny, his girlfriend, has warned me, "You gotta be careful with Ronny. You know he has four personalities at once." Right now I am getting a look at gangsta Ronny—Saint.

"It's not fair, it's not fuckin' fair," Ronny says, hitting the side of a building in frustration.

"I know, I know," I tell him.

"Shit, I gotta go. I gotta go talk to my homies about this."

Ronny takes off abruptly. I can't remember where I parked my car. Darius rides back by and I ask him to help me. I don't want to wander around alone.

"I need to find my car, can you—"

"Yo' ride is a Prius—yeah, I know where it is."

I had forgotten about hood intelligence. Darius leads me to the car. I give him five dollars and he rides away happily.

I go home that night, thinking about the LAPD. I don't say anything to Mark. I really don't want to deal with his reaction. I have also gone silent because we have been fighting constantly. It's not about gangs; it's about counterterrorism. It's clear that there is an insane amount of money being spent protecting Los Angeles from (drum roll here) ter-rorist activity. I am finding this all laughable—except for the fact that there has been what the LAPD likes to call mission creep. The war against terrorism has slowly started to include talk of the need to "fight urban terrorism in our communities." Increasingly Mark has been talk-ing to me in his "official business" tone of voice about terrorism on the streets and in the neighborhoods. It doesn't help that while I am driving home after Ronny has abandoned me, I hear Mark on the radio discuss-ing how terrorist organizations are raising funds by selling counterfeit purses at swap meets. He is about to be interviewed on PBS's *Frontline* by the correspondent Lowell Bergman, my longtime hero. I don't know whether to feel proud or angry or embarrassed.

"Hi, honey, I'm home from the swap meet," I snap in lieu of describing my day in Nickerson Gardens. "I think a terrorist just tried to sell me a counterfeit Prada bag." Mark ignores me as I continue. "But I'm not worried, 'cuz I heard what you said on the radio. I'm so relieved that this is what my tax dollars are being spent on."

"Y'know, you don't even know what you are talking about," Mark begins, with exaggerated patience. He has adopted the tone of a math teacher explaining division to the class idiot. "This is not a small thing. We are talking about millions of dollars being funneled into overseas accounts. This is what is financing terrorism across the globe."

I really think I am about to lose my mind. "You want to explain to me why it is so important to watch swap meets carefully, while patrols have been cut in East LA and there was a big shootout in Nickerson Gardens two days ago?"

"Here we go," he mutters. *"Poor black woman."*

This phrase had its origins in a major fight that was still a sore spot for Mark and me. A month earlier, I had arrived home drained after spending time with the family of a young homie who had been shot near Athens Park in South Los Angeles. It was unclear whether he was an active member of any neighborhood. All that was certain was that a sixteen-year-old boy would be facing the rest of his life paralyzed from the chest down. I wanted nothing more than to curl up in my husband's arms and cry. Instead, I was greeted by the sight of Mark hurriedly making arrangements to leave the house.

"You can order something from Emilio's," he instructed. "They'll deliver. Shannon already circled what she wants on the menu." All I saw was the uniform and all I heard was his officious tone, so I started screaming:

"Where are you going?"

"Will you control yourself?" he whispered. "I don't want Shannon to hear you yelling." This was all I needed to hear to raise my voice another decibel level.

"Stop telling me what to do! Stop being so controlling!" Then in a triumph of intellectual reasoning, I added, "You're acting like an *asshole!"*

"Calm down." This was the "license and registration voice" I knew so well. In the past, Mark had told me stories of soccer moms swearing a blue streak when he stopped them for speeding. He would ignore the profanity while adding charges to their citation. As the women screamed he would write, "Driving without a seat belt," and "Brake light out," and "License expired"—all visible offenses that would add to the ticket's grand total. He was maintaining the same pleasant tone with me while I screamed like a banshee.

"Look, I'm not supposed to tell you this," he began.

Here we go, I thought. I wasn't fooled. This was the sweetener. All cops used this with wives and family. You were let in on some important, inside information—so inside it was probably just being reported on the local news—to help you understand why your husband, boyfriend, father was running out the door. When Mark and I were newlyweds, the long-suffering wife of the chief of operations advised me, "Honey, get used to being alone. They're gone all the time." I had absolutely no intention of accepting this reality.

"Just tell me where you are going," I repeated, now using a normal tone of voice.

"There's a guy who killed two cops in Colorado and they think they've got him trapped in Long Beach. So the LAPD has set up a command post along with the Long Beach PD to get him. We've got thirty men on overtime and I've got to get there as soon as possible." That only enraged me further.

"You don't have to go to this."

"*No?* This is my job." Mark was just starting to show signs of agitation.

"No it's not. Your job is to run the counterterrorism bureau and babysit John Miller. Please just tell me how someone who may or may not have killed two cops in Colorado relates to counterterrorism. Please. Tell. Me."

The mention of John Miller was not good. By tacit agreement, Mark and I stayed away from the subject of the man who was, on paper, Mark's superior. Early in his tenure, Bill Bratton had brought along Miller—who was his best friend—to head up the counterterrorism bureau, which had been designed and implemented by Mark. Bratton frequently pointed out Miller's wide-ranging experience, which included a stint working as

Barbara Walters's co-anchor on *20/20*. This did not exactly endear him to the troops. But Miller was a good guy who constantly sought Mark's counsel and acted responsibly, given his limited law enforcement experience. Despite all this, the favoritism evident in his appointment was a particularly vicious thorn in Mark's side and a topic I generally avoided. But not tonight. Mark looked at me sharply.

"Look, you know, it's about the murder of a cop. I've got to go."

"You're all a bunch of maudlin idiots. You're gonna spend a lot of taxpayer money on overtime hunting this guy down because he killed a cop. Meanwhile, a mother was shot and killed in South Los Angeles last weekend. Was there one hour of overtime spent on her? No. Because it was a poor black woman. You don't fucking care."

"Look, I've gotta go." He walked over to kiss me good-bye and I ignored him.

After he left, Shannon came down wide-eyed. "You and Daddy were having a fight?" She was half-questioning and half-observing.

"Yes, and I don't want you to get scared. We were just fighting over the way the LAPD investigates certain cases with lots of energy and ignores other cases—particularly those involving poor people." The ongoing brainwashing of my only child diverted me from my fury. Mark rarely interfered in the education of Shannon; for that I was grateful. When I had come into her life, she was attending a summer camp run by Calvary, a fundamentalist Christian group. This was a desperate choice, made at the last minute, after Mark was unable to enroll Shannon in a school-sponsored summer camp. I had known Shannon precisely two weeks when she announced, "I have something wonderful to tell you." I narcissistically waited for the declaration that she would love for me to be her new mommy. Instead I had to check my facial expression when Shannon continued, "I found Jesus." It took all my self-control not to ask, "Was he lost?" and smile while thinking, *I have gotta get to work on this kid.*

That had all changed. Recently Shannon had arrived home from school and announced that it was important to be honest and say she was an atheist because people who were agnostic were just afraid to tell the truth. She also believed George W. Bush was probably the Antichrist. But right now she was focused on my anger at Mark.

"Do you mean how Daddy doesn't care about gangs and you do?"

Shannon was well aware of the never-ending argument about how much money was spent on counterterrorism and how little was spent on gangs. While Mark was tasked with spending $50 million in government grants, negotiating how money would be allocated—City Fire, Information Technology, Emergency Response—I was working with community-based organizations that were lucky to get by on $100,000 a year. Greg Boyle did not receive *any* government funding at Homeboy Industries to support his work on job training, tattoo removal, mental health services, drug counseling, and education. From that night onward, whenever we argued about gangs and counterterrorism, Mark would try to end the conflict by joking, "Poor black woman."

"Dad doesn't always understand what people go through—especially people in Watts. They are poor and they commit crimes. That's wrong, but it doesn't make them terrorists."

"When we went to the Watts Towers you told me lots of people there weren't gang members. Is that what you mean by 'poor black woman'?"

I was happy to settle for this small victory. Shannon and I moved on to the take-out menu.

A few days after the swap-meet argument, however, Mark and I continue to argue.

"It's not 'poor black woman' and you know it," I say. "It's the inequity of the whole situation. You should have been with me two days ago with Ronny. The LAPD is just hassling people in Nickerson Gardens for nothing. And they don't even understand the gang problem."

It only increases my fury when Mark responds, "Look, the gang problem has been around for a long time. It's not gonna get better—and after 9/11 we need people to feel safe."

"It's wrong," I insist. "People are *not* afraid of terrorists. They're afraid of getting killed. They're afraid of Florencia and the Rollin 60s. In the hood, the Twin Towers don't mean the World Trade Center. They mean the county jail. That's what's real—18th Street is real." But I know we are arguing about money and what Mark had said on the radio and the emphasis on counterterrorism because we really don't want to talk about the elephant in the room.

Mark is afraid.

And, even though I didn't want to admit it, so am I.

It had all started about a week earlier, when a gang interventionist named Mario Corona told me, "There's a rumor on the street your husband is LAPD."

I never volunteered that I was married to a cop, nor did I hide it. I also knew that street intelligence on outsiders was pretty limited. The neighborhoods knew about one another and who came into their territory, but they knew very little about people in the outside world. I was never involved in any arrest. I kept telling people nothing was going to happen to me.

But Kenny Green had told me the story of Gil Becerra, and it had an impact. Gil Becerra had functioned as a gang interventionist. He had impressive bona fides—he had been in the US military and on the streets. None of this had saved him from what occurred when he got in between two rival gangs, trying to negotiate a truce. He was beaten and left for dead. He sustained multiple broken bones and now had permanent back injuries that made it painful for him to walk or stand up straight. But for me, the critical issue lay in the phrase "gotten between two rival gangs."

I was convinced that as long as I didn't plant myself between warring neighborhoods or interfere in gang activity, I would be okay. I also was careful never to go into a violent situation without someone from a neighborhood along for the ride. When Mario told me about the rumor, I told him I was always careful. He listened patiently but warned me again.

"You gotta be careful. If these guys find out that you're married to someone who is a cop, they'll kill you."

Mario

> Everyone belongs to a gang—the LAPD and the Bloods and
> Crips and even the fuckin' Boy Scouts, there's no differences.
> We all the same.
>
> —Darius

For several weeks Mark and I live in a state of détente. We carefully avoid talking about gangs or counterterrorism. We celebrate Shannon's twelfth birthday. It rains incessantly, but when the weather clears I announce I am going out to do some interviews. I've started to compile a series of gang life histories and I don't want to lose any of the new connections I've made. Mark asks me to reconsider.

"I'm concerned about you going out at night. There's been a spike in violence," he begins.

"No. You said you didn't want to stop me from the work I love." I knew that whenever people from the neighborhoods had been cooped up because of bad weather, there was invariably a frisson of gang activity when clear skies returned. I just wanted to see what was going on.

"You leave me when you go to work, now it's my turn," I say on my way out to meet up with Mario Corona, the gang member turned social worker who was part of the staff at the San Fernando Valley grassroots agency Communities in Schools.

CIS operated out of a small building with cinder block walls that looked like it would not survive the next major earthquake. Located in Pacoima, it was a DMZ right in the middle of a hotbed of drug dealing and gang activity, staffed with outreach workers who possessed long histories in the neighborhoods and devoted themselves to gang prevention and intervention. It was headed up by Don Quixote reincarnated as a kickboxer, Blinky Rodriguez, and a social worker turned Sancho Panza, Bobby Arias. Together they traveled from City Hall to school sites, preaching the gospel of leaving the gang. Blinky, in particular, could walk the talk. He had one son locked up in Corcoran State Prison and another son dead, victim of a drive-by shooting.

"I've paid dearly—with my life—for the gang problem," Blinky would insist. "I remember going with my wife to see my son, lying on a slab in the morgue. And I can't even talk to my other son, he's in solitary confinement."

That Blinky had experienced a Job-like set of sorrows, no one could dispute. However, there were rumors about Blinky—that he was connected, that he was part of the Mexican Mafia, that he collected taxes— a street-level form of extortion. "If those rumors are true," he sighed, "then why am I always so fucking poor?"

Still, despite all the second-guessing, I felt grateful to Blinky and Bobby because they had brought me to the party. Early in 2002 I had conducted an evaluation of the CIS intervention program, and while there was room for improvement, the outcomes were positive—the areas where they worked showed reduced rates of crime. After the evaluation, we continued our relationship: they included me at meetings and connected me with gangbangers all over the San Fernando Valley.

Blinky had credibility with the neighborhoods in and around Pacoima. In the aftermath of his son's death, he sat down with representatives of roughly seventy-five gangs in the San Fernando Valley and brokered a gang "truce." One of the moving forces behind the negotiation was a shot caller representing the Pacoima Criminals, Mario Corona. The truce was credited with reducing gang homicides in the Valley. More importantly, Blinky had acquired a powerful new ally— Deputy Chief Ron Bergmann of the LAPD.

The agency that was Bergmann's favorite "crime-fighting tool" operated in a constant state of chaos. There was after-school tutoring and case management. Then there were the former gangbangers and *veteranos*, who worked to stop retaliation and gang violence. These street interventionists planned funerals for gang victims and joined forces with the mothers of children who had been killed in drive-by shootings, chanting, "No more bullets flying! No more babies dying!" After a homicide, Blinky would counsel grieving family members not to retaliate while arranging for a burial plot to be donated. This occurred at a high pitch, in crisis mode, all at once. And then there was Mario.

Mario Corona stood out in the fray. He was tall, soft-spoken, and possessed an almost Castilian courtliness. Blinky suggested we work together. I showed up at CIS braced to meet a rough-and-ready gang member and instead, in walked Sir Galahad. He was my tour guide through the barrios of the San Fernando Valley, a place I knew nothing about. South and East Los Angeles were notorious for gang activity. But there was a whole other world of violence in the San Fernando Valley that buzzed on pretty much below the radar.

Mario spent several days driving with me through "the Valley." Here, the gang problem wasn't located in the projects as it had been in South and East LA. Instead, there were huge apartment complexes, low rent and government subsidized, that housed different neighborhoods, serving as a staging area for criminal activity. Mario took me to talk to the homies kicking it at Parthenia Park, alerting me to the fact that there were sixty-eight apartment complexes bordering the park, many of them sheltering gang families and the homies who drifted from unit to unit. I quickly learned that every neighborhood provided housing for its homies; gang members didn't end up in homeless shelters. Instead, if they were careful to maintain ties, they could always ask for help from their homies, in exchange for work. This quid pro quo ensured that there would always be lifeblood serving the neighborhoods. I learned this not from the leadership of gangs, but from hanging around with the foot soldiers—the individuals on the lower rungs of the totem pole, angling to get ahead.

Parks were often the site of wars between the rival gangs or between the police and the homies. But, at other times, they also provided a respite from the action. "It's important for kids to have a park so they won't run the streets," Mario explained. "When I was Big Spider—part of my neighborhood—I spent all the time on the streets. I got jumped in to the Pacoima Criminals when I was thirteen, and I never looked back."

He was the eldest son in a single-parent family, with a mother who worked all the time. His story sounded achingly familiar.

"I never knew my dad, he was always incarcerated," Mario told me. I had quickly learned that "incarcerated" could mean three days in county jail or a life sentence in Folsom. No one talked about being in prison or in custody. No one differentiated a local lockup from a maximum-security prison. Instead, this five-syllable word covered everything. I had also learned that incarceration and drug abuse were the two major reasons homies did not know their fathers—and Mario was no exception.

"I came here illegally when I was three," Mario told me. "I didn't have papers, and no one cared. I went to school and I was a really smart kid. I got good grades on IQ tests and all that. But I was always running the streets after school. My dad wasn't around—he was back in Mexico—and it was just my moms and me. Everyone kept warning her that I was in a gang. She didn't believe it." He admitted to me that he was identified as a leader within the Criminals. Involved in violent crime early on, he made the rounds through the juvenile halls and probation camps of the LA County system. Eventually he graduated to Los Angeles County Jail—CJ, as he and every other homie referred to it. This story was becoming fairly typical. I was wondering if I was going to meet any gangbanger—past or present—unacquainted with the juvenile-justice system.

This was exactly what juvenile-justice advocate Carol Biondi had taught me when she explained about camp-bangers. "You can't imagine the damage the camps do," she insisted. "The staff is so busy filling out paperwork, they don't spend time with the kids. In the camps at Challenger, they have a fight club 24/7." Mario was no exception: the camps were his training ground.

"I was just doin' what I had to do," he offered, a terse explanation for a youthful life of crime.

I knew he wasn't telling me everything he did coming up through the neighborhood. Instead, he showed me pictures that were strictly gangsta. The shaved head, the tattoos, the look of fierce combativeness. I knew there was more.

"But through all that, I thought, I wanted to go back to school. I really did. But I had to be straight to go to school. I couldn't kick it with the neighborhood. I thought, well I'll just try one class."

Mario was intelligent and charming. I could just imagine teachers responding to him. He soon confirmed my theory, explaining, "Teachers liked me." He negotiated the long slow climb, through community college and a bachelor's degree at Cal State Northridge. There were the inexplicable detours.

"I never missed class. Never. Except for once. There was a knock on my door and I answered and the next thing, I felt heat."

He had been shot at close range in the side of the neck; he showed me the scar. When I asked Mario why, he said, "I don't know. I don't fucking know. All I know was I saw the light. You know how they tell you when you're gonna die you see the light. I saw the light but I said, I'm not coming."

This was a much-rehearsed and repeated line of Mario's. It was invariably met with gasps from the audience when he spoke in public. Strangely, it never had the desired effect on me; it always felt a little too staged, too practiced. I did not find this part of his story authentic. I knew he was leaving things out.

What Mario did not leave out of the story was his next stop after finishing college: graduate school at USC, where he earned a master's degree in social work and became the poster child of the university, which featured his grinning face on its website. "You too can make a difference," read the tagline over his biography. Mario was a winner. He was living proof that things could turn out more than okay. He was twenty-eight years old, at the top of his game. He hadn't simply aged out of the gang; he had left voluntarily, a shot caller walking away from the neighborhood. He joined CIS full-time, with a fancy title, director of job development, and a small salary paid out of a grant from the US Department of Labor. But his passion was working with youth, and we spent several hours driving around the neighborhoods of Pacoima.

After spending several hours with Mario, I got in at about 3:00 a.m. Mark was waiting up for me. We both wanted to stop fighting—so we agreed to disagree. Instead, we had reached a truce of our own, and in the days that followed, I worked hard to preserve the balance between us. On the phone we talked about what we were going to have for dinner, not what Crips or Bloods or the Avenues were up to. And we were typical parents, worried about Shannon's school performance and academic demands. At Paul Revere Middle School, she possessed an aversion to math and a strong facility for English and social studies. The DNA might have been absent, but she was turning out to be my daughter in so many ways. A few weeks into the spring semester, her English teacher passed out a class assignment for a term paper that would include a research question, a literature review, and interviews with two people. I was furious.

"She's only in eighth grade for God's sake," I complained to Mark. "She will burn out at the rate she's going."

Mark was much calmer about the project until Shannon reported her research question: "Why do people join gangs?"

"No," he said very quietly.

"I'm so proud of you, I'm so happy you want to do this. That's a great question!" I ignored Mark completely and threw my arms around Shannon.

"No. No, no, no. Think of another question," Mark said.

"Let me talk to Dad, sweetheart, and then the three of us can discuss this."

Shannon ignored both of us and continued blithely on. "I want to interview Mom and I want to interview a gang member." After her announcement she went happily up to her room, taking the stairs two at a time while Mark glared at me.

"She can't do this. She can't. It's not safe. It's not even safe for you. You're gonna drag her to go see someone from 18th Street or MS-13 or the Rollin 60s and the next thing I know, you'll both be dead."

"What are you talking about?" I wasn't even angry. I was shocked.

"All right. I know I'm overreacting. And I know you won't do that. And I know I can't stop you from going out. But you're an adult and she's a child and she can find another research question. She doesn't need to go and talk to any gang members. It doesn't need to involve danger. I don't care. I don't want her doing this. She's trying to figure out what you're doing, she's trying to understand it, and this isn't the right way. Something could happen to her or to you while you're with her."

I was actually pretty impressed with Mark's psychological insight. I knew Shannon wanted to comprehend what was driving me out—night or day—into situations that involved weapons and bullets and drugs and rap music and other strange, exotic, and unnamable dangers. But I was having a hard time understanding my husband's terror.

"I'm glad you understand about Shannon. But I want to know, what is frightening you?"

"You know what I'm afraid of." Mark looked downward, studying the floor carefully.

I was angry and frustrated and started to cry. "I don't understand, I don't. All I feel is you trying to control me."

"I've lost everyone in my life. I'm afraid I'm gonna lose you."

I had never felt so unutterably a marital failure as at that moment. While I had empathy to spare for the homies in the neighborhood, I had failed to remember my husband's terror. It was thirty-four years in the LAPD combined with a lifetime of loss.

The first time Mark and I went out, we exchanged the G-rated versions of our personal histories. I laughingly told him I had been married and gone through "the worst divorce in human history." I should have kept my mouth shut. Instead I learned, elliptically, that he had been married more than once. A month later he came to my house for dinner and told me the more detailed version of his personal history. His first wife had died after twelve years of alcoholism and a terminal case of cirrhosis of the liver. His second marriage, a rebound after the devastation of the first, ended after two brief years. His third marriage, to Shannon's mother, had been a happy union until a lump on his wife's collarbone turned out to be a rare form of cancer that killed her within six months.

And still this was not the end.

Six months into our relationship, Mark and I were talking on the phone one night when I asked him about his mother. These questions were pretty de rigueur for me, the child of psychotherapy. "She died when I was fourteen," he told me.

"What happened?"

"She died from burns and smoke inhalation. She had an accident and burned to death."

"I'm so sorry. How did it happen?"

"I'll tell you another time."

What could be so disturbing that he'd have this much trouble talking about it? I wondered. I was the orphan of a man who had died of cancer. There were only so many ways Mark's mother could have burned to death. A kitchen fire? An auto accident? Trapped in a burning building? Perhaps there had been a fire and Mark had escaped while his mother had not. The real answer was more disturbing than any of the scenes that ran through my head. A few months later, sitting on my patio, Mark explained.

"My mother was an alcoholic. She drank until she went to sleep. She started in the morning and drank all day. Usually she was asleep by the time we got home from school. But one day I was home with my sister and another girl. We were playing records in my sister's room. I noticed something strange about the light coming from underneath my mother's door. It wasn't right. I opened her door and saw that she was on fire. She was drunk and fell asleep while she was smoking. The cigarette dropped and caught her nightgown on fire."

He paused for a moment.

"That was when they didn't worry about whether or not nightgowns were flammable," Mark continued quietly.

"I ran in and tried to save her. I kept trying to put the fire out and hold her and her skin started coming off on my hands. My sister called for an ambulance and finally one got to the house. I had to ride in the ambulance, sitting next to her body. They took her to the hospital and she died a few days later. I couldn't save her."

I was ready to start arguing with Mark about Shannon going to meet with gang members when I remembered this conversation. It didn't take a rocket scientist to understand why Mark tried so hard to control me. And Shannon. It was time for me to stop. Stop being so defiant. Stop being so insensitive. Start seeing that Mark was scared too. He had lost so much already. He didn't want to lose Shannon and he didn't want to lose me.

"Honey, I know you're afraid. And I *am not* going to let anything happen to Shannon. I would never take her anywhere dangerous. And I would never take her out at night. We'll go after school to CIS and she can talk to Mario. He's a social worker, he's the real deal. He was in a gang but it was fifteen years ago. He's perfect. She'll probably fall in love with him. You can even come with us."

It was the last line that got him. I *never* included Mark. That was just bad juju all around. But after my offer, Mark visibly relaxed.

"I don't need to go."

"Look, you can go to CIS if you go during the day . . ." He caught himself. "I mean if you're taking Shannon—not you, you alone . . ."

"I know, sweetheart." I smiled.

"Just during the day. I don't want her there when the sun goes down."

"You got it."

A week later we drove out to CIS. I stayed in the lobby talking to Blinky while Shannon interviewed Mario behind closed doors. An hour later she emerged with eyes as big as saucers. She was enthralled.

"I told her she was wearing the wrong colors. She's wearing her mama's colors, she should be wearing my colors, USC." Mario hugged me and whispered, "She's really special." He promised he would be at my class at UCLA to talk about his life in two weeks. I felt like I had been delivered.

Being brought up in a Greek household, the notion of an evil eye was consumed along with my morning oatmeal. You should always be careful—according to the evil eye—because if you don't remember it when things are good, *something bad will happen.* I forgot about all of this once I started spending time with gang members. There was no need for the evil eye—these gangbangers had it encoded in their DNA. If that weren't enough, sometimes it appeared on their tattoos. You didn't have to worry about something bad happening—it always *was* happening. Only good outcomes shocked gang members—when someone went to a party and didn't get shot, when someone actually got and kept a job. When someone managed to kick drugs. But I had reason to believe. To forget about the evil eye. Things really were better. Mark and I had reached a new level of closeness. And Shannon had begun to understand my work.

Mario offered Shannon a portrait of redemption. He talked to her about his childhood and teenage years and how his life had changed. A week later she came home from school and reported, "The teacher was so interested in my paper. She asked me all kinds of questions. She said it was great."

I was full of myself.

Shannon and Mario developed an ongoing relationship via e-mail. He advised her about schools. She was a shy girl and felt comforted by this smart, sensitive young man who responded to her appropriately, like a big brother. Mario appeared and spoke to my class—four hundred undergraduates listened to him, so silent you could hear their breathing. We continued working together, interviewing homies throughout the gang-infested sections of Pacoima.

"I don't mind your going out with Mario; he's smart—although there's something about him, I can't put a finger on it," Mark told me.

I laughed but asked what he meant.

"Something just goes off inside of me—call it cop's intuition." Still, I went to meet Mario about an hour after that discussion and Mark packed me a snack. I shared most of it with Mario until we stopped to talk with three young homies, all at the edge of thirteen kicking it on a street corner, outside Section 8 housing. It was eleven at night. They should have been home asleep and instead they were smoking bud and hanging out.

"Hey, Spider," they called out to Mario.

Mario and I got out of the car.

"This is my homegirl, Jorja. I call her Mama because she's got a little girl. She's helping out at CIS. She wanted to talk with you."

It was heartbreaking. The three of them had no parents, no family to speak of. One lived with a foster mother, one lived with his sister, one lived with his mother, who "isn't home all the time. She do drugs." Who cared for them? This was the cartoon of gang activity. I kept hearing Greg Boyle's voice in my ear: "Kids who join a gang aren't running toward something. They are running away from something."

"Did you go to school today?" Mario asked.

The three heads all hung down.

"No, man, no." The three were in middle school. It was unclear when they had last gone.

"We gotta do something about it. How 'bout we all go out and get something to eat and we talk about you goin' back to school?" Mario asked kindly. The five of us trooped off to Denny's, and the three boys attacked the Grand Slam specials as if consuming their last meal on earth.

There were many nights like this with Mario, who worked far beyond his hours and his job description. His official work was to try to teach gangbangers "job skills." But, in fact, he was always on lookout in the community, watching for the youngsters in danger of nosing over the line. He sometimes called to talk with me about DCFS and how to keep the kids out of the system. It was a never-ending nightmare that we shared. I felt comforted that he was out there and got used to phone calls from him at all hours of the day and night. Most of the time the news was bad. However, in late January he had left a message, excited. The security detail at the Academy Awards had contacted him. They wanted him to train kids to work as "stagehands" behind the scenes. "I'm gonna train some of my homies, Mama," he told me. "Show them a different life." The local paper got hold of the news and decided to run a human-interest story on Mario.

Still, there were things about Mario that did not add up. Mark started laughing when I told him Mario was getting ready to buy a house. "Oh yeah, that's what a social worker can afford on $2,000 a month," he observed.

"But it's in Pacoima, for God's sake," I told Mark. "Not Encino or Sherman Oaks."

And then there was the Mercedes that he drove. But that too was easy to explain. It was an old sedan, a diesel, dug up from a used-car lot for $3,500. Finally a former student who was now a USC professor, Annalisa Enrile, called to tell me that Mario was running a club in Mexico. "It's a real bangin' club, Jorja," she laughed. "We should go down to Baja and check it out." I was so preoccupied trying to figure out what I could say to make this fly with Mark that I forgot to ask how a gang interventionist was buying a house, driving a Mercedes, running a club, and planning to go to law school. It didn't add up, but I wasn't working my mental calculator until I got the call.

The call invariably comes on a Friday night or over a weekend or right before vacation. The call never comes during business hours. This time was no different. The voice mail was time-stamped 3:00 a.m. and the message came from Bobby Arias. "Call me," he said tersely. "It's about Mario."

There was a whole world contained in those five words and it was not good. It was either going to be guns or drugs. There was little else to fuck things up in the neighborhoods. Someone was shot, someone OD'd, or someone had been caught dealing. I called Bobby back and when I heard the tightness in his voice I waited for death.

"I want you to hear this before it hits the news," Bobby warned.

"Oh God." I braced myself.

"Mario's been arrested."

This was when all the fragments of Mario's life pulled together. He was arrested on suspicion of possessing a pound of methamphetamine—obviously not for use but for profit. The meth was found taped to his chest, underneath his clothes. The surrounding information was even more disturbing. None of this had happened in the darkness of night. Instead, Mario was arrested on a sunny afternoon, a little before three. Joe Curreri was the LAPD captain who announced the bust, adding that Mario had long been under suspicion.

I thought back to my interview with Joe Curreri over a year before. After calling Bobby, I turned to Mark, who was watching the replay of the arrest announcement on the local morning news. The last frames showed Mario leaving the police station, having posted bail.

"I guess your friend Joe Curreri is happy," I said ruefully.

"Come on, sweetheart," Mark cajoled me. "Did you look at the charge? Suspicion of transportation of narcotics. For God's sake, that's not a small thing. He's a drug dealer. He ruins people's lives. I felt it—there was something about him."

I thought about this. Mark knew a lot more than I did. He had been assigned to narcotics for several years and successfully worked under-cover—posing as a drug dealer. I laughed when he told me this, until he showed me his mug shots from his "arrest"—his all-American looks transformed with hair grown to his shoulders and a Fu Manchu mustache and beard.

"I guess I'm just worried. And I don't want this to bounce back on all the good people who work so hard," I admitted. I was listening carefully to the news report. I knew there was no one who would help Mario or Blinky or Bobby. Ron Bergmann had retired a few months before, leaving CIS without its greatest defender.

"Listen to Curreri. He has already tried Mario and convicted him. He appears to have forgotten about—what's that pesky little thing the LAPD loves so much—the Bill of Rights?"

Mark shrugged and listened as the report continued that Mario had been under surveillance for more than six months.

On Monday, there was more news involving Michel Moore, the new deputy chief of Valley Bureau. Moore was not a favorite around our house. With Bergmann gone, the LAPD rumor mill had predicted that Mark would finally, deservedly be promoted to deputy chief, taking over command of the Valley. Instead, the position had gone to this rather brash commander while Mark languished in the counterterrorism bureau, watching over John Miller. Moore had been on the job a few months when Mario was arrested. After he bailed out, an informant had revealed that Mario had allegedly been part of a transglobal drug-distribution network. Evidently, the rumored ties to the Mexican Mafia did not prevent Moore from calling Blinky and asking him to convince Mario to turn himself in to the LAPD. Blinky put a call in to Mario, who resisted, complained, and then acquiesced. Blinky drove him over to Valley Station to be booked on new, even more serious, charges. He remained in custody, bail pending.

And there I was looking like an idiot—the role model I had introduced my daughter to, in jail. Mark had figured it out. And once I thought about it, I knew Mario was guilty. While I recognized that Mario was smart, I had forgotten that the neighborhoods recognized talent.

Mario was gifted—and people responded to that. Whether it was the barrio or USC or gang intervention, Mario had the golden touch. And when he talked about changing his life, you wanted to believe. But in rewinding the story and listening to his words, it is unclear just exactly when Mario started to change or why. Mario insisted, "I had adults who helped me, especially teachers." In the human-interest story that was his life, there was always a former professor willing to comment about his brightness, that "something special," the spark in him. But how on earth did he get better? I was a good teacher and earned wonderful evaluations, but I knew a few hours in a classroom and the ministrations of a caring instructor were never enough to change someone's life. There had to be something more.

And now the authenticity of Mario's change was murky. It was all lost in the confusion of his arrest and the news of his possible deportation. No one wanted to touch him with a ten-foot pole. Once in custody, the police had tossed his house and found a 9 mm handgun, not registered. This was added to the case against him. In court, Mario entered a plea of no contest to two major charges: transportation of a controlled substance and being a convicted felon in possession of a firearm. He was sentenced to nearly three years—thirty-two months—in prison; his deportation remained open to negotiation.

All of this left me shaken—and angry. It now seemed like a miracle of good timing that I had agreed to work as the gang policy advisor for the mayor of Los Angeles. I had been recruited by Maurice Suh, the brilliant and enterprising attorney who was deputy mayor of public safety. Maurice was so enterprising that while I was moving into City Hall and taking the photo for my official ID, he announced he was resigning his position and going back to private practice. "I've got school tuition for three kids," he told me. It was a late night and his City Hall office was crammed with packing boxes. "Watch out," he told me. "Everyone here is venal, corrupt and venal."

Just where do you think you are, Sparky? I remember thinking as I listened to Maurice. He was working for a politician—Mayor Antonio Villaraigosa—who was being described as a potential vice presidential running mate if Hillary Clinton won the Democratic nomination for president. He abandoned me with one final admonition: "Watch your back. They'll throw you to the wolves first."

Thank you very much, Maurice. Still, maybe I was better off working with policymakers. Maybe I could help people more by working to change laws and create programs. Maybe it was time to stop running the streets. And then came my first assignment: figure out how the mayor could distance himself, as far as possible, from Mario Corona. *Join the club*, I thought to myself. There was a photograph of Mayor Villaraigosa with a group of gang interventionists, including Mario, on the mayor's website. I suggested that it be removed, as soon as possible. USC had set the bar pretty high; the university had erased all traces of Mario from its website two hours after the press release concerning his arrest. Still, dealing with the Mayor's Office was nothing compared to what I had to face at home. Mark was smug, but I tried to ignore that. How was I going to tell Shannon?

At dinner we began our nightly sharing. When I first came on the scene, upset at the non-existent level of conversation in the Leap household, I demanded that everyone bring a share to dinner at night—something interesting, something new, something they learned. It could not be a work report or a test score. That night my share was Mario.

"I have something to tell you that is very sad and frustrating," I began.

Mark kept eating while Shannon looked curious.

"The LAPD stopped Mario and they found him with drugs. He wasn't using. He had a lot of methamphetamine—"

"Crystal meth," Mark helpfully supplied. I glared at him.

"He had a lot of meth on him. He was getting ready to sell it."

The room was silent.

"My Mario?" Shannon asked, already knowing the answer. She was trying not to cry.

"Yes, sweetheart."

"What's gonna happen to him?"

"Well, he's going to prison. And they are trying to figure out whether or not to send him back to Mexico."

I had already offered Shannon a sort of verbal primer on immigration when I explained that Mario was here on a visa, that he was legal but not a citizen.

"Do you think he did it?"

I knew in my bones he had done it. That was the answer to the house and the car and the $100,000 student-loans payoff. But I was not going to be responsible for fostering my daughter's cynicism. The world would take care of that.

"I don't know, sweetheart. It doesn't look good. But this is America and—George Bush notwithstanding—you are innocent until proven guilty."

Mark rolled his eyes.

And then Shannon asked, "Can I write him?"

TEN

Fear Rules over Love

My hood is my family and my family is my hood.
—Ronny Dawson

Events with Mario leave me shaken. A week later, Ronny calls and apologizes for abandoning me that day that now feels like it took place a million years ago. The afternoon he left to find his homies, he was picked up in an LAPD gang sweep and spent a week in county jail. He asks me if we can get together. I may be working for the mayor, but I am still moonlighting in the neighborhoods. I meet him the next night.

"When did you get started with the neighborhood?" I ask.

"In middle school," he begins. "I wandered into doin' stuff." Ronny is calm and thoughtful.

"I guess it was the stuff I did after school that got me in trouble—like fights, bein' the lookout, informin' people where the police were at, and so I was put up into the Bounty Hunter Bloods. And y'know it was easy, 'cuz no one at home was payin' attention. It was nothin' but dysfunction and I saw a lot of violence. So I got violent." The words skate over a frozen pond of trauma. When Ronny was nine years old, a shooter from the Crips killed his favorite cousin, Anthony.

"He was special, my cousin. He wasn't in the neighborhood. He was goin' on to college. But he was part of my family. So they killed him. This is when I started learnin' about the rivalry between the Bloods and Crips. I guess that was when I first really felt pain in my life—Anthony was only sixteen when he was gunned down. Then three years later my granny died—so from nine to thirteen—those years was really rough for me. And my daddy wasn't around."

"But who were your role models? Who helped you learn to be a man?"

"I admired people, growin' up, and some of them were dope dealers. Some of them were killers and gangsters, but they all had this aura, this persona about them, and I would think, Damn, I wanna be like that when I grow up. But I never wanted to be a shot caller, I didn't wanna kill anyone, that was not one of my goals, I just wanted to be respected and liked by the girls."

After his granny died, his older sister assumed custody of Ronny, but she was no match for the teenage boy. Ronny's first arrest had already occurred when he was ten years old, and he was constantly in trouble from that point on. He makes no excuses.

"I was responsible for my troubles. My sister was young. She trusted me to be at home and take care of her kids and my sisters by myself. I learned to always look out for them.

"While I was with the kids, my older cousins would come by and sell drugs out of her place. I helped them. That jumpstarted me—when I was fourteen, I started sellin' drugs myself. I already had a good reputation in the neighborhood and I was up for helpin' out the homies. Gettin' money was the icing on the cake. I still participated in violent stuff. From fourteen to eighteen, I was gettin' shot at a lot—I got wounded, really bad, for the first time when I was sixteen when I came home from my basketball game and cut through the wrong neighborhood." At fourteen Ronny went to probation camp for the first time.

"When I went to camp I saw my enemies. A lot of the dudes were big, grown men laughin' and tellin' me, 'We're not gonna fuck you up, little nigga. We're gonna give you a pass.'" But his next trip to camp, at fifteen, marked a change.

"The emotional standpoint hit me harder. Now I was thinkin' about what I was doin', what kind of role model I was—I was thinkin' about my little cousins and nephews—how do I look to them? I knew I had to get out and make somethin' of myself."

"Were you changing?" I ask.

"No, I was maturin'." It's a sophisticated nuance, and I wonder how far Ronny would have gone if he had been emotionally supported and educated. As if reading my mind, Ronny continues.

"After I got out, I started goin' to school. I got off probation for the first time—it took me a minute to get off of probation because I used to always go to court alone. My parents were about the last people I would call. I was alone." I know what Ronny means by "a minute"—it's the hood paradox. A minute means a long time, something that feels like forever.

His resolve dwindles. Eventually, Ronny drops out of school and returns to drug dealing, working for his cousin who operates the Fifth Avenue of crack. When another gang member tries to muscle in on his profitable corner, Ronny's cousin shoots and kills him. The Bloods retaliate and kill one of Ronny's nephews. This is all part of a series of ongoing feuds and shifting alliances, the Bloods constantly fighting between themselves. This is never all-out war. There are fewer Bloods than Crips and their numbers must be preserved. Still, the drug economy causes frequent conflict between Blood sets.

"This is how a huge beef began between my family and my neighborhood. It's still goin' on," Ronny tells me.

I struggle to figure out the difference between Ronny's family hood and his neighborhood. The Bloods have always been a very loose network of independent groupings—called "hoods," never "gangs." The hood controls a discrete geographic area, with sets claiming even more specific streets and city blocks. These streets or projects give the sets their names—Ronny was from the Bounty Hunter Bloods—a set that claimed the Nickerson Gardens housing project as their territory. The Bounty Hunter Bloods gang is composed of several different sets—including Ronny's family, the Hillbilly Gangsters.

"My family was poor and people would make fun of us—my mama was a crackhead and we had accents, so people would call us hillbillies. We started sellin' dope and makin' money so we called ourselves the Beverly Hillbillies. Then my cousin put the *G* at the end of it and we became the Hillbilly Gangsters. We started all havin' babies and that would make people cousins. We were popular 'til the drug murders occurred. People said we planned it, makin' up rumors—callin' us the hillbilly snitches. There was this other circle of people who were strong, they had fear in the projects, no respect. My family was respected and loved. But fear rules over love—even though love is strong. The neighborhood put a green light on my family, the Hillbilly Gangsters."

The green light is the point of no return. A neighborhood receives a green light when it has broken a code of gang life. Kenny Green once tried explaining this to me. He started laughing when I asked how a green light was recorded, explaining that nothing is written down; gang members learn the rules verbally and through relationships. There is a code of silence—that encompasses loyalty and respect toward all things hood.

"Let's say your neighborhood is shooting and they kill a child. Then they get the green light. You can't kill a little child or a baby. Or if someone in your neighborhood gets caught snitching, then your neighborhood gets a green light." Kenny is going through all of this in painstaking detail. He is a scholar of the hood.

It is always open season on any neighborhood that has been greenlighted. The other gangs can shoot to kill with impunity. Here in the Wild West, no breach of the code goes unnoticed. Outsiders are constantly watched. While I am with Ronny, my cell phone rings. It's Big Mike, who tells me that I've been spotted in the projects.

"You know they watch when anyone new shows up," Big Mike cautions. "Be careful, Little Mama." I feel safe but I try not to think too hard about the surveillance under way in the projects at this moment. Ronny is showing me where his homies have carved their initials into the cement of Nickerson Gardens, with the Cs in their names carefully crossed out. This is because any reference to Crips, however oblique, must be undone as part of the Bloods' practice of "affirmation by negation." The Bounty Hunter Bloods avoid certain words—they won't say "cuz" or "cousin" because it sounds like "Crip." Instead people are referred to as "relatives." Back in the day, homies tell me, the Bloods liked to wear Calvin Klein jeans: the words symbolized "Crip Killer."

"The whole time the situation with the green light was in the air," Ronny recalls, "I wanted to go on missions, but I was torn. It wasn't like I hated my whole neighborhood—I really loved some of the people in it. But my family kept sayin', 'Fuck everybody.'

"So I decided to leave the family and go to my hood, by myself. This was when I really fell in love with my neighborhood—they embraced me. You're my nigga, you're my friend—and they gave me guns to protect myself."

From what I can decipher, Ronny left his own family set, identifying with and representing the Bounty Hunter hood. This change is further complicated when he is arrested, no longer a boy. He is a man, charged with possession of a firearm.

"I was eighteen and it was my first time going into the Men's Central County Jail. I felt weird, I felt lost. I had heard all of these rumors about county jail. I made it through processin' but believe me, it's not a walk in the park—you got your gang activity right there in the jail—you got your Sureños so you got racial tension and gang tension and a lot of the dudes in my hood were aware of my family members and the people in the projects and I was scared—these dudes were a threat to my life. "

At this moment, Nickerson Gardens is no longer part of Ronny's reality. Instead, he is my walking, talking guide to the California penal system.

"The prison structure is better for keepin' things cool between the races and the gangs. In county jail there's no structure, it's a lotta dudes that wanna make a name for themselves. And there's trouble because of the age difference—in county jail there's more people between eighteen and twenty-four, while in prison there's men in their twenties and thirties and forties. This makes it a lot smoother, they dominate. CJ operates the way younger men operate. I remember I was nervous, walkin' down the hall to my cell. Everyone's bangin' on their cells, sayin', 'Where you from?' I had to answer really strong. You can't say nothin', and you can't be soft. I hadda say it loud, 'Bounty Hunter Bloods.'

There is defiance in Ronny and there is fear.

"I can say it now—the blacks in jail are crazy. We take on whoever is there. And someone—a non-affiliate—doesn't get to avoid this. A lot of them get their ass whupped—dudes look at them like they their bitch. If a non-affiliate gets into a fight with a gang member—another gang member jumps in, that's the way the blacks operate. The Latinos—the Sureños—structure it a little bit better—most Southsiders don't fight in jail, but the blacks fight all day long. I always think, this is trainin' for us—we know that a race war could pop off at any given time, we need to get fear into other people. And you gotta be tough in county jail 'cuz if you go to prison it's gonna follow you—it's like your ghetto report card. You got your reputation—and you see that same OG dude that you was disrespectin' when you come to prison and it's like damn, where are my homies at now? You gotta remember, LA only has two county jails but California has thirty-six prisons. I have dreams about prison, they're nightmares."

Whatever his nightmares, after his first trip to jail, Ronny became a frequent guest of the county—a side effect of his new enterprise: drug dealing.

"Y'know in the hood, this is how we make money—you wanna get yourself established, start a business, buy a house—then you gotta do a drug deal. So I got out of jail, I decided to do some dealin', save some money. But every time I started to be productive, I would get arrested. I know what to expect. It's a breeze—I got rank, I'm not a nobody. Everything's cool. But then jail is still jail—I'm gettin' disrespected by the deputies—they strip-search me whenever they feel like it. For the life, we live—jail is inevitable—and we learn. The older homies in jail schooled me. 'I expected more out of you,' they would say. I was held accountable to act in a certain way. I grew in jail."

Ronny's role models are gangbangers. His family is a hood. His mentors are older homies in county jail. This all sounds overdetermined. But of course, there is more. While he is locked up in county jail, he learns that his mother has lung cancer. He reacts with love and fear—the two go round and round in Ronny's head and he is frozen.

"We had prayer circles in jail. All races invited, blacks, Hispanics, read a few Bible Scriptures, pray for people who are sick, pray for people going to court in the morning. Everyone in jail respected the prayer circle—there's no talkin' loud, you can't flush the toilet during prayer circle. I liked it. I tried to pray for my mother," he tells me, "but still, nothin' comes out. Nothin' comes out—even now."

Tears trail down his cheeks. This is the only time I have seen Ronny cry—when he talks about his mother. She died three months after he was released from jail.

"She was so young when she got sick and she was sober for six years. She was only fifty-four when she died," Ronny says quietly.

I am not surprised. My age. I know there is a part of Ronny that relates to me like a mother. Calling. Checking in. Asking for help.

Ronny never visited his mother in the hospital, adding to the credit line of trauma. Her death starts him on a downward spiral.

"I couldn't sleep, I couldn't eat, I couldn't think—I kept havin' flash-backs—I wanted to leave the hood but I didn't know what to do."

Ronny is dealing with unfinished business. Most of the men and women trying to leave gang life experience post-traumatic stress disorder. Public health experts estimate that probably 80 percent of gang members on the streets suffer with some form of PTSD. Ronny was no exception. His daily dose of violence, grief, abandonment, and loss would test anyone. But instead of going to a therapist, Ronny returns to the street, gangbanging after another one of his cousins is shot and killed.

"I was close to Tyrell and we lost him. I didn't know how to control myself. I pretty much didn't care anymore. I really hadn't gotten over my mom's death either. It was drugs and guns then—doin' them, sellin' them. It was just crazy shit going on—shoot-outs, stayin' up for days gettin' high, back and forth, me and these dudes against the dudes who killed my cousin. I was sleepin' with one eye open. I did everything you could imagine, and I finally got caught and wound up in prison for a year. Destiny, my girlfriend, went to drug-treatment program. We both had to clean up or we would die." Ronny believes the arrest saved his life.

"Everything happens for a reason," he tells me. "That day or the next day—I coulda done something that woulda killed me or put me away for life. I felt I was rescued from myself. I remember in jail, waitin' for the prison bus to come in. When it did, the prison guard made us strip buck naked, put us in these paper suits, I was sittin' on the bus and thinkin', 'Damn, I am really going to prison.' On the bus, everybody's talkin', people eatin' their food. I didn't want nobody to think I was worried. I am with people who got fifty years, sixty years, life without the possibility of the parole. Then we pulled up to the prison, and it looked like a big-ass private military base. They strip-searched us, gave us prison clothes, and it's like, God, I'm really in prison. And anything can happen, your life can be taken, gunshots, prison riot, you look on the wall and see big signs that say, 'No Warning Shots.' That was an eye-opener."

Ronny does easy time. He lives in a dorm and watches cable TV.

"I was learnin'. Everything in prison is based off politics and it's petty. It's about control and keeping the violence down. But I tried to stay out of trouble. When it was over I knew, I wasn't gonna go back. And I gotta be careful 'cuz when I get out of prison, my PO tells me I'm on a gang injunction. I never knew it. I'm fucked."

Being served with a gang injunction is a rite of passage for so many of the people I know. It is the cornerstone of the "suppression" approach to gang violence and about as far from community-based gang intervention as you can get. The injunction process begins when the court issues a restraining order that prohibits specific gang members from congregating. Congregating is said to involve three or more gang members (there's that magic number) in a given place at a given time. Law enforcement insists that this is a sound public-safety strategy to end gang activity in communities, enabling citizens to "enjoy quality of life."

The City of Los Angeles took gang injunctions for a test run in the mid-1980s, with the first official injunction being served against the Playboy Gangster Crips. Despite legal challenges and concerns about mistaken identities, by the time I am hanging out in different parts of Los Angeles, gang injunctions are in full throttle, with sixty-five injunctions having been served on fifty neighborhoods. The injunctions name names—identifying people who are members of specific gangs and decreeing that they cannot congregate in public places. Additionally, these individuals are not allowed to carry lethal weapons, including screwdrivers and pocketknives. The name of anyone served with a gang injunction is placed on the CalGang database, where it lives on in perpetuity. There is no way out. In Los Angeles, where eleven thousand names appear on the database as supposedly "known" gang members, exactly three people have managed to have their names deleted. I am only half-joking when I tell people that my name probably appears in the database.

It is Kafka in the hood. There is no way out. And there is no way to know when and if you have been actually served with an injunction. Instead, most homies learn they have been named on an injunction when police or FBI raid different gang hot spots or once they've been locked up. Ronny was no exception. He was lucky his parole officer told him.

"I don't know why they're usin' these injunctions. The injunctions don't do nothin' except make the hood stronger."

Ronny is not alone in this opinion. I strongly doubt the usefulness of gang injunctions, and I am in good company. No less than the US Department of Justice and the Office of Juvenile Justice and Delinquency Prevention have found that although injunctions may have some effect on gang activity in small towns, their impact on established gangs in large cities is zip, nada, nothing. Even Mark has told me that, while the LAPD "officially" supports injunctions, he is part of a small group of commanders and deputy chiefs who disagree.

"We all know that the injunctions don't do a thing," Mark remarks when I tell him what Ronny said. "Ronny is right—injunctions may actually backfire and make the gang more coherent. They don't make things better. You can bet they probably make things worse by strengthening the ties between gang members—you drive them underground and they have to conspire to get together. And what's worse, it becomes like a self-fulfilling prophecy." I smile when Mark says this. For once we are on the same side.

This is a good thing, because by this time I am being called up by public radio and asked to comment on "the effectiveness of gang injunctions." A local news program contacts me, and before you can say "research evidence," I am miked up and blithely denouncing gang injunctions. Two days later I am taken out to the woodshed by a City Hall functionary because I am not allowed to make such comments while serving as the mayor's gang advisor.

"We need to all be on the same page," the enraged deputy mayor tells me. "The mayor supports gang injunctions." There is speculation that the mayor, mulling over a run for governor of California, is trying mightily to distance himself as far as possible from his ACLU roots. I feel like I am starring in season five of *The Wire* and life is imitating art to a point of insanity. While I love the people I meet in City Hall, I am ready to go back to UCLA—and life as a gang anthropologist in the streets—when my one-year appointment ends.

Once I exit the Mayor's Office, the ACLU asks me to work as an expert witness on gang injunctions. They have filed a class action suit against the City of Santa Ana. When I see the area designated as the target of the injunction, I cannot stop laughing. It is a lovely suburban neighborhood that includes antiques shops and the Chapman University campus. Peter Bibring, the ACLU attorney handling the case, is amused by my reaction.

"A lot of people think gang injunctions really are the first step toward gentrification. They want to kick the gangs out to drive prices up," he tells me while convincing me that the ACLU has a strong case. "We can use your help."

I have to declare a side. The trouble is, I've been invited to work as the senior gang policy advisor for Lee Baca, the sheriff of Los Angeles County. I don't know how I am going to do this. But when I voice my concerns, Baca tells me I have a right to my own opinion. "I don't want you to be a yes-man," he reassures me. I couldn't care less that he's using the wrong gender. Baca possesses true integrity.

I begin imagining what Ronny would say to Lee Baca about the impact of injunctions. It's a fantasy I keep to myself later that evening in Nickerson Gardens. Ronny spins out stories of what he did when he was young. He tells me he doesn't know if he will live more than five more years. He accepts this life as his fate. He waits.

ELEVEN

Teardrops

Why wasn't anyone ever there to tell me not to do this,
not to go into the gang, not to bang, not to get a tattoo?
—Natalie Flores

I keep thinking about Mario. In the feature film running in my brain, I see the signs that he hadn't left his neighborhood. The biggest sign, the one I should never have missed, was his refusal to remove his tattoos. Mario's ready excuse was that he just hadn't gotten around to it—he hadn't found the time. But in retrospect I realized it was more than that. The tattoo is the covenant, the pledge of life and loyalty to the neighborhood. Some look crude, betraying their street or prison-made origins. Others are more complicated, rendered in multiple colors. Almost everyone I know in this world has them, and no one talks very much about them.

In anthropology, the decoration and piercing of the body is a big deal. There's even a scholarly journal, *Ornament*, devoted to tattoos and body piercing. But I always felt that the act of getting a tattoo represented a meeting of art and masochism. The pain and permanence scared me. Under ideal "professional" conditions "in a street parlor," the modern process of tattooing is sterile and involves electricity and speed. The electric tattoo machine works by infusing an area of the skin with ink using a bar of needles. The needles are electronically driven in and out of the skin anywhere from 50 to 150 times a second with what is hoped will be a minimum of pain. When tattoos are more crudely made with hand-held needles, whether in the hood or in the prison system, the tattooing process, called "pinning," is excruciating, and the end product often crude. Homemade tattoos were "born" in prison and progressed beyond pinning. Inmates, ever innovative, would put together prison-made tattoo machines from everything available: strings from guitar class, ink from art class, smuggled needles, and the motor from a Sony Walkman to power the process.

The first tattoo I had ever seen looked very crude indeed, small block letters appearing on the lower arm of our next-door neighbor, Dora Kaufmann. She gave me books and told me stories about Auschwitz. At eight years old, I connected tattoos to something dark and evil. The gang tattoos I later saw—machetes dripping blood and death's heads with gang names written underneath them—did nothing to dispel these feelings.

I first learned about tattoos from Fabian Debora, a former gangbanger who used to buy drugs from his earnings as a tattoo artist. Fabian has graduated from the neighborhood in many ways. He is now an extremely talented artist whose paintings have been shown in art galleries. His artistic sensibilities are apparent as he talks to me about tattoos.

"Tattoos send a message," Fabian begins over Chinese food at Paul's Kitchen in downtown LA. "They may tell what side of Los Angeles you are from or the story of your life. Some homies get tattoos for the art form, some do it for rank, sometimes it happens at a party, some do it in prison."

Fabian has a sleeve—a full tattoo—down his left forearm. He tells me that it is his autobiography—portraying the struggles of his life, with his inner child, with death. The words "I've tried" and "Fuck love" are all portrayed, along with death watching over him. There is a clown with a gun, trying to commit suicide, and a female clown. His right arm bears no tattoos. "These are the two parts of my life," Fabian explains.

There are other tattoos Fabian has had removed: the huge "eyebuster" with the letters LA that adorned his neck and the small teardrop near the corner of his eye. The teardrop tattoo is universal among Hispanic and African American gangs, and I ask Fabian about its meaning.

"The principle behind the teardrop is to symbolize pain." Fabian speaks carefully. "Three definitions come with the teardrop: you have lost someone close to you, you have hurt someone crucial to you, or you have spent time in jail or prison. You get a teardrop for each term served. Sometimes homies have tears running down their cheek—that means much time served."

Fabian cautions me that there are obvious tattoos you cannot get. I learn that only when you have acquired a certain rank within the neighborhood is it appropriate to have a tattoo on your stomach or chest. He adds that black gang members have a totally different system. "Their symbols are different. And they don't use Spanish; they might use Swahili."

I wanted to know more about tattoos in the black neighborhoods, so I offered a veteran African American gangbanger, Maniac, lunch in exchange for a little street education. He turns down the meal, but we meet in Leimert Park on a sunny afternoon, where Maniac checks out the area around him carefully before talking.

"Every neighborhood has a tattoo," he begins. His voice is soft and the words come out in a sing-song rhythm; I am listening to Mr. Rogers on crack. Every neighborhood works out its own symbol or group of letters, incorporating the gang name into the design. The name is intertwined with skulls or crosses or swords or eagles. "Florencia" most often appears written out in block letters—preferably across the neck—usually followed by "13." The Bloods also focus on a body location, spelling their name out on the knuckles of the right hand. 18th Street sticks to basics—the number 18 says it all.

"Once you get tagged—tattooed—that means you're committed," Maniac tells me. "It means you're committed to the neighborhood until you die. It's the same for every hood. This way we're all alike. You see the tattoo—it means you're not a wannabe. It means you've been put up."

Tattoos are the gang's universal language—and the rules are identical whether you are black or brown. Part of being active in a neighborhood means getting your gang's name tattooed in as many body locations as humanly possible. The tattoo needs to be visible, announcing affiliations and loyalties. In addition to this, however, certain symbols are shared between all the neighborhoods—black and brown. And none is more notorious than the teardrop.

"Every time you go to prison, you get a teardrop, y'know, the teardrops you see goin' down from the corner of the eye," Maniac says deliberately. "But you gotta look close to get it. It always means death, like a brother has died. If it's empty inside it means that someone you love has been killed. Or it can mean that you got the tattoo because you've done a murder. If the tear is filled in, it means that the person—like a brother—died but it wasn't because of a murder. Maybe it was a car crash. Maybe they OD'd. If the top of the tear is empty but the bottom is full, it means retaliation. You got someone. But mostly the tear means you killed someone. A tear for every murder. If you get the tattoo while you are in prison, that means you murdered someone while you were incarcerated."

I am exhausted by this commentary. Is anything in gang life simple? It's also becoming clear that the sheer volume of material gang members are required to master far exceeds the information in lecture notes and readings required for my graduate course in juvenile justice. The information is subtle and intricate. It constantly shifts and changes as gangs subdivide and new neighborhood sets form. On top of this, very little is written down. Every gang member is required to memorize all relevant knowledge, including at least part of the bookkeeping for drug deals. Some degree of brainpower is required to function successfully in a neighborhood.

Removing a tattoo is one of the major signs that someone has decided to leave gang life. It is also a commitment of enormous proportions, and no one takes it lightly. Because of this, several gang-intervention agencies offer free tattoo-removal services before developing or providing any additional programs. The gangbanger who gets rid of his or her tattoos also leaves behind their former self, denouncing ties that are emotional as well as physical. It's a scary move—the child is leaving their family behind and beginning a new life. With tattoo removal, there is always loss. Along with this emotional weight, the physical process of tattoo removal is not for the fainthearted.

I learned this early on, watching a two-hundred-pound homie blink rapidly while breaking into a sweat during a removal session at Homeboy Industries. Typically, the black or dark-colored inks are easiest to remove and go away completely. I inwardly cringe when I see someone with colored inks and elaborate designs.

"That's gonna fuckin' hurt," one homie explained to another homie, eying the multicolored FLORENCIA-13 adorning his neck, while they both awaited treatment.

Once in the treatment room, wearing goggles, I watch while Victor Perez, the volunteer physician, works with a heavy laser gun balanced on his shoulders, ready to blow away the shrapnel of a wayward identity. "By getting rid of this tattoo," he reassures the Florencia homie, "You're gonna feel better about yourself." When he is finished, Victor introduces me to Rosa, who tells me, "I decided to get rid of all my tattoos the day my four-year-old told me she was gonna get tattoos just like mine."

The next person who comes for tattoo removal is Carlos, whose right cheek is adorned with wedding invitation–style calligraphy spelling out the words *Fuck Your Hood.* I wonder who has RSVP'd during his eight-year sojourn in prison and why he would wear profanity on his face. Other tattoos are easier to understand: The names of children. The date of death of an adored mother. Homies constantly ask me if I have kids and if I have a man. When I tell them I do, they ask why I don't have any tattoos. I shrug and try to think how I can explain that, right now, I can barely handle my name change. For twenty-four years, I had possessed one last name—my first husband's—and built an identity around it. This was my tattoo. I wish I could have laser treatments for that. Both Shannon and Mark had assumed I would change my last name. I had acquiesced, but it still felt strange.

After Carlos finishes, I sit on the floor outside a classroom at Homeboy Industries next to a thin, silent homie whose facial expression clearly warns, *Don't come near me.* Of course, this acts as an instant invitation. I find out that his name is Luis, and while I work to disarm him, asking him questions and telling him about myself, I notice that there are tattoos on his eyelids. For several minutes I try to imagine what it's like to get that soft, nearly translucent skin tattooed. But while one part of my brain feels pain, another part is slowly making out the letters. One eyelid says FUCK and the other says YOU. I am breathless with the suggestion, with its location, and with the mechanics of its removal. Later in the day we check in. Luis has found out that the tattoos cannot be removed. The risk of damage to his eyes is too great.

"At least," I weakly console him, "it doesn't say the name of your gang."

"But how I am going to tell my little girl?" he asks.

I have no answer for him. His eyelids fall somewhere outside the entire etiquette of tattoo removal, which is surprisingly straightforward. Sleeves—tattoos that extend from the shoulder to the wrist—along with other prime locales for gang tattoos (the neck, the head, the cheeks) must be removed by laser if they are gang-oriented. If you have a tattoo on your skull, it is easier to simply grow your hair. Longer hair invariably serves as an announcement that you're no longer active. Neighborhood loyalty is communicated through the practice of daily head-shaving. This accentuates the fierce look of the individual, and tattoos stand out dramatically against the baldness of the skull. Rarely are tattoos removed from the chest or upper legs, because they can be easily hidden with clothing. The chest is a particularly painful region. And other body parts can be left alone.

"I knew a guy who had tattoos on his dick," Patrice, a former gang member, tells me. "Can you imagine having tattoo removal there?" She and I both start giggling when she confides this. "I never got tattoos. DeShawn wanted me to—he wanted me to get a tattoo and I told him fuck you. No way. And now he's back in jail. What would I do if I had his name tattooed on my breasts or—" She hesitates, leans in, and whispers, "—On my pussy like he wanted." I know DeShawn has caught a murder charge and that he's probably guilty. I had seen him the week before in South LA near Athens Park, and he told me he was on the run.

While Patrice's account makes me squeamish, what really bothered me were the facial tattoos. "They get them on the face to look menacing or scary," Fabian tells me. But he adds, "There might be other reasons, I don't know." It takes several months and painstaking discussion to uncover the stories of five different men—all with extensive tattoos on their faces—who finally admit they were sexually abused by a male adult when they were children. It's as if they were trying to make visible the stigma they felt. This is not a large enough research sample to satisfy the rigorous methodologists at UCLA. But I am now even more disturbed when I see someone with his face tattooed.

Then there are "the lips." Maniac had already cautioned me, "Don't ever ask a black homie 'bout the lips—they don't have the lips." He was right—I had first noticed the striking design on Latinos from the neighborhoods. The lips invariably appeared on someone's neck, and the first few times I saw them I was convinced that they were actually red lipstick marks. Fabian had explained that the red lips were the sign of a "significant other." Another homie, just back from a long lockup, told me the lips were a symbol of "the last kiss of my lady before I go to prison." Other gang members scoffed at this and insisted that the lips formed the shape of the number 13, which signified the thirteen letters (and one space) in "Mexican Mafia," or *M* being the thirteenth letter of the alphabet. Felipe Mendez, a former gangbanger I had befriended, told me, "They mean someone's a player." But I preferred the idea of the last kiss—it was romantic and tragic and one of the rare examples of men exhibiting the kind of erotic passion typically associated with women.

But tattoos were dangerous in a different way. When arresting and booking an alleged gang member, law enforcement officers routinely insist that each suspect strip down so that all body parts can be photographed. I have sat through far too many court trials where the damning, oversized photographs of gang tattoos were paraded before judge and jury. They are the embodiment of the idea that *you just can't leave the gang*—and they seal the deal in the minds of onlookers. Most of the time, the impression left by these photographs is dead-on.

But one day in court I *knew* that the person whose tattoos were being displayed had left the neighborhood. The US attorney was gazing intently at a photo that she then held up for everyone in the courtroom to see—a naked chest with an enormous tattoo of MS-13.

"Alex Sanchez kept the tattoo of MS-13 on his chest, close to his heart. He has never left the gang," she insisted. "He was still affiliated, still active; in fact, he was a shot caller and he would never remove this tattoo."

I knew—along with almost everyone else in court—that this was not the truth. Alex Sanchez had endured a series of painful treatments to remove tattoos from his head and neck. His attorney countered, "The tattoo is over the cardiac region. To use laser treatments in this area is painful and extremely dangerous."

No one was looking at either attorney. We were all looking at Alex.

I had been on close terms with Alex Sanchez for several years while he established and built up Homies Unidos—a gang-intervention agency that worked with the neighborhoods operating in Central Los Angeles, primarily MS-13. Alex's curriculum vitae was a wonder to behold. He had been an active member of MS-13 and had been extradited once to El Salvador for a parole violation, successfully fighting a *second* attempted extradition. He had renounced all gang ties and had been granted political asylum once it was revealed that he had been systematically harassed by the LAPD. Now he was fifteen years out of the neighborhood and a strong candidate for the California Peace Prize. His agency received grant funding from the City of Los Angeles and the California Wellness Foundation.

I had been working with Julio Marcial, a Wellness Foundation project officer who grew up in the Pacoima barrio, avoided the neighborhood, got a college education, and wore a suit and tie but never forgot who he was. He asked me to evaluate Homies Unidos and I agreed—but I had my Trojan horse, my ulterior motive. I wanted to hang out with the guys trying to leave MS-13. I was finishing my evaluation plan and called Alex to talk about it. He laughed and said, "I've got to go switch out a transmission with my brother-in-law. The one in my car isn't working. I'll call you in the morning."

I didn't hear from him in the morning, but this did not strike me as odd. Time was fluid in gangs, as in community-based organizations. Midday I got a text from Celeste Fremon that read, "Alex Sanchez WTF?" Celeste was a successful freelance journalist who was "present at the creation," covering gangs in general, and East Los Angeles and Greg Boyle in particular, for over twenty years. She was completely plugged into the Los Angeles gang community. Celeste knew I was away—on a working vacation in New York—and if she was texting me, it wasn't good. Three phone calls later I learned that Alex had been arrested under the RICO statute, charged with racketeering and conspiracy to murder and was being held in federal detention, unable to see anyone but his lawyer. All I could think was, '*Not Alex.*'

Even before I started working on the evaluation, Alex and I had spent a lot of time together appearing on panels, attempting to answer the unanswerable questions: "How Can We Stop Gang Violence?" or "What Intervention Strategy Works Best?" Our names were listed as "gang intervention" speakers and constantly recycled both locally and nationally. I also visited Alex at Homies Unidos, checking in with him while I interviewed homies in Rampart Division—one of the least understood, most gang-impacted areas of Los Angeles.

Rampart was a strange hybrid of community activism, gang violence, and police brutality. It was part of my personal history. I had been baptized, rather unsuccessfully, at St. Sophia Greek Orthodox Cathedral—right in the heart of what urban planners called "the Byzantine-Latino corridor." It was also an area Mark knew well—he had served as a captain in the notorious Rampart Division of the LAPD, site of some of the worst police corruption in recent times. But most of us knew it as the Bermuda Triangle of Los Angeles—everything disappeared into Rampart. It was where Nora Ephron rhapsodized that you could order the best pastrami sandwich in America. Most of California organized labor had offices in the area, as did Constance Rice's highly effective civil rights law group, the Advancement Project. The streets were alive in Rampart—with families, children, and activity around the clock. There were vendors selling chorizos, fake social security cards, and "real" passports. It was also a great place to buy crystal meth and to order a hit. Or so I had been told.

Alex had set up shop right in the middle of Rampart—down on Olympic Boulevard—in a crowded warren of offices where Homies Unidos offered tattoo-removal services and parenting classes. Running the agency and lecturing in public, Alex was chronically overworked and overscheduled. If he had time to be active in MS-13 in the midst of all these never-ending activities, he was a much better professional than I. Taking a break after a morning spent with homies, I met Alex and his colleague, Susan Cruz, for lunch, and while we ate Korean barbecue, they talked about their days in MS-13. They described it as a horrible experience that taught them what really needed to be done to stop the violence. Now they just needed enough funding to help. We spent most of lunch discussing what was required on federal grant applications. At the end, we touched on what was going on in the streets.

"MS-13 is warring with 18th Street. It's getting more and more violent," Alex told me. He and Susan also talked with me about the changes in the streets, insisting that there was a new generation, a younger generation, without limits, without hope. After lunch, I went out to talk with two homies from MS-13 and it was clear that Alex and Susan were right.

I spent several days after that with one youngster, Luis, who shared a birth date with Shannon. He had dropped out of middle school and was thinking about going back. He had not been jumped into a gang "yet."

I asked him what he did every day, and he was evasive. "A few things," he would say and then tell me he had to leave soon, could I kick him down with a few bucks? While I obliged him, I kept wondering, *Where is the prevention program for this guy?* He talked a little bit too much about the older homie who was his friend, and I let him ramble until he revealed himself. He was my daughter's age. And he had a mentor. The mentor was teaching him about crystal meth. I saw Luis two more times. The second time he showed me his MS tattoo and told me he had been jumped into the gang.

"It's a family, miss," he explained, using the unfailing politesse of every Hispanic gang member I had ever known. "My mother is gone, my father I never know. I know this. I know my neighborhood. MS-13 Normandie clique." One week later Luis was dead.

I needed to see Papa, my therapist. The losses were beginning to pile up. I was having nightmares—there were too many homies who died before their lives had begun. The next time I am with Alex, speaking at yet another gang conference, we talk about Luis. I confess that Mark and I have had problems and we are both in therapy. "He needs it, I need it, I guess we all need it," I told Alex. "I can't be married to anyone from the LAPD without both of us going to therapy."

"I know," he told me. "I go as much as I can. I wanna be a good husband and father. Thank God I have Kaiser." We sounded like two middle-class suburbanites discussing our relationship issues. Half an hour later, I listened to Alex speaking, unprepared for what he would say.

"I go to see a psychiatrist for my PTSD and my rage. I need it," he announced, unabashed, in front of five hundred people at UCLA. "This is the hidden cost of gang membership. I do it because I want to protect my children from this madness and I want to find out who I am. We all need therapy."

Now, months later in court, listening to the case against Alex, all I could do was snort when the US attorney, a Sarah Jessica Parker clone wearing a diamond big enough to cut open a dictionary, talked about the "double life of Alex Sanchez."

So there was Alex Sanchez, in a white federal detention jumpsuit with 110 letters of support from law enforcement and academics and community leaders and Latina mothers. There was $1.2 million in the bank as guarantee for bail and, in a breathtaking moment, the political activist Tom Hayden coming forth and offering up his home as collateral for bail. After his marriage to Jane Fonda ended, Hayden had moved to Mandeville Canyon, living in this house with his wife, Barbara, and their enchanting son, Liam. He wrote a book on gang intervention entitled *Street Wars*, and was constantly sending e-mails decrying George W. Bush's tactics in Washington and the LAPD's tactics locally.

"Same old Tom," my husband would mutter. "Always complaining about the LAPD."

I thought about the man Shannon was learning about in US History that semester—the young activist and anti-war protestor who authored the Port Huron Statement. I was ready to start berating Mark when I remembered that just a few months earlier, both he and I had been to Tom Hayden's house as part of a small group talking with Virginia congressman Bobby Scott about the Youth Promise Act and its future in the federal government. Alex had been there.

Now there was a crisis. If Alex Sanchez could get into this much trouble because of past associations and alleged phone conversations, after devoting himself to gang intervention and violence prevention, what is the future for gang members who simply want to leave their neighborhoods? I keep thinking of Chino, tattooed up and down his arms, who is illiterate and undocumented and can barely care for himself let alone his infant daughter. What chance does Chino have if someone of Alex's stature and sophistication falls?

After the bail hearing, I walk over to Homeboy Industries—a few blocks from the federal courthouse. I talk to Joanna while she is having a tattoo-removal treatment. Victor Perez is working on the multicolored tattoo of her gang name, Dark Eyes, and another tattoo that says, LOVE MY HOOD FOREVER.

"This hurts like a motherfucker—I'm never gonna get another fuckin' tattoo again," Joanna says with a laugh. But I am far away, remembering the gang lieutenant who insisted, "They get their tattoos removed so when they go to court and you bring out the pictures, they can say, It's not me! Then after their case is settled, they go out and get new tattoos." This did not make a lot of sense to me. I had not heard of homies getting "re-tattooed" after they endured the pain of multiple laser treatments.

There were too many outsiders who believed the idea of "once a gang member, always a gang member." The people who made this their mantra wore uniforms and carried guns. Some of them were school administrators who presented kids with an "opportunity transfer" off their campuses at the slightest sign of trouble. Some of them wore robes and listened to complaints and then were perfectly capable of throwing someone back in jail for failing to fill out the proper form. A lot of them were probation officers who obsessively followed their caseload, watching and waiting for someone to do something wrong rather than applying a calculus of intent and accident.

I was beginning to see that tattoos involved more than ink and pain. There were mental tattoos—and most of them were not on people from the neighborhood. This was what plagued Alex, whose bail was denied that afternoon.

Joanna's latest crisis temporarily drives Alex Sanchez out of my thoughts. After her tattoo-removal treatments, she introduces me to Clumsy, or Carlos, her cousin who has just been released from prison. Carlos is nervous, twitchy, and looking very institutionalized. Joanna is trying to help Carlos settle in. This involves getting him a job at Homeboy Industries and a new place to live, out of Florencia territory. Carlos served a seven-year stretch in prison for attempted murder; he is viewed as a good soldier who did not roll over on his partners in the crime. Such loyalty makes him a valuable commodity.

"They don't want to let go of Carlos," Joanna begins. She nudges Carlos and assures him that I am coo'—nothing will happen if he talks to me.

"My neighborhood does not want to lose anyone," he explains. "They want me to stay. And it's bad. My mother is Florencia, my father is Florencia, my wife is Florencia. They don't want to let go of me. And my PO doesn't believe me, he doesn't help, he is waiting for me, trying to get me to fuck up so he can violate me and send me back to prison."

Joanna, in a frenzy of informal case management, asks me if I can help find Carlos somewhere to sleep, just for the night. Her behavior mimics my frantic efforts the night before to find my cousin Nick, whose drug use has been an ongoing anxiety for me. His ex-girlfriend and I stayed out until midnight, chasing him in and out of bars in Silver Lake, trying to convince him to go home with one of us. But the parallel only stretches so far. My cousin is a doctor, with a six-figure income. Carlos doesn't even have a social security number or a driver's license. What he has is the name Florencia-13 tattooed across his neck, an alphabet choker referred to as an "eyebuster." I keep looking at Carlos and thinking that if his tattoo removal is successful, he will look like an undergraduate sitting in one of the classes I teach at UCLA. He is boyishly handsome, newly animated, excited about his first apartment. He is also trying to escape a death sentence of the streets.

Two days later, Elie Miller, the Homeboy attorney and head of a self-described "legal ministry," calls to tell me that Carlos has been arrested. She asks me to tell Joanna, but I can't find her. That evening, Joanna texts me. She is in the hospital with Marcos, who has come down with pneumonia. I am home, reviewing Shannon's math homework with her. Our biggest struggle is eleventh-grade calculus. Shannon's adolescence is a complete failure—she is neither moody nor rebellious. Instead, she appears to be evolving into a rather unique individual— obsessed with indie music and the vintage clothes she purchases at local thrift shops. She has also taken to spending large amounts of time after school volunteering as a tutor and office assistant at Homeboy. I feel she is safe there—she hangs out with the homies in the curriculum office and helps them with their charter school homework. She has befriended an older homie—Raul—and they have grown close. She teaches Raul the fundamentals of calculus. He advises her about life and warns her never to get a tattoo, telling her, "Women should not have tattoos, because they are the beauty of the world. Their beauty should not be spoiled."

I feel reassured when Shannon repeats Raul's advice to her. Two of Shannon's cousins already have tattoos. Neither Mark nor I want to see her get one, although we have already told her that after she turns eighteen, it is her decision to make. I tell Mark he should be happy—an

OG may actually prevent our daughter from following a youthful trend. He is silent for a moment.

"Great. Now the homies are helping us raise our daughter. What's next? Are we adopting one?"

I wonder if it's a good time to tell him later that one of my favorite couples at Homeboy, Quentin and Ana, have asked us to be godparents for their baby.

I wait.

TWELVE

The Lost Boys

Where would we be if we kept chasing the wind
Around the streets love to stay high as a kite
After the cord snaps and send it flying
Up, up and away
Riding the freedom of gravitated euphoria
Itsgoodtoknowyou.

—Quentin Moore

"It's rough out there," Screech tells me, "I gotta protect myself."

It is spring 2008. In the past six weeks two more gang members have been killed. Screech—who asks me to call him by his "real" name, Kevin Williams—has taken to traveling with a gun, strapped, everywhere he goes. He is also jumpy, erratic, and quick to anger. When I tell him to leave his gun at home, he stops talking to me. Three days pass without my seeing him. Instead, my cell phone rings at all hours with calls from his wife, Elena.

"I'm so worried about Kevin," she tells me, her voice pitched high with anxiety. "I wake up in the middle of the night and he is standing at the window, staring out at the street. I tell him to come to bed, but he won't come. Sometimes he leaves—I don't know where he is going."

All this is happening at the start of a major evaluation project. I have teamed up with two brilliant colleagues at UCLA, Todd Franke and Tina Christie, to design a longitudinal study of former gang members who come to Homeboy Industries for help. The three of us have just been awarded enough money from the John Randolph Haynes and Dora Haynes Foundation to fund the first two years of what will be a five-year study. Julio Marcial, who has the soul of a researcher, ultimately comes through with funding from the California Wellness Foundation to help with the remaining three years. It is a dream come true. But now the real work begins.

I meet Kevin Williams during the proposal-planning stage of the study, and he quickly involves me in all aspects of his life—gang activity, love, and danger. He is talkative and funny, with mocha-colored skin and gray-green eyes, the star of a gang-intervention class sponsored by the Los Angeles County Department of Human Relations. "Spreading Seeds" is a popular course with an unfortunate title: half its attendees have already fathered multiple babies. But oddly enough, its blend of new age mysticism and indigenous teachings appeals to homies, whether black or brown. Kevin attempts, carefully, to explain the class to me.

"I'm learnin' that to move beyond the present, you gotta understand the past—and the oppression of people of color." But when I ask Kevin about his personal history, the radical speak suddenly disappears.

"I guess I'm seein' I always wanted a family," he admits. "I never met my father. I know who he is. He was a Black Panther. Then he got locked up. I could find him but I don't wanna. There's nothin' he could do for me right now. When I was comin' up there was no older figures except who I met on the streets. They were gangbangin' and stuff—I learned their trade, I could see they were makin' money offa drugs, but I wasn't sure this was what I was gonna do. But they were kinda my family, ya feel me, that was it. I didn't have anythin' else."

Kevin is one of my lost boys—he belongs to no one, not his neighborhood, not even himself. Although he tells me he is an Eight Tray Gangsta Crip, he shows no signs of the blind allegiance to the gang I have witnessed in so many others. He reassures me that he is free to talk with me "any night," offering to drive to UCLA and meet on my turf. He defies the stereotype of the gang member—if such an individual even exists.

Criminal justice experts, law enforcement professionals, and policymakers have worked overtime to define gangs and describe gang members. Ultimately, most agree that a gang consists of any group that gathers together on an ongoing basis to "engage in antisocial or criminal activities." When determining the minimum size for gang activity, the magic number is usually set at three. Gang members "identify with one another based on geographical location, clothing, colors, symbols and names. They communicate their gang affiliation through hand signs and graffiti. Law breaking activities enhance the gang member's credibility, creating fear in the community and providing an ongoing source of income." This is what gang experts believed—and I was included in their ranks. I had written those words in 2007 in a book chapter called "Defining Gangs," and they represented the reasoning of minds far more scholarly than my own. There was a laundry list of gangster traits: someone who is violent, someone who is antisocial, someone who intimidates and preys upon the weaker members of society. But I knew that, no matter how exhaustive the list, something was still missing.

Getting to know people like Kevin, along with Ronny and Joanna, reinforced for me what was already obvious: there is no typical gang member, no one-size-fits-all. Instead, there is something of a pattern. The father is absent. The family is fractured. The neighborhood is calling. But just when I think the pins are lining up, something doesn't fit.

While his father was MIA, Kevin's mother tried to provide. She was gone most days, working full-time as a medical aide at a nearby convalescent hospital. When she was home, she was always critical, always watchful.

"She was on me alla the time," Kevin remembers. He mimics the high pitch of her voice: "*Be home after school, it doesn't take that long for you to catch the bus, call me and let me know that you got home.* She was always sayin' things like that. But I was fourteen, I was already out. One day she came home and I wasn't there and when I got home we started fightin', hittin' each other. I'm thinkin', There's no point in this. So I call 911 and tell them, 'My mom is beatin' up on me.' The police took forever to get there and then after talkin' to her, they got me in cuffs and they took me to the police station—Seventy-Seventh Street. I was hotheaded, on the ride there I was like, Why the fuck you takin' me to the station? My mom is the one you should be takin' to the station.

"I wound up in Los Padrinos Juvenile Hall. We went to court and my mom showed up and said, 'Any child I raise, if they try to hit me, they still wouldn't be alive when I got done.'" But despite his mother's open admission of child abuse, Kevin was reclassified from child welfare client to delinquency case.

"This happens all the time," Carol Biondi tells me when I ask her about Kevin. She is my go-to person with good reason. Despite her well-groomed beauty, affluence, and Hollywood connections, Carol is the full-time watchdog of the Los Angeles County Department of Probation. She walks the camps and halls, organizes a Saturday newspaper class at Camp David Gonzales, harangues authorities, reviews legislation, and serves on the LA County Children's Commission. She is the real deal.

"You get a kid who's in the child welfare system," Carol explains. "They say something inappropriate and they get labeled a delinquent. In this case Kevin mouthed off to the cops and they decided he belonged in Probation. It's that simple. And that wrong."

"That's how I caught my first juvenile probation case," Kevin confirms, "for doin' nothin'."

One thing is obvious: somewhere along the line his mother ceded Kevin's parenting to the County of Los Angeles. "There's no one gonna be there for these children," Big Mike has already warned me, and Kevin is living proof. As I get to know him, I see that the all-too-familiar pattern took hold once he was released from juvenile detention.

"I get home and I'm livin' in one neighborhood territory of the Eight Tray Gangstas—ETGs—but I'm supposed to go to my school in 67 NHC territory. And I got big problems. I'm not *in* the neighborhood—but it's where I'm from and people just see *that*. And I feel like I'm kinda part of them."

In this alphabet soup of the absurd, Kevin faces multiple threats. The ETGs command the largest black gang territory in LA—a little over two and half square miles of real estate in South Los Angeles. As part of this, there is ongoing conflict between the ETGs and the Rollin 60s Crips dating back to 1979. This rivalry extends to all "Rollin Os" gangs and to all "NeighborHood" (NH) gangs including the 67 NeighborHood Crips (67 NHC) whose turf contains Kevin's middle school. Despite continuing efforts to negotiate peace treaties, the rivalry remains lethal.

"People were jammin' me up all the time, askin' me, 'Where you from?' I had to answer, and I got so I could get along with everyone. I didn't wanna belong to a neighborhood, I just wanted to get along." Kevin chose street diplomacy as his problem-solving strategy.

The smarter homies, like Kevin, often possess some sort of personal charisma rendering them capable of crossing boundaries. Despite claims about how strongly the neighborhoods cleave to geography, there are always the informal ambassadors who can negotiate the lines of gang territory. Their acceptance, however unstable, depends on force of personality and the ability not to offend anyone. But there is a price to be paid. Acceptance can be revoked at a moment's notice. And, if you can cross boundaries and be a "get along guy," you are never going to move up the food chain of the neighborhood. It's the shooters who do well, the guys who are willing to kill.

"There's soldiers and there's talkers," Big Mike has told me.

It's clear that Kevin is a talker. So is Ronny, who explains his ability to go beyond borders in the neighborhoods.

"I had the love of my hood but I wasn't gonna give up on friends who claimed other neighborhoods—they were my brothers too. I told the people in my hood the truth, I wouldn't leave my friends." Unlike Ronny, Kevin does not blatantly declare his independence. Instead, he uses a different strategy to "get along."

"I was cool with people from warring neighborhoods 'cuz I could do stuff, fixin' cars, installin' radios. This guy, Larry Walls, taught me mechanics and computers. He and his wife were there for me. If I had a problem they would come to the school. I wrote down they were my grandparents on my emergency card."

Kevin is inventive—what does not exist, he creates. He makes the Walls his family. But Larry dies suddenly, there is no insurance, and his widow goes to live with her daughter in another state.

"Yeah. That's what happened. All of a sudden, I'm alone."

Then, Kevin is shot. He is precise about when. Most homies keep time by their arrests and lockups. It is childhood milestones courtesy of the juvenile justice system. There are no photographs or report cards or bronzed baby shoes here. Few gang members possess a social security card, and their birth certificates are misplaced, lost. Some are undocumented. Kevin's only scrapbook is his body. He recalls his ages via scars that bullets have left.

"I got hit when I was seventeen. After I got shot, I couldn't go back to school. I was at Jordan High but my enemies were there so I got put on a home-study program. I tried home study for a minute."

Formal schooling ends for Kevin. There is no counseling, no experts are called in; he is finished, done. He connects with a series of homies and attempts check fraud, burglary, and auto theft. Every effort ends with Kevin reclaimed by Probation and weaving through three halls and one camp. Recounting this, Kevin smiles.

"I turned eighteen in there. When I got released, I really started gangbangin'. There was nothin' else to do."

Until then, Kevin hadn't formally joined any neighborhood: his status was murky. Researchers describe such youngsters as "wannabes," kids on the periphery of the gang, flirting with membership, performing criminal acts, and building their credibility until they are asked to join the neighborhood. They become "foot soldiers," carrying out missions, led by the shot callers and the *veteranos*. This model portrays the progression of gang life as orderly. In reality, very little adheres to the clear-cut stages of gang membership laid out in scholarly articles. Day to day, in the neighborhood, there is no specific process—only matters of violence and timing and pain. Most homies join a neighborhood on impulse. Kevin was no exception.

"I joined the hood 'cuz of my brother. I had taught him alla this stuff, and then he comes and tells me, 'I'm gettin' put on.' I was like, 'You're not gonna get put on before me, I'm gonna get put on before you, I gotta protect you.'

"Put on" in gang vocabulary is the initiation process. It's identical to being "jumped in"—a phrase often used by black gangs. It is only a beginning, however. You are still required to prove yourself by "putting your work in." The process of Kevin and his brother being put on is vicious; both of them are beaten bloody by five different gang members.

"My brother isn't really a banger even to this day—and I still am feelin' bad about this. He doesn't have it in him. But we got in. Guns and shooting—it was our life." Kevin's voice softens. Big Mike has warned me that guns are everywhere. Every homie is strapped. Kevin explains, "I feel lika man when I gotta gun. Ya get up in the morning and ya put on your gun. It's whatcha do.

"You look up, you're strapped and you already a gangbanger," he continues. "It's dirty. Before I got in, the picture of the gang is beautiful, but once I got in, these guys wanna make you be a killa. The things they gonna do to you—to make you be a killa—you don't know. I thought that we were just gonna have meetings. What a joke. *What you gotta understand is that they really do stuff to you.*"

I do not press Kevin about the "stuff."

"No one understands—in the neighborhood—they hurt you. They keep you scared. They want you under control."

So this is the romance of the gang. This is not *The Godfather.* No one is bathed in the coppery light of brotherly attachment. The neighborhood is the abusive father, heavy on shame and intimidation, parceling out respect. We sit quietly for a moment. Kevin's head is down. He is trying not to cry, but he fails. His tears fall. The moment is leavened with regret and humiliation.

It is a while before I see Kevin again. Elie Miller e-mails that he has been arrested for armed robbery. He gets a year in county jail. Lockup marks a critical passage for Kevin, including a lesson in racial disparities. Felipe Mendez, a gang interventionist in East Los Angeles and former gang member, had already explained jail politics to me.

"If you are Latino or Hispanic or whatever, the worst part of county jail is reception—it smells like shit, you're naked, you feel like you're gonna throw up. Then once you go in, Southsiders have their spot. You're set. But the blacks—they are at it from the time they get in. They don't know what the fuck they are doing."

Once he is out, Kevin unknowingly confirms Felipe's description, offering up a primer on the black experience in jail.

"In jail Sureños get along and take care of each other—no matter what their beef on the street. But black gangs—we go to jail—it's the same as on the street. Neighborhood Crips—NHC—they are fightin' the 60s, 90s—they all gonna have the same enemies and they gonna get along with the same people. Let's say a neighborhood shot up somebody on the street—let's say a Hoover stabbed an Eight Tray, then they come in and it starts right away. Right there. In jail. I pretty much stayed out of it until one night there was a riot, I jumped up into it and I wound up in the jail hospital.

"I'm thinkin', What the fuck am I doing? I decide I'm gonna get *out* of the hood and *into* school while I'm in there. After my seventh month, I got in school, I wasn't gettin' jumped, I'm learnin' a lot."

In jail Kevin earned his high school diploma. But once he's discharged, he can't find a job. Scrambling for a place to live, Kevin needs money. He starts selling crack and weed.

"I had to make a livin'," he tells me defensively. "Then one night at my brother's house I saw Homeboy on MTV. A light bulb came on and I rushed down to see Father Greg—I remembered him from camp. I started workin' and I met my girlfriend, Elena. We were together for a month. Then I had to go back into jail. I went somewhere that I coulda avoided. Instead I listened to my homies—from the neighborhood." This is a story I hear again and again—wrong place, wrong time—and the pull of the gang. Kevin was locked up again, for a violation of his probation, serving five months. When he was released, he returned to Homeboy Industries and married Elena.

"I know it's not all perfect. I know what I got against me," Kevin says, thoughtful. "I wanna make money. This makes me wanna do certain things, like slangin' or goin' back to the neighborhood, that I gotta fight within myself. It's strange—I gotta fight myself to be a man."

I hear an echo in Kevin's words. My other lost boy, Ronny, could be Kevin Williams's twin—except he is a Blood and Kevin is a Crip. Still, each possesses all the pieces that should lead to success, but nothing comes together. Both are charismatic, charming, and very smart. Both have long-term relationships with women who provide them with stability and financial security. And yet something is missing.

A month later, Ronny comes to work at Homeboy and immediately endears himself to the staff. Hector Verdugo, the head of security at Homeboy, takes him under his wing, suggesting that the two of them go to school together. When I ask Hector if he is serious, he laughs.

"I can see the two of us holding hands, skipping along, at community college, then at UCLA. You can help us get in."

Hector then quietly adds, "No, I mean it. I'm serious."

I want to believe him. The idea of Hector, the responsible leader from the Homeboy management staff, studying alongside Ronny, the favorite son of the Bounty Hunter Bloods—is irresistible. I ask Hector why he has chosen Ronny.

"He's just so fuckin' smart," Hector tells me. "And he can get along with everyone."

Hector leaves after we finish talking about Ronny. I am alone for a few minutes when a beautiful young woman comes to the glass door of Greg Boyle's office at Homeboy. She is crying and has a split lip and a small bruise on her cheek that she insists came after she fell over a chair while walking in the dark. It is Elena—Kevin Williams's wife.

Elena works as assistant chef to Patty Zarate, the head chef at the Homegirl Café, one of the businesses that provide jobs for homegirls as well as a small revenue stream at Homeboy Industries. She is hardworking and fearless. When the crew of waitresses at Homegirl refuses to wait on LAPD chief Bill Bratton, Elena dons an apron and struts over to him.

"No one wanted to wait on you," she announces, "but I said I didn't mind. And I'm gonna take your tip."

Elena was born in Guatemala. When she was a year old, her father abandoned the family. Her mother moved to Los Angeles to work as a domestic, leaving Elena behind with her grandmother.

"I loved my grandmother," Elena recalls. "She was the only mother I knew—my real mother, I had never seen. But when I was fifteen, my grandmother died. My mother sent money for me to come to California, to live with her. I didn't have no one else. So I left." It was a tortuous journey, led by a coyote.

"The things I saw on that trip," she tells me, "you cannot imagine. I don't know how I lived through it."

She arrived in Los Angeles and learned that her mother had remarried and had two more children. There is tension, fighting, and Elena ends up being kicked out of the house. She stays with friends who are part of a neighborhood.

"I didn't have money and I didn't want to be a hooker. So I fell in with a neighborhood—MS-13—and they told me I could make money by faking auto accidents." She is actually relieved when she is arrested. After giving evidence on MS-13, she receives a suspended sentence and goes to work at the Homegirl Café. When she and Kevin marry, they represent the dream of leaving the neighborhood, transcending the pain each had experienced to find something of meaning. Almost everyone at Homeboy marvels at the strength of their commitment to each other. But there are a few skeptics.

"Fear wins out over love," Ronny warns me.

Now Elena is crying while she rubs her bruises and asking me to text Kevin. Maybe go and talk to him. I am ready to kill Ronny and Kevin, although not necessarily in that order. But I turn and ask Hector to explain all this to me.

"Kevin listens to his boys, his gang. He fights—too much," Hector tells me. I already suspect that Kevin has been going back to his neighborhood and mixing it up. He gambles with violating probation. Elie has been e-mailing me to get a hold of him, warning, "Kevin Williams has already missed a court appearance and is on two grants of formal felony probation; his next stop on the merry-go-round may be prison."

I call Maniac, who along with teaching me about tattoos is one of Kevin's homies. We meet up again at Leimert Park in South LA. When I get there, he reassures me that Kevin will come into Homeboy in the next few days. Maniac is calm where Kevin is manic. He is not handsome but carries himself with quiet confidence, assessing me carefully through the lenses of his wire-rim glasses. He tells me that Kevin will eventually leave the neighborhood. I ask him why he stays.

"If you've gone up in the gang, you don' wanna give up the status. You're used to it; it's feelin' good. The shot caller is jus' like the CEO of a corporation—he's got alla things that give him rank. He knows if he retires, it's all gonna go away. Maybe he can handle it. But probably he can't. He's gonna stay in his job till he dies. That's me too." He smiles at me. "I guess I'm inna state of transition. I wanna get out, but I don't know if I can live without my status, my perks."

We spend several hours talking. Maniac exhibits what Kevin and so many others lack—gravitas. He also possesses a cold center and the ability to perform a kind of detached calculation about the life around him. "I did my research," he tells me. "I found out what the best gang was. It was the Rollin 60s. And I made up my mind I was gonna join that neighborhood."

He makes his decision sound like he was picking a college. In the higher-education analog, the Rollin 60s are the equivalent of Brown University. Not as high profile as the Harvard and Yale of the hood—the Grape Street Crips and the Bounty Hunter Bloods—but insular and powerful.

"They are a dangerous gang," Mark tells me later when I describe the exchange with Maniac.

"He'd be happy to hear you say that."

As I say this, I cannot help but think about the rather perverse long-term relationship Maniac carries on with the LAPD.

"They all know who I am," Maniac laughs. "When they stop me, they always say, 'Hey Maniac, how ya doin'?' Just that way, those words."

Maniac is smart. He is careful. Whenever he is stopped and searched by the police, he is holding absolutely nothing. Despite belonging to a neighborhood for more than a decade, he has never served time in prison. About once a year he gets locked up. Briefly. It's always a quick trip to county jail on minor charges: possession of marijuana, discharging a firearm in a residential district. Only once is it serious—attempted murder—but even then the charge does not stick. He is Mr. Clean Hands.

"I don't get emotional," he explains. "If someone in my neighborhood gets killed, and everyone is sittin' around cryin', smokin' dope, drinkin', talkin' about the homie, I don' lissen. I go do my business, arrangin' for things to happen. I gotta get a job done."

He is calm and matter-of-fact, all business. Kevin is not this guy. Kevin is a confused, miserable mass of trouble, and it's getting worse. In the days that follow, he doesn't come into Homeboy Industries. He tells Greg he needs to make more money. He goes out on casting calls for TV shows, hoping to get hired as an extra, playing a gang member. Kevin is in for the easy fix—music videos, film roles—none of it is realistic and all of it is just around the corner. He keeps saying he has left his neighborhood. He is lying—to Elena, to me, to himself. Kevin stops answering my calls. This is when Elena calls me in fear, begging me to help her find him.

It's clear that he needs some structure. Greg finally decides to try Kevin out in the Homeboy Bakery. A few days later, I check in with Elena to see how she is. She tells me that things are better at home and then asks, "Come see Kevin—he'll be at Homeboy in an hour."

I find Kevin late that afternoon, parking the Homeboy Bakery delivery truck. He is decked out in his uniform—white shirt and pants. He looks happy.

"I'm workin' at the bakery, I'm feelin' good. I'm workin' on my rap CD. Now all I gotta do is get into school. Things are gonna get better, Jorja, I feel it."

I smile and tell him that this all sounds good, that I am happy for him and for Elena. It's one of the first times I don't feel it.

THIRTEEN

The Streets Will Be Me

I try to think about what I'm gonna do when I leave the
neighborhood. I can never think what it looks like.
—Louie Mora

I am thinking about Kevin and Elena while I sit in the middle of the
new Pico-Aliso projects, watching Fabian Debora paint a mural on a
back wall. It is an incredible piece of art, with vivid colors, portraying a
mother and child. He is painting this in the place where he used to deal
crack cocaine and engage in violence on a daily basis. But before painting the mural, Fabian had to reach out to members of his old gang—
Cuatro Flats—to secure their permission to paint.

"I have to show the proper respect to them," Fabian explains. "If
not, they will paint over my murals. They may even try to shoot me. I
am a little nervous. I may have to take some of my relaxing pills."

Fabian is the poster child for redemption. In his days with Cuatro
Flats, in between gangbanging he developed a reputation as a talented
tattoo artist. He started out creating tattoos for members of his own
neighborhood, but soon even members of other neighborhoods began
visiting. The converted garage in his mother's house served as a neutral
zone where rival gang members sat quietly waiting until Fabian took
the next customer. He was the kind of homie whose talent and charisma
enabled him to engage with rival gang members. "I would just sit and
work on the tattoos. I wouldn't talk. All the neighborhoods knew that
and they'd come to me. They just wanted a good tattoo." Fabian and I
have spent a lot of time talking about tattoos and art. His designs were
complex and fanciful, interweaving gang names with scenes of indigenous life—the letters for "Cuatro Flats" would be entangled in the hair
of an Aztec god. To keep going, he began dipping into crystal meth.

When the ratio of time spent doing drugs to time spent drawing tattoos flipped, Fabian was a full-fledged meth head no longer designing anything but the madness in his brain. But even his meth-fueled paranoid delusions were fanciful until the night he ran wildly to the middle of the I-5 freeway, trying to chase "death." The California Highway Patrol found him gripping the concrete wall that served as a center divider. The CHP stopped oncoming traffic to allow him to get across the road. Once safe, he ran desperately to avoid the three-year prison term for violation of drug probation that awaited him. "The next afternoon I gained a moment of clarity and remembered what Father Greg had wanted for me, to enroll in residential drug treatment." Fabian had already failed multiple attempts at outpatient drug treatment. But the next day, he enrolled in his first and only course of inpatient drug rehabilitation at the Salvation Army drug treatment center. Fabian now heads up the substance-abuse program at Homeboy. But his real passion is his art, which is no longer limited to the small canvases of body parts but has expanded to fill entire walls.

I stare at Fabian's painting, hypnotized, when he sits beside me and says, "I feel good. I didn't have to take any of my relaxing pills. I am glad to be able to give this back to the community. And I want to apologize to all of the mothers here. It is part of my recovery. I am thankful I survived all of this. I could have died. But my art has saved me."

The next day, I'm far from East LA, out trying to locate an address in Compton, currently the per capita murder capital of America. I pass Piru Street, birthplace of the Pirus, or the Piru Street Boys. I'm looking for Trayvon Jeffers, who is part of the senior staff of Homeboy. It takes time to find Tray. There are no addresses here, and GPS operates via word of mouth. Finally, I find Tray's aunt's house, where he meets me on the porch.

I have gotten to know Tray at Homeboy, but it has been only recently that he feels comfortable meeting me in Compton. His paranoia hangs out along with the two of us. It is one part PTSD and two parts street anxiety. Despite his protestations that he has left his neighborhood, I'm not so sure.

"I understand you're doing things—that you go back to your

neighborhood sometimes. And I know you don't want to trust me. But you can."

I'm taking a risk. Tray looks momentarily angry, but then speaks. "It's takin' a lot for me to open up—people can take advantage of you. Sometimes I can open up to it—sometimes I can't. I try to check myself before someone else does."

We start talking about leaving the neighborhood.

"It's just so fuckin' hard, it's so hard. And you gotta have a reason to stop. To go away from the neighborhood . . ." Tray drifts away, thoughtful.

I try to read the silence. Tray was usually laughing, a jokester, the life of the party at Homeboy. People responded to him with affection. "I love Tray," Hector told me. "He's a stand-up guy." But his girlfriend had called me, crying, because Tray kept texting her that he was going to kill her.

"You know, I'm supposed to stay away from here," he tells me. "But I can come during the day. No one is out. They're all sleepin'."

Tray slowly opens up while we walk the streets, talking about what he did as a little boy. How his grandmother had taught him to stuff nickel and dime bags of heroin.

"My granny's been doin' heroin since I was born; my mother's gone from PCP to cocaine to heroin. She's got HIV now, but she's still an addict. I never really knew my father. I first went to foster care when I was seven. My daddy was gone. I think he left my mom when she got pregnant with me. My mom was usin' even then. The neighbors called social services and that was it. They came and got all of us. There were six of us kids—all with different fathers. They couldn't keep us together, so they had us in different places. I was always in trouble when I was a kid—fightin' and skippin' school. The foster moms would start out likin' me, but then they wouldn't want anything to do with me. They would wind up calling social services sayin' get that kid out of here. Of course, the last one had sex with me before she called social services."

I'm not surprised. Tray is proud—puffed up with the sexual conceit of a man remembering an early conquest. "She wanted me. I had sex with one of my teachers too." This happens at Markham Middle School, the lowest-performing middle school in Los Angeles and a focal point of black gang recruitment. "I liked the teacher but I didn't do so good at school." This is an understatement. His educational history is a sham— and includes an endless list of high schools—Manual Arts, Fremont, Crenshaw, Gardena—even an "opportunity transfer" to Palisades High, the school, I think ruefully, that Shannon is now attending.

"School didn't last," Tray tells me. "I started bangin' when I was eleven. Robbin'. Fightin'. Doin' drugs. I was in camp when I was twelve, in between all the schools, and I went to—y'know—all the usual ones."

Tray recites the names of twelve different camps—the stations of the cross, homie style. He fathered a daughter at sixteen. But the summer before he turned seventeen, Tray hit the big time: he was jumped in to the Compton Piru clique.

The Piru Bloods claim both territory and celebrity connections. The late rap "mogul" Suge Knight, founder of Death Row Records, claimed a connection to the gang. Tracing the sets and subsets is like playing a weird version of "six degrees of Kevin Bacon." Still, Tray tries to explain it to me.

"The Pirus are a gang under a gang, an alliance under an alliance. The Pirus got sets which got subsets." What I understand from this labyrinth is that Tray was a Blood. I start asking about his old life, telling him to just nod if he has ever experienced something I bring up.

"Drugs."

Nod.

"Guns."

Nod.

"Robbery."

Nod.

"Rape."

A half nod.

Tray was shot several times. At nineteen, he wound up in the ER at St. Francis Medical Center in Lynwood, where a nurse told Tray about a gang-intervention program that recruited active gang members and trained them to be paramedics. Tray emerged as the "Earn Respect" program's success case. He was quoted in an *LA Times* article about his achievement, explaining, "It's like going from hell to heaven, all we need is a chance."

Less than a year later, Tray was back in hell. Arrested for the attempted murder of a police officer and a John Doe—an unidentified individual. A deal was struck.

"When I went to prison, I thought I was invincible, but I wound up with two strikes. I already had one strike when I was sentenced and then I got into a fight when I was in there and then one of the guys in the fight, y'know . . ."

"Died." I finish for him.

I keep thinking, *I don't want to know, I don't want to know.* I didn't want to associate Tray with a cold-blooded killing. But I couldn't ignore this. The cat had dragged the dead mouse in, and there it sat, in the middle of the floor.

There is no remorse in Tray's eyes. And he is one of the good ones. He is at least trying to leave the neighborhood. I feel nauseated.

"I was bad. I was still fightin' demons. I just kinda went into a nose-dive when I got out of prison. I couldn't find a job, so I started sellin' drugs." We continue walking.

"Everything feels hard," Tray admits while nodding in acknowledgment at a group of homies. He is a promiscuous greeter, calling out to everyone he sees. Women like Tray, they are flirtatious. They wave their cell phones at him and say, "Call me," or roll their tongues around their lips suggestively. Several make derogatory comments about me while miming how they will provide oral sex. One is less subtle. "I will suck your cock anytime, baby. White girls don't know how to suck cock, baby. She too small for you, baby." Tray puts his arm around my shoulders protectively. I repeat my internal mantra: *It is daytime, I am safe.* We are deep in Pirus territory.

After prison, Tray wound up at Homeboy Industries. He was unusual—one of the few African Americans working at the old office in East Los Angeles. And yet his physical grace and gregarious personality won everyone over. Tray fell in love, got his first apartment, and had a fiancée who had given birth to twins on Christmas.

"I loved workin' at Homeboy but it took me a long time to settle down. I was still with my neighborhood. I'd lie—and still bang, pretend I wasn't slangin' when I was, pretend I wasn't usin' when I was. I started goin' to AA. I said I wasn't going to deal. And then, you get weak. You deal, and you say, I won't taste, I won't do it. Then I relapsed, everything was goin' downhill, and finally I got it! You need to be sober—because when you're not sober, everything goes downhill. I believe now. I pray. I wanna be a good father to my girls.

"I can be at home—and I hear someone's gonna party—and I wanna go. Then I gotta say, 'I'm grown.' Reality sets in—I gotta think—I got the twins. At first, I wanted to do it for other people and now I wanna do it for myself. I kept thinkin' I didn't grow up in a messed-up home. I was denyin' the truth. But I did. It was a crazy fuckin' place. And it helped me a lot of ways—I know how to survive. That's how I feel like I know I can relate to so many people. I came from the roughest situation. This has made me the person I am today. The streets will be me."

Tray is wistful. He talks about the father he has tried to find. He wants his daughters to know their history. But he ends our visit telling me he has "business." He can't walk me back to my car.

I hold him tightly and tell him I love him. He smiles, his face goofily happy.

"Everything's a fight in my life. I'm glad you're here."

One week later my phone rings. It's Hector. "Tray is gone. He was shot and killed Saturday." There is a silence between us that is long and filled with sorrow.

In the days that follow, the story of Tray's death unfolds in a typical manner. He was shot during the day, at a Bloods reunion picnic. No, he was shot at night, after the picnic. It was because of a fight. No, it was because the shooter was high on a combination of four tabs of acid and a bottle of red wine. No, it was because his former gang had set him up.

"I thought you told me Tray left the gang," Mark says to me later that day when we are out walking.

I shrug, because this is impossible to explain. You can never leave the gang.

I am standing at Tray's gravesite at Inglewood Cemetery. My paternal grandparents are buried two "lanes" away in the same "memorial park." There is a press of people surrounding a solid oak casket with brass handles. Tray is buried in his Homeboy shirt. His mother is high and crying, screaming, *"Who's gonna be the ball bearings? Who's gonna be the ball bearings?*" It takes several moments before I realize she is asking who the pallbearers will be. His fiancée is sobbing and it looks like there are at least a hundred people representing—wearing all manner of red, from red knit stocking caps to red sweat pants and sweat shirts. The men have their sleeves rolled up and bare their tattoos—menacing and proud. There are young women dressed in clinging red jersey dresses—attire for clubbing after-hours, not praying at a gravesite in broad daylight.

I am crying and feel as if I will never stop. The homies throw gang signs and chant, "Pirus, Pirus, Pirus."

An unidentified woman comes forward and begins to hump the casket. She is in ecstasy and as she writhes I can hear her words.

"You can never leave never leave never leave."

You can never leave the gang.

FOURTEEN

Intervention

We're the ones in the street, riskin' our lives every night.
And no one respects us, no one understands that we are out
there. If we weren't, there would be blood runnin' through
the streets.

—Khalid Washington

Gangbanging is not limited to the streets: policymakers, foundations, and law enforcement all over California are arguing over the most effective ways to reduce gang violence. Many believe that "hard-core" street intervention is the answer. The Mayor's Office funds these efforts to the tune of $6 million, while Homeboy Industries, focused on long-term intervention, continues to struggle. I am inadvertently drawn into the fight. The first year of the Homeboy study is under way, and the preliminary data is promising. But I am also completing an evaluation for the Weingart Foundation on the Unity Collaborative program of "ambassador" street intervention, and its outcomes are strong. At this point, I am completely confused over what—if anything—is the "answer."

As the debate rages, Julio Marcial organizes a Violence Prevention Conference for the California Wellness Foundation, with an eclectic cast of characters. LAPD deputy chief Pat Gannon arrives to describe the department's collaboration with the Mayor's Office gang-reduction program. Blinky Rodriguez is there—ready to talk about Communities in Schools. Julio has tapped me to head up a panel examining the effectiveness of street intervention, asking, "Do you want to come out in support of hard-core intervention or are you gonna be completely critical?"

I don't know.

To further confuse matters, the conference opens with its keynote speaker: Father Greg Boyle, who worked with gang members before it was fashionable. Over twenty years earlier, when he started the small

storefront agency that would grow into Homeboy Industries, he received death threats, not invitations to symposiums. He was accused of
"sheltering" gang members. But now even the cops want to hear what
he has to say. Greg doesn't discuss street intervention at the conference.
He focuses on the need for kinship and the importance of job training
and comprehensive services. He is funny, insightful, and restrained. But
a week later, at dinner with Mark and me, Greg is anything but.

"I think the ideas guiding hard-core street intervention are ridicu-
lous," Greg insists while we drink Laphroaig on the rocks. He is not like
any priest I have known. "Go out to anyone in their community and ask
them if they want a truce with the neighborhoods so they can 'live with'
gang members and the answer is *no!* No one wants to live with gangs.
They want them gone from their community. No one wants to negotiate with them. I don't know why the police advance this point of view."

He and Mark talk at length about the law enforcement mentality,
and for once I sit silent. At the beginning of our marriage, I could never
have imagined this scene. Mark and Greg, independent of me, enjoy a
strong bond and a true friendship. I think about how my brother Tony
recently reported, "When I tell people you're married to a cop and work
with a priest, they ask me if I have another sister." However, Greg's
words snap me out of my reverie.

"I think the street interventionists operate like a SWAT team," he
insists while Mark laughs.

"Yeah, but you gotta remember, in places like South Bureau, the
LAPD has grown to respect these guys. They've built relationships with
the street interventionists over the years. They're not snitches—they
won't betray anyone in the neighborhoods—but they help one another
to try to stop the shooting. You gotta be realistic about this, Greg."

"I am realistic. I think the police are settling for a short-term fix
instead of a long-term solution. On top of this, don't they realize that
it's the people who've worked with gang members over long periods of
time who are responsible for the drop in crime—this hasn't happened
overnight. And it hasn't happened because of the interventionists."

Everything Greg is saying makes sense, but his is not a popular view.
Following the lead originally set by Ron Bergmann, the LAPD has combined suppression with street intervention, and gang-related crime in

Los Angeles continues to drop. Gang violence has not disappeared, but almost everyone agrees that things are under control. Overall crime is approaching a thirty-year low. It is hard to argue with such success, but Greg Boyle does. He insists that it is a mistake to attribute the drop in crime to the efforts of the LAPD and the street interventionists. *Has the emphasis on street intervention worked against real change*, I wonder? Greg does not.

"We *had* the opportunity for real change. Here we were on the brink of tearing this thing wide open and inviting anyone with a pulse who has their life together to be involved with these folks. Instead we create this rarefied group—the street interventionists—who claim that gang members will listen only to them. What are they talking about? We shouldn't be telling gang members to listen to someone. Our task is to listen to them."

There is an undeniable truth to this. I practically have ASK, DON'T TELL tattooed on my tongue. It's probably one of the reasons people trust me. I don't want to tell them what to do. No one can be convinced to leave the gang. This lesson appears lost on both law enforcement and the practitioners of street intervention who believe outreach will solve the problem.

"Oh, come on," Greg laughs. "Just what *is* all this nonsense about possessing a license to operate? There's no such thing. You need all hands on deck—everyone helping—that's what makes the difference. From after-school programs to job development. And everything in between—including mental health services."

"But you have people who say street intervention works," I counter, still agnostic.

"I think it works, but it doesn't help. Remember, not everything that works, helps. But everything that helps, works."

Khalid, however, has other ideas. I meet him in South LA a week later. We spend the afternoon together, kicking it, while I wait for two homies I'm supposed to interview. They never show up. Instead, I ask Khalid why he thinks street intervention is the best way to deal with gang violence.

"Whether it's Greg Boyle or the LAPD, they don't know what we're really dealing with," Khalid begins. "We got real trouble in the neighborhoods—and the only thing that is keeping the peace is the intervention goin' on in the street. We're the only ones these gangbangers listen to. We're stoppin' the violence and gettin' the neighborhoods to practice mutual respect."

But the exact meaning of mutual respect between gang members remains unclear. I suspect it's the street version of a non-compete agreement. Several people from the neighborhoods have offered me their opinion that truces aren't negotiated to keep the peace; they exist to allow gangs to sell drugs or "product" in different areas. But Khalid never mentions drug dealing. Instead, he talks about rumor control and violence interruption. But I think, *Why is it that no one who practices street intervention is discussing how to help people leave the gang?*

While we talk, Rashad Davis walks in and Khalid announces, "Here's who you wanna talk to." Rashad was once a shot caller for a Bloods set and still looks the part. Beyond this, he behaves like someone who is still active. He never wants to be photographed and rarely appears in public.

"Rashad is the real deal—he's not one of those Hollywood interventionists—they wanna work for the mayor and get their picture in the paper. Fuck that. Rashad has taught me, y'know, operate below the radar." While Khalid chatters away, Rashad barely speaks. I ask Rashad what he thinks, but he remains noncommittal, telling me only, "What keeps the peace are the truces." I leave, still confused.

That night I call Celeste Fremon.

"All I hear about are the truces, the truces, the truces," I tell her.

"What I want to know," Celeste sighs, "is where are these truces? Has anyone seen them?"

She was right. We constantly heard about the peace treaties and truces—who negotiated them and who agreed to them. But there was never a witness, never an outside observer. The interventionists would announce that different neighborhoods had made agreements, drafted treaties, and entered into "the truce" or "the understanding." And these agreements lasted as long as they lasted, until the violence started up again.

The next night, I spend six hours with Kenny Green, who promises to explain more about street intervention and the truces. We hang out in the Harbor—a place that sounds like a naval destination and is pretty

much unknown outside the neighborhoods. Before leaving home, I tell
Mark where I am going.

"That is one of the most violent parts of LA, and no one knows
about it." Sometimes it helps immensely that Mark is part of the LAPD.
We share a shorthand about gang hot spots and problems.

"Did you take your BlackBerry?" he asks. When I start laughing, he
becomes irritated. "You need to take your BlackBerry and you need to
take identification. Am I gonna have to tell you this every time you go
out?"

Every time you go out. At last we have arrived at this.

"Why do I need identification?"

"In case something happens to you."

"I'm gonna be with Kenny."

"What if something happens to him?"

Mark is right, but over the past few months I've noticed that he no
longer tries to stop me from going out. He tries not to be controlling.
At the same time, I am actually beginning to delight in life at home. We
have finally left Westlake Village and moved back to West Los Angeles,
actually turning a healthy profit when we sold our house in the gated
community. Shannon is settled into an overcrowded but diverse and
lively charter school. And I am now "Mom," not Jorja. But the streets
still call me. Tonight that call takes me to somewhere I have never
been—the southernmost tip of Los Angeles.

Kenny is my guide, as he has been for so many years. He is over
six feet tall, with high cheekbones, copper-colored skin, and an arresting presence. His charisma is matched by his intellectual curiosity. The
latter leads him to routinely travel beyond the hood, to cultural events.
Two nights before, he had texted me from Royce Hall: "@ UCLA listening 2 Deepak Chopra." Kenny was once an active gang member, but he
talks very little about his former life in the Harbor area. Occasionally his
rage flares and I witness traces of the past. "Kenny was a badass," a ten-
year-old homie once told me. "I wonder why he left the neighborhood."

But Kenny and I rarely talk about the past. He is consumed with
changing the lives of the "little homies" that he sees. While he left his
neighborhood a decade ago, he lives in the same area, working as an
interventionist and all around go-to guy for social services. If someone

has a job interview or needs tattoo removal, Kenny delivers them to their appointment.

We drive around late at night, through different areas, stopping occasionally to talk with homies. Prostitutes flirt with Kenny shamelessly. There are also more reserved figures—including Pelham.

"You'll find out that people go around sayin' that Pelham is responsible for most of the product in the area—and his family has been doin' this for a long time," Kenny says as he introduces me to a nondescript African American man in his early forties who could pass for a thin, wiry basketball coach. Kenny doesn't talk but I already know that Pelham sells crack cocaine, and "special" customers can drive down an alley and pick up their order at an open window. A little after 11:00 p.m. on this particular night, I watch the In-N-Out Burger of crack. While I sit with Kenny, three BMWs make the trip down the alley, and I think of my cousin Nick. The scene lends new meaning to the term "drive-thru."

"That's for the large orders," Pelham tells me. "For the smaller orders, I have runners." The runners are young, and on cue, one walks up to Pelham, Kenny, and me. He eyes me suspiciously.

"We don't like outsiders here," the little homie warns. "We steal their money, we beat them up."

Kenny starts laughing. "Listen to this youngster. He sounds just like me. I used to do the same thing when I was his age."

"Quiet down, boy. She's a friend. She's coo'," Pelham explains.

There is an unspoken question and it's always the same: Is she police? Kenny, just like Big Mike, vouches for my credibility. He knows I will never reveal anything I hear on the street, with one exception: child abuse.

Of course, there is little chance of this. I rarely see homies with their baby mamas or their children. No one invites me to come over to his crib. Like gang members all over Los Angeles, many homies in the Harbor really don't live anywhere. They crash together at different apartments. The homies who actually possess a permanent address find themselves operating a crammed safe house, six or seven people to a room, often without heat or electricity. There is literally no place for visitors. And of course, there is always criminal activity. I may not be police, but no one wants me to know what they are doing. Instead, I meet homies on the street or in local parks where the outdoor basketball courts are always in use. Hoops go on 24/7 in the hood. I see youngsters playing all hours of the day and night. They look carefree.

But not even the basketball games escape neighborhood tensions. There are ten-year-olds wearing Nikes with red or blue shoelaces. The colors are subtle, nothing overt. But everyone watches carefully—it's a matter of life and death. No one wants to make a mistake with what they're wearing. It's not just that red represents the Bloods and blue the Crips—all these shades reinforce the hood esprit de corps. The colors are everywhere—it's a badge of honor. Kenny tells me to look at the piping on their baseball cap brims. These kids are young—in the last year of elementary school.

"I don't worry about the kids who show up every day and play. They are okay," Sean Robinson tells me. With his polo shirt and whistle, he is readily identifiable as the local park director. But he also has both ears pierced and his forearms are sleeved. He sees me studying his tattoos, which are all decorative and not gang-related.

"I grew up here, I know what's goin' on. If the kids show up every day they're fine. If, all of a sudden, I notice they're gone, not comin' to play, not comin' out, I know they're gettin' into trouble."

Trouble can mean all kinds of things. Three days earlier, two young homies broke into his office and stole eighty dollars from his desk drawer. Sean did not call the LAPD. Instead, he called Kenny. Kenny found the two youngsters, got the money, and told them to quit stealing. It's local justice, and the authority figure doesn't wear a uniform. When I ask Sean about the theft, he laughs.

"They're just youngsters. Why would I call the police? God only knows what would happen to them then. So I get Kenny. And he takes care of it. And he makes sure these youngsters will learn the lesson not to steal. In a good way." It's clear that Kenny Green is the long arm of the law in the Harbor. But Kenny is very careful to explain that while he maintains his street credibility—his license to operate—his former life is long gone.

"My days with the neighborhood happened when I was just a young-ster," he tells me. "I said good-bye to all that a long time ago."

"But what made you able to leave the gang? How did you let go of your neighborhood?"

"You never leave the neighborhood—you just stop participatin'. I guess I'm like an alumni. I graduated. But I still check in with my old homies—we visit—it's not a lot different than you."

Over and over again, homies equate leaving the neighborhood with graduating college. So where do I fit in? I "graduated" UCLA three times—ending up with my PhD in 1988. But I am *still* there. I have now been on the faculty for nearly twenty years. Does that make me an OG of sorts? This may be my own version of "you can never leave the gang." I am beginning to understand that leaving—like joining—is not a hard-and-fast process.

Kenny and I meet up with Dead Eye. He is out of prison just six months, and I would bet my two-bedroom cottage that he still bangs. He makes $1,000 a month at Starbucks. Along with this, he catches a few shifts unloading cargo at the Wilmington docks.

"I need work," Dead Eye complains. "I'm not makin' enough money at Starbucks. It's bullshit, man. I can't serve another fuckin' latte." I am trying hard not to laugh at the visual of this 250-pound tatted-up gang-banger working as a barista, but Kenny doesn't blink.

"So stop bangin' and look for a better job. Full-time." Kenny spits out the words. Dead Eye tells Kenny he will "check it out." He leaves, saying he needs something to drink.

"He's still active," Kenny observes.

"Why doesn't a job stop anyone from hangin' out with the neigh-borhood?"

"If it's only part-time, if they got nothin' else, they're gonna keep bangin'," Kenny tells me. "Just a job isn't enough. They need help."

"It's quiet right now," Dead Eye observes when he returns, nursing a beer. The smell of bud is in the air. Kenny is the lead announcer tonight, and Dead Eye is the color commentator.

"There's not much going on," Dead Eye begins. "Tonight's an in-junction night. The cops come through to enforce the gang injunctions, right on schedule, Wednesday, Thursday, Sunday. So on those nights, we all stay in. The other nights they don't come out here. Then we come out to play." He doesn't bother to correct the pronoun, adding, "On injunction night, we come out but we gotta be out alone—there can't be three or more together. They bust us."

There was a major overhaul of public housing in the mid-1990s. Farther north, in East LA, the Pico-Aliso projects were demolished. Here, on the east side of the Los Angeles Harbor, the projects that were home to many African Americans were leveled, pushing residents into areas traditionally inhabited by Latinos. In a miscarriage of urban "planning," this renovation of public housing caused gang warfare. Over the past decade, battles between the neighborhoods in the Harbor had claimed many lives.

"This is ground zero for hate crimes," Kenny says soberly. "Like I told you a while back, it's the blacks and the browns." I have heard these words already. A year before, at Hollenbeck Middle School, where I have worked evaluating a gang-prevention program, Felipe Mendez and I had talked about racism, in and out of prison. Felipe is a sensitive man. But I could tell by the three tears running down his left cheek that he'd had multiple prison stays. When I asked him about how the races operate in prison, he was embarrassed to admit he sometimes still followed the rules of behavior.

"If you give someone black the can that you're drinking from—you can never drink after them," Felipe explained. "Or if you give them some of your food, you can never eat from the same plate. When you get out from being locked up, the rules stay the same." It sounds like the prison version of apartheid, and it is alive and well in post-racial America.

Compared to the relative stability ensured by prison politics, the atmosphere in the Harbor is far from tranquil. No one abides by any rules. This little sliver of gang territory, unknown and overlooked, is where the browns and blacks fight incessantly. They don't eat from the same plate. Instead, they try to kill each other.

"The gangbangers out here don't get a lot of attention," Kenny told me. "And we don't get a lot of resources."

Someone shoots from between two parked cars. It's a random shot, to whom it may concern, and everyone slowly looks up. I crane my neck to see, and Kenny reaches over and pushes me down. There is one more blast of gunfire before the street goes quiet. Later that night, I cannot sleep. It's a delayed reaction, and I recognize it as a nascent sign of PTSD. Greg Boyle frequently refers to "our PTSD," as if discussing a difficult family member.

After spending time with Kenny, I am convinced that things are slowly changing—maybe even starting to get better. I tell this to Ronny a week later, when we meet in Watts. Ronny, however, disagrees.

"There's a lot goin' on, but you just don't know about it. There are still people dyin'. But here's what happens. The LAPD don't record nothin'. If they don't record nothin', they don't report nothin'. If they don't report nothin', it's like it never happened. Simple."

I didn't subscribe to the conspiracy theory of LAPD statistics, but I knew that more crime was occurring than was being reported. And oddly enough, a criminologist who consulted with the National Institute of Justice—the research arm of the Department of Justice— confirmed Ronny's theory, albeit confidentially.

"Bill Bratton relocated gang crime—that's what happened," she explained. "You look at the city of Los Angeles and crime went down. Go forty miles due east to the Inland Empire and they're talking about a gang epidemic. This isn't resolving the problem—it's relocating the problem."

What this particular criminologist, along with many others, has noted is that gang violence is no longer exclusively urban. Suburbs have grown more socioeconomically diverse—making way for gang migration. Researchers have identified "chronic gang cities" and "emerging gang cities." In my own non-scientific universe, I receive more and more calls from gang-prevention and -intervention programs in the Inland Empire, a region centered on two cities, Riverside and San Bernardino, that sprawls out until it reaches Los Angeles County, connected by the freeway systems of Southern California. Kenny and I talk about the spread of the neighborhoods two weeks later when we go out again.

"The gangbangers goin' everywhere," he remarks while we watch a basketball game in Banning Park. There are a few homies out drinking forty-ouncers and smoking bud. Shots can be heard sporadically. Homies who are blown or angry shoot up houses and parked cars with casual abandon, trying to avoid the living. "But the other problem," he adds, "is that we can't stop the guns—they're everywhere.

"These youngsters," Kenny continues. "They got someone to give them guns but they got no one to teach them to be a man." I want Kenny to talk with Kevin Williams. Nothing is working with Kevin. Neither

Greg nor Hector has been able get through to him. Maybe an African American former gang member can connect. I ask Kevin to meet Kenny at these basketball courts the next day. Kenny and I both show up.

There is no sign of Kevin.

"Maybe he should just move out of the neighborhood, maybe that's what he needs—to leave LA," I begin.

Kenny disagrees. "You can't be a part-time homie. You gotta heal the community you tried to destroy. Otherwise you'll never have any peace. You gotta live next to the neighborhoods, work in the community—let people see you livin' there. It's a sign of respect."

I think about Big Mike as he says this, but I keep quiet. These days Big Mike is working night and day in Jordan Downs. Despite the downward trend of crime in Los Angeles, gang violence doesn't decrease in the projects. But once he finishes counseling and intervening and organizing and preaching, Big Mike climbs into his tow truck and drives back to Cherry Valley, in the Inland Empire. He chooses *not* to live in the community he serves. Until recently, the same applied to Bo Taylor, who labored in South Los Angeles but lived in Riverside County. In a way, each of these men is the mirror image of the police officers fighting crime in Los Angeles, who scramble into their SUVs at end of watch, driving off to Santa Clarita and Stevenson Ranch, far from the communities that they pledge to protect and serve. Kenny Green is an anomaly.

I don't know who is right. I'm stuck trying to figure out what would be best for Kevin.

Big Mike calls while I am with Kenny and tells me that Marlo Jones, aka Bow Wow, the interventionist who once worked for him, has been arrested for burglary. "I'm glad Bo fired him," Big Mike tells me. "I hate to say it but Bow Wow was just no good. Bo knew it. I knew it. Aquil knew it. Now he's locked up where he should be. I just wish Bo were here to help with handlin' this."

Bo Taylor has been dead a little over six months—after a long struggle with cancer that included alternative therapies and trips to Tijuana. Too much has happened. Mario. Bow Wow. Even Alex Sanchez, who is still being held by the Feds, waiting for an appeal on the denial of his request for bail. The motives and activities of the street interventionists are constantly under suspicion.

I'm not worried about gang intervention being a front for criminal activity. I'm worried that it is only palliative. It helps in the alleviation of symptoms that are responsible for a great deal of pain and suffering. *But it doesn't heal in any permanent way.*

Kenny and I talk about Bow Wow and the future of intervention. I try to call Kevin, but he never answers. We wait.

One week later, I drive down to KUSH, a gang-intervention program whose acronym stands for absolutely nothing, in Watts. I have asked Kevin Williams to meet me there. I am still hoping that he will attach to a former gangbanger. I keep thinking the right father figure can help Kevin. Maybe he needs an African American role model. Someone other than Tupac Shakur, for God's sake. Every black homie I know looks up to Tupac—the martyr of hip-hop. Ronny has told me, "If he lived, Tupac would have been bigger than Dr. Martin Luther King."

The interventionists meeting at KUSH are still recovering from the journalist Anderson Cooper's visit the week before. The CNN cameras focused on the agency, broadcasting interviews from its headquarters— an empty house directly across the street from Nickerson Gardens. Today, one bedroom serves as a makeshift meeting room where the interventionists huddle around the table. There is no discussion of gangs. Instead, everyone is talking about money. Big Mike is in a state of financial panic.

"I jus' don't have enough fundin'—I can't help these children. I'm livin' in Cherry Valley. It takes me a coupla hours to get into town, and I'm usin' a lotta gas. I don't have any fundin'. I don't know how much longer I can go on."

I am speechless. The loss of Big Mike would be devastating for Jordan Downs and South LA. His role in things should be expanding, not dwindling.

More interventionists arrive and the bedroom at KUSH quickly fills up until people are sitting on the floor. I call Kevin, but he does not answer. I call Elena, who tells me he is gone. After I let Kenny know that Kevin is not going to be meeting us today, we relocate to the William Nickerson Gardens Recreation Center.

"This is the only recreation center in the projects," Big Mike observes. It is also the place where, a few months later, an interventionist will be shot and paralyzed from the shoulders down. But this happens during the dark early-morning hours—now it is light and the place looks like your average community homework-center. The room is equipped with a bank of computers along one wall, awaiting kids for after-school tutoring. The problem is that it's now 4:30 p.m. and no one is here. We meet in the tidy stillness.

"I need money. I told the Mayor's Office but they don't wanna give it to me. They say I'm too small, my agency isn't big enough. And even if they give me the money, I don't know if I want it. They might think I'm a snitch, my life is gonna be in danger." Big Mike is worried about the immediate future. In three months, it is rumored that forty thousand prisoners are set to be released from California prisons. It is estimated that half of them will descend on Los Angeles County. This is an old rumor, but the interventionists are on edge.

"Our lives are gonna be in danger, 'cuz we gotta lotta dry snitchin' going on," T. Rogers volunteers. "Dry snitching" occurs when law enforcement compiles bits and pieces of information from informants until it adds up to a case. Everyone looks uneasy. The interventionists walk a fine line; they are at risk if their relationship with the police is seen as collaboration. Their attitude swings between bravado and fear. But like Rashad Davis and Blinky Rodriguez, they believe "we are the only ones who are out there. Without us there is gonna be blood in the streets."

I am tired of this refrain, but I also know that it is true. I am learning that street peace and justice extends down a spectrum—from the truces I don't see or understand to violent retaliation when there has been child abuse. But things are happening within these disenfranchised communities at a grassroots level. There are OGs and community organizers who are beginning to work at healing their streets from within. Although the LAPD has worked hard in recent years to rework its tarnished image and build community relationships, here in South Los Angeles, mistrust of the police remains. In Rampart, there are still protests against police brutality and suspicion reinforced by the violence that erupted during the May Day melee—the incident in MacArthur Park in 2007 where LAPD used excessive force to break up a lawful immigration demonstration. People who live in these communities don't always want to deal with law enforcement. Sometimes they would rather deal with the inter-vention worker who takes the place of the "beat cop." I don't voice this opinion today while I'm sitting in Nickerson Gardens. But later, when I get home, I am brought up short by something Mark says.

"You're so interested in the interventionists—don't you realize they're the law enforcement arm of gang intervention? They have to go to an academy. They have to get special training. And they're the only ones who feel qualified to handle violence in the community."

I am speechless. Shannon is greatly amused.

"Dad is right. All you have to do is take out the word 'intervention-ists' and put in 'police' and it's practically the same."

Suddenly, I am too tired to think about all of this. Then Shannon tells me, "Uncle Chris called. He said Nick is in rehab."

FIFTEEN

Business

Rule Number One: Shut the fuck up.
Rule Number Two: Shut the fuck up.
That's how you do business.

—Felipe Mendez

I am sitting in a restaurant in Chinatown, waiting for Joanna. She is late and I use the time to problem-solve. For once, my dilemma doesn't involve a gang member. Instead, it's family. My cousin Nick has left the Betty Ford Center after two days and no one knows where he is. I am trying to figure out who to call when Joanna walks in and the room shape-shifts into a confessional. The trouble is, I'm not a priest.

"I've gotta tell you something."

"I know," I say levelly.

"What do you know?" she asks, suddenly suspicious.

"Just tell me."

I wait.

"I'm hustlin' again. I can't go to Homeboy. I can't even look G in the face."

Joanna doesn't openly admit to drug dealing. Hustling is code for all street enterprises: drug dealing, fencing stolen goods, even selling handmade jewelry. But Joanna's eyes fill with guilty tears. She wants to know how I knew and is surprised when I show her my field notes, where I have graphed my suspicions.

Drugs are the quickest pathway to financial stability. I think Joanna strug-
gles to survive financially and is tempted to hustle. She has told me she doesn't
have money. But at Bullet's graduation from fire training, she is wearing a
beautiful outfit and ballet flats. Her nails are freshly manicured and Marcos
wears a new outfit. Joanna films the graduation ceremony with a small, expen-
sive video cam. I think she is dealing.

"Mama, you're on it," Joanna observes, the closest she'll come to admitting my notes are accurate. "That's what we wind up doin'. Bullet's gone to rehab and I don't know what else to do. I've got no money. People in the neighborhood—my family—they told me they were gonna help me when Bullet left and then they didn't do anything. And I can't make it. I gotta get my hustle on."

I ask her how much money she makes from dealing, but Joanna remains cagey. "Don't ask me that. I already feel like shit."

I wonder just how much this is. Angel Duarte has already bragged that he makes $4,000 a month tax-free from dealing, but I think he is exaggerating. Sudhir Venkatesh, author of *Gang Leader for a Day*, did the math while studying the Black Kings gang in Chicago's South Side, finding that the average foot soldier made about $3 a day. While I think the net may be higher in Los Angeles, it is not lost upon me that no one I know is getting rich dealing drugs. They are just getting by. But I don't ask Joanna. Part of me doesn't want to know. Instead I tell her that she should go to Homeboy and talk to Greg about money.

"I don't want to." She is adamant.

"Why?"

"I'm probably just too proud," she says. "And I know Father Greg cares about me—the trouble is once we got Bullet into rehab, Homeboy really started havin' trouble with money. Homeboy doesn't have money. I don't have money. We're all fucked. I just don't know what to do about money. That's the truth. So I hustle a little. I gotta get by."

I'm trying to figure out just how drugs figure in gang life. Joanna insists that drug dealing is how some of the larger neighborhoods—like 18th Street and Florencia—finance operations: it puts their foot soldiers out on the street. Listening to her, I begin to believe that these "soldiers" are the neighborhood sales force. A moment later she adds to this account, saying that the proceeds also enable the neighborhood leaders to buy cars and houses.

"My grandmother owns her own house," Joanna explains, and I imagine a sweet Mexican woman carefully paying off a small mortgage on a monthly basis over the years. I later learn that her grandmother was a notorious drug dealer who owns three houses "free and clear." However, when I ask about the mechanics of drug dealing, Joanna shuts down. "I gotta go get Marcos from preschool," she tells me, then leaves.

Ronny turns out to be a more willing guide to the everyday life of a drug dealer. There was talk that he had been groomed to be a shot caller but lacked both interest and ambition. The neighborhood underachiever, Ronny excelled at street dealing. He still possesses the easy smile and relaxed manner of a natural salesman, sharing the story of his career trajectory and its slippery slope into dealing. Ronny had managed a crack house and a "rollin'" corner where business was good. But after a six-month visit to county jail, he stayed out of the business for a year. He desperately wanted to be legit—but no job materialized.

"I thought I would be okay, but I couldn't get a job. Then I started sellin' marijuana—little nickel and dime bags. I was the best weed seller in the world. But y'know, I wasn't sellin' much, just a half a pound a day. It was cool. One day, I had like a hundred bucks and I said fuck it, let me buy a quarter pound—no more little bitty two ounces of weed, I'm gonna sell a lot. I kept on sellin' more and more till I got caught for possession and I went to jail, my first drug case."

Of course, once free, his employment prospects hadn't improved.

"When I got out of jail, my brother had his own drug spot rollin' and my cousin had his. My brother said, 'I don't wanna getcha right back into selling drugs.' But I wanted to hang with my cousin—he had women around—so I started sellin' dope ten days after I got out. My cousin got me a job doin' inventory. I still was sellin' drugs but I was goin' to work too, plus I had me my first little car. I would go to work in the daytime and sell drugs at night. My life was balanced. But then things changed. I started sellin' crack cocaine—the money was faster. I quit my job. Weed had been fun and it involved women. Crack cocaine was male-dominated and it was for reals, not fun. I was workin' for somebody who was a really good person. . . ."

Is he serious? I think, hoping my expression doesn't give me away.

"The individual who ran the business took care of me—I was able to do what I wanted to—I was hands-on and independent."

I struggle to understand how Ronny, who reads the Bible on a daily basis, could tell me a crack distributor was a good person. Over a decade ago, crack cocaine had laid siege to and basically decimated the African American population in Los Angeles and San Francisco. At one point, half the families in South LA were reportedly "in the system" as clients of child welfare, courtesy crack cocaine. Even today, many feel the black community has never quite recovered—including the African American men who drew extensive drug sentences. I can't stop myself from reminding Ronny of this.

"I know what crack did to people—to my family. But I would sell drugs to my family. If they needed money—I would give it to them. If they had no money, I would give drugs to them."

I stop myself before I tell Ronny what else I think. He watched his mother destroy her life on crack cocaine, but that is not part of this narrative. Instead, we talk about the money drugs brought. They also brought other changes.

"Sellin' drugs required things. It required guns, it required more attention to the streets, so basically it was time consuming with both my actions and my mind—I had to be worried about it all the time. But it brought me status too. I started to get a little more rank in my neighborhood. You could fight all you want, you could be brave all you want. If you don't got no money or no gun in the projects, you don't got no rank." This was the curriculum vitae of a successful gangbanger: drugs, money, guns.

Still, Ronny was not a major drug distributor. He could not shed any real light on who controlled drug distribution and how this played out in the neighborhoods. The truth about the relationship between gangs and drugs was a dicey thing. There was a mythology that gangs controlled drug sales, operating through an entrepreneurial, highly structured bureaucracy more intricate than the IRS. This all played into the drama of conspiracy and gang corporate structure that had people in the suburbs quaking in fear and law enforcement assembling task forces to "take back the streets." Newspaper headlines and TV docudramas fed the narrative of the lethal, drug-dealing gang "organization." Two decades of research, however, had begun to offer another perspective. While some studies continued discussing "corporate" gangs, other research showed that drug dealing formed only a small piece of neighborhood existence. Several studies revealed that the smallest, most numerous gangs were preoccupied with loyalty and territory, not product. Instead of violent, organized groups, the neighborhoods were barely capable of what Greg Boyle often referred to as "disorganized crime." As early as 1996, on the tail end of the "decade of death," the National Youth Gang Survey questioned three thousand law enforcement departments nationwide and found that the vast majority believed that gangs were incapable of either managing or controlling drug distribution.

This was what I was seeing in Los Angeles. There was no real connection between drugs and the neighborhoods. In fact, it was more the exception than the rule that the folk I knew pooled their earnings for the gang. Instead, the more enterprising homies told me that they saved their money for their baby mamas or their families. The vast majority of gang members or people trying to leave the neighborhood, like Joanna, sold drugs to "get by." Despite what she told me about financing foot soldiers, her current efforts were fairly typical and less exciting—they had nothing to do with Florencia-13. Drug dealing occurred on impulse and was part of a grab bag of criminal activities like theft, burglary, check fraud; anything and everything was on the table in the struggle to make a living.

Meanwhile, the mythology of the corporate gang was kept alive by law enforcement, which force-fed the public misleading statistics. What bothered me was the distortion by numbers: when an individual who belonged to a neighborhood committed a crime for their own reasons, the police immediately labeled the crime "gang-related." This led to higher statistics about gang-related crime and little understanding of what was really going on in the streets. *It wasn't about the neighborhood, it was about poverty.*

The corporate-gang myth also obscured the truth about drug distribution. For that kind of information, I needed to talk to someone who knew the logistics of drug dealing in LA without being in the business. I begin to consider whom to interview and I feel like I am on a fool's errand. When I share my questions with journalist Celeste Fremon, she urges me to talk to Felipe Mendez. "He is incredible and he knows the business. Y'know, he's out of the life," she remarks. "Felipe has changed so much. And he was a serious character. He was a *real shot caller.*"

Felipe and I had grown close since I had completed the evaluation of a Los Angeles School District gang-prevention program at Hollenbeck and Markham middle schools. It was an intense project that had consumed huge amounts of my time and had broken my heart. So many of these young kids were going to be lost to gangs, and there was little this program could do about it. As the gang interventionist assigned to the program, Felipe served as a combination key leader and mentor to many of these fledgling gangbangers looking for a role model. He was also one of the most intelligent homies I had ever encountered. Medium height and very slim, with hair he wore in a ponytail, Felipe exuded a quiet strength that both men and women found irresistible. He was a natural leader in any endeavor, legitimate or illegitimate. He was the one who knew the rules—to stay quiet and watch your business no matter where you were. He had risen through the neighborhood ranks rapidly, trusted and well respected. And yet, Felipe had turned his back on everything and exited. He stood out, a living rebuke to the idea that you could never leave the gang.

I knew there were scars. Felipe possessed rage and regret, guilt and anxiety and God only knows what else. But along with this backpack full of demons, Felipe was brilliant. Listening to him, I morph into an MBA student in a course taught by a master professor.

"Tell me about your work." I could be straightforward with Felipe. He'd always respond.

"When I was eleven years old, I realized that I wanted things. When you're little you get told—you can't have this, you can't have that. But I wanted things. And I started then, at that age, going to get them. First I got them the easy way. And the easy way was illegal."

This is an understatement. By the time he was twenty years old, Felipe was sitting in Avenal State Prison for possession of a controlled substance with intent to sell. He had fathered four children and had overseen a drug-distribution network before he was even legally eligible to drink. Once he was released, he distanced himself from the neighborhood. "I got serious about making money, and when you get serious, you can't gangbang anymore," Felipe explained. Here he was—the walking, talking counterargument to the mantra that gangs were corporate organizations devoted to drug dealing and revenue.

Felipe tried to go legit—saving his money and eventually opening a restaurant. He was Stringer Bell—the intelligent, ambitious drug-syndicate operative in the HBO series *The Wire*. I was not surprised when Felipe told me how much he loved *The Wire*. He talked about his methodology.

"We would buy fax machines," he explained. "Then we would completely hollow them out—just take out all the guts. We would stuff the drugs into the fax machine and then ship it UPS and Federal Express to houses or offices to where someone took delivery." I marvel at the innovation. But I also wonder why someone as smart as Felipe would join a neighborhood.

"I grew up around it—my mom was in it and my dad was in it, my grandfather was in it, and you kind of feel destined to it. I got jumped in to it when I was thirteen years old. This is a tradition among Latino gangs in the projects—you went through the ritual of getting involved in gangs."

"If you felt destined, how did you get out?"

"I got out when I was about twenty-five. It's kind of hard to say exactly when I got out, but there was a point when I stopped. It's like you say, 'I definitely do not gangbang.' You start to grow out of it. For me, drug dealing kind of pulled me out of it. I had to get serious. Now, there's different . . . what's the word?"

"Perspectives," I fill in. Felipe has always asked for help with his vocabulary.

"Perspectives. I think an outsider would see slanging—drug dealing—as gangbanging. But I'm not worried about gangbanging, I'm worried about money. And I started to reflect about growing up, my family life compared to the family life on TV, those thoughts of my family line, your grandparents, my parent, myself—how did I end up this way and how can I stop the cycle?"

It's hard to reconcile the thirty-two-year-old man in front of me with the thirteen-year-old boy who was jumped into VNE. But the neighborhood fit his identity perfectly. Varrio Nuevo Estrada, also known as VNE, is one of the oldest and largest Hispanic gangs in Los Angeles, its members identify as Southsiders, or Sureños. Founded in the early 1940s, VNE traces its roots to the Estrada Courts project—a Los Angeles City housing development in Boyle Heights. Within Estrada Courts, VNE developed a fiercely violent reputation, which ultimately resulted in a gang injunction being granted, ordering VNE members to cease associating. This did not stop the neighborhood's spread to include multiple cliques in the Antelope Valley of northern Los Angeles County and the Inland Empire. The neighborhood was both feared and revered. Felipe was proud to belong.

The gang provided stability for Felipe, who spent most of his early years in "the system," parented by Children's Protective Services. His father died while incarcerated when Felipe was four years old. His mother suffered with severe mental illness. Their apartment in the projects featured a revolving door of police officers, boyfriends, drug dealers, social workers—all who stayed long enough to indulge, arrest, or remove Felipe and his younger sister, Lilita, from the household. When I asked Felipe what had kept him sane through all of those years, he did not hesitate before replying, "Lily."

"I had my sister," he continued. "When we were in some foster home we would push our beds together and go to sleep with our pinky fingers touching. Nothing else, just our little fingers. And I could get to sleep. Y'know, this makes all the difference in the world, to have someone I can fully trust, whether I'm right or wrong.

"Look at us now," Felipe laughs. "We're still living together."

Felipe has a daughter and Lilita has two sons. Both of them are no longer with their partners. Instead, the brother and sister rent a house in Lincoln Heights. Of course, domestic life is somewhat less than idyllic. Lily suffers from depression. The local schools are overcrowded and underperforming. One of Lily's sons is failing sixth grade. Their landlady is intrusive, "checking" on them all hours of the day and night. There are family arguments. But Felipe tries to mediate. Constantly.

"I imagine this is how you were in the neighborhood," I tell Felipe.

"I was kind of a negotiator."

"If you were born in Brentwood, you would have been an attorney."

"Nah," he says.

"Yeah," I say. "What do you think lawyers do? They negotiate. They mediate."

"Yeah, that's what I used to do in the varrio when some of the *veteranos* would try to scare the youngsters—y'know, intimidate them. I reminded them, 'You can't do this. You gotta remember where you came from.' I guess that's why I ended up being an interventionist. You work with the varrio, you talk with them."

Later, when I relate this to Mark, he is not surprised. "There's your story," he remarked, something he has taken to saying whenever I talk about Felipe. "He is the success case of the neighborhood. Felipe has the story you want to tell." I marveled at Mark's endorsement and then it struck me—they were alike—each of them quietly magnetic and occasionally tyrannical. And both of them were highly intelligent. I gradually began spending more time with Felipe.

A few weeks later I discover that although Felipe has left the neighborhood, he maintains ties to the place where he more or less grew up. Along with Ramona Gardens, Estrada Courts is the only old-school project still standing in East Los Angeles. Just like the projects in South LA—Imperial Courts and Jordan Downs—Estrada Courts was constructed between 1942 and 1943. It owed its construction to the boom in wartime industry work and the eventual return of war veterans to East LA. Spread out over thirty acres, Estrada Courts is composed of just over four hundred one- and two-bedroom units. It borders the San Bernardino Freeway and is dotted with colorful murals, some of which were featured in the music videos of Tupac Shakur and, more recently, the Black Eyed Peas.

I first visited Estrada Courts when I was in college, on a politically correct date with someone who took me to see the murals and eat Mexican food. I still remember the mural painted by Danny Martinez, *In Memory of a Homeboy*, and feel strangely nostalgic when Felipe talks to me about the VNE homie memorialized in the artwork. But when I recall the "charm" of the projects to Felipe, he laughs. "I can tell you what it was *really* like then." We are talking about this while we spend the afternoon walking through Estrada Courts. The silence is almost eerie.

"It's so quiet," I observe.

"It's not like it was when I was coming up and part of my barrio— there was shooting every day. I mean every day. We had base heads, but they were part of the neighborhood. They would stay awake in the early morning hours from three to five while all of us homies would be sleeping. They would watch over things. Nothing really happened from six to ten—people would be getting up and taking their kids to school."

But in the past decade, VNE had pretty much disappeared from Estrada Courts. First there was the injunction, then, with the advent of CLEAR (Community Law Enforcement and Recovery), the LAPD's "weed and seed" strategy, violent gang members were locked up. It's no surprise that CLEAR was heavier on the weed part of the equation. Felipe readily told me, "They really got the neighborhood out of the projects." CLEAR was also aided and abetted by the Clinton administration's "one strike" housing policy mandating that a family be removed from public housing if one of their members was convicted of a violent crime.

Now, in the quiet daylight, there were a few grandmothers, a handful of drunks, and a man selling fruit.

"I guess CLEAR changed everything," I say.

"No. What has really ripped the community apart was glass." Felipe was reinforcing everything I already thought about the impact of crystal meth—glass. "You never knew what the homies would do with it though, because glass would make you talk. One homie could put it in a cup of coffee and then give it to another homie—like it was sugar. Except it would make them say all kinds of things. They could find something out and use it against someone." It was interrogation via getting high—no waterboarding required.

"I would never deal it in the projects," Felipe insists. "I knew that it was doing crazy shit to the community. What can I say? Business was good." Felipe never acknowledges guilt. But I have noticed that he spends an inordinate amount of time in Estrada Courts. He talks about "mentoring the youngsters" and "building up the community." Ever the businessman, he still makes a little money on the side, in charmingly legal ways. He runs a crepe concession stand at street fairs and concerts, employing homies who are reliable and willing to work a twelve-hour shift. Shannon sees him when she goes to daylong music festivals to see indie bands. Felipe watches out for her and gives her free food.

"I'm glad I got out of the life. Look at what happened to Louie."

"I know," I tell Felipe. "I can't stop thinking about him. When is he gonna get out of prison?"

"I don't know, homegirl," Felipe tells me. "I just don't know."

I had believed that Louie Mora, like Felipe, was ready to leave the neighborhood, particularly once he fell in love with Veronica. When she got pregnant, he rarely left her side, awaiting the birth of their little boy. The relationship confused me. Veronica was beautiful. But Louie Mora—there was no good way to describe it—was the most ridiculous-looking gangbanger I had ever seen. He was Alfred E. Neuman in tattoos, with a set of teeth that would make an orthodontist cry. Strangely, he was a member of the Avenues, a gang that took its name from the less-than-poetic designation of a series of streets in Northeast Los Angeles beginning with the word "Avenue" and ending with a number, like Avenue 64. The Avenues was an established neighborhood, allegedly controlled by the Mexican Mafia and not amenable to police intervention. They dealt both drugs and drive-by shootings with alacrity.

"The LAPD could never get a grip on them," Mark told me. We both knew Avenues territory quite well. Shannon rode horses nearby. Mark would watch while she practiced her trot at a rickety barn that shared space with the LAPD equestrian team, I would get my hair cut nearby in Glassell Park, and then the three of us would eat pizza at a local Italian restaurant.

A few blocks away, the Avenues controlled both territory and distribution of their product by practicing excessive violence against anyone who ventured into their area, particularly African Americans who the neighborhood wanted to relocate ASAP—preferably in a cemetery. The *LA Times* ran several features amid community outcry about "black on brown" crime. The Avenues caught the attention of the federal government and the Los Angeles DA, Anthony Manzella, who prosecuted them for "hate crimes" based on federal law.

All this time, I would take Louie Mora out for pizza in Eagle Rock and try not to stare at the AVENUES tattoo six inches high on the back of his skull, which he refused to cover by growing his hair. I thought he was pretending to be part of the neighborhood. Besides, he insisted, "I don't wanna bang. I just wanna be with Veronica." But once the baby was born, there were problems.

Veronica would come into Homeboy Industries, crying. Louie had gone out gangbanging. Louie had not come home. Louie had gotten drunk. Finally, Louie came into Homeboy and I begged, "Please stay home. What you're doing is dangerous." Greg and I both sat on either side of him while Greg cajoled him.

"Here we are, the president and vice president of the Louie Mora fan club," Greg began. "We want you to stop. We want you to stay at

Homeboy, where you are safe. We want to make sure you don't go back to the gang." Louie listened but promised nothing.

In September I took a working vacation. Mark and I flew to Switzerland, to attend a World Health Organization conference on violence prevention. While speakers discussed the worldwide epidemic of violence, back in Los Angeles there was a huge gang bust of the Avenues that involved the FBI and videotape and RICO charges of racketeering and conspiracy. I thought of Alex Sanchez. I was beginning to wonder why these things kept happening when I went on vacation. Louie Mora was one of the people caught on tape. The *Los Angeles Times* described him as a "notorious drug dealer."

"It's very sad. He's going away for a long time," Greg told me when I called him to find out what happened. And now, six months later, Felipe and I were still talking about Louie Mora.

"I think he's gonna be in prison forever, Jorja," Felipe says flatly. "You don't know how hard it is to leave the neighborhood. It took me a long time to finally let go. And we have to watch out for the youngsters. They can't even *start* gangbanging."

"But Louie had everything ... and he loved Veronica ... why couldn't she stop it?" The rush of words comes out before I even know what I am saying.

"I don't know. I just don't know," Felipe answers.

I think of Joanna. She is alternately open with me, then guarded. Felipe is more straightforward. He is also willing to risk himself. A week later, when I meet him for lunch, Felipe tells me he has something to show me.

Three new poems.

"I am tryin' to get in touch with how I feel. I guess this is how I do it. Y'know, I learned in the gang-intervention training we all have PTSD. We all have trauma."

Felipe is the exception. Poetry is rarely the homie defense against emotional pain. The majority seek the treatment most readily available: 24/7 self-medication.

SIXTEEN

Self-Medication

Pulling back on the plunger
sucking up any compassion, love or life
that's left in my body.
Emptiness swallows me whole,
blood running down my arm like a tear on my mother's
face reconfirming her own thoughts of failure,
re-inflicting the pain and abuse my father once laid upon her.
Now dead from the same poison I yearn for.
Memories running through my head like blood through the river of
    my veins.
Nothing left to live for is a thought that invades my mind.
    Like soldiers in a
foreign country, reeking of broken promises, dirty stairwells and
    nights that
never end.
Sickness interrupted.
Sunlight embraces my face, thoughts of my own children
flutter through my mind like
butterflies on a sunny day.
New hope found in a child
clinging to the cracks of his father's broken heart.

                                 —Joseph Holguin

In late summer, Kevin Williams spirals downward. Fabian Debora tells me he suspects Kevin is using crystal meth.

"I know you are close to him, so I thought you might want to know. Some people saw him at a party and said he was blown out of his mind." About an hour later, Hector Verdugo tells me that while Kevin was working the Monday-night shift at the Homeboy Bakery, Elena went out with some girlfriends. Kevin accused her of cheating on him, and there is gossip that he beat her up.

"They've got a strange relationship, those two," Hector remarks.

That night Elena calls me, crying, and says, "Kevin is having so much trouble, he tried to . . . to hit me." She chokes the words out. "He says I'm doing crazy things—things I would never do. He thinks I'm having sex with alla his friends."

Things get worse. Two weeks later I sit in on meeting between Greg and Kevin McNally, the bakery supervisor.

"Kevin is a mess—I suspended him five days for no call, no show on Monday morning." McNally chooses his words carefully. Running the bakery is not an easy task; he tries to maintain order and produce baked goods while managing a group of homies from multiple cultural backgrounds and rival gangs. But it's Kevin Williams's inconsistency that's on his mind today.

"I can't do without him, but he's not showing up," McNally says. "He's suspended."

Kevin misses a week of work, and the following Monday he comes storming into the office where Greg and I are talking.

"They won't let me clock in, G," he says angrily. "I just wanna come to work!"

Greg soothes Kevin, but it's a temporary fix. He tells Kevin to go sit outside in the lobby and wait until our meeting ends, pretending we have things to discuss. Once the glass door closes, Greg and I both simultaneously start talking.

"He's crazy and manic—," Greg says.

"I can't believe what's happening—," I begin.

Both Greg and I had hopes for Kevin and Elena. But now he's presenting with the Siamese twins of gang problems: mental illness and substance abuse.

"I think he's decompensating," I offer.

Greg nods. "He keeps talking about people at Homeboy dissing him. It's paranoid," he adds. "Y'know, whenever we talk, he's still very sweet with me. But I don't know what he will do to someone else."

A few minutes later Greg calls Kevin in and tries to get him to see a therapist. Kevin refuses and leaves. For the next three nights, Elena texts me, terrified that Kevin is out with his neighborhood. He misses a second week of work at the bakery and his fate is sealed. I am with Greg and Hector when they tell Kevin he is fired. Kevin screams, "Fuck you!" then storms out.

I am suddenly frightened. I think of Tray. Is Kevin going to be next?

"Don't worry," Hector tells me. "He's gonna be back. He's gonna leave the neighborhood again—eventually. This is what they all go through. They go back and forth, all the time."

Greg is less certain.

"He's been shot at a couple of times," he muses. "I'm sure he's using drugs, but you know there's something else—there's something off about Kevin. It's psychiatric. I truly think he is mentally ill." Greg goes on empirical evidence. If someone abandons Homeboy "voluntarily"— not because they are arrested or killed or locked up on a parole violation—Greg believes something is wrong with them. Why would anyone willfully reject a helpful and hopeful environment? It is a sign that they are not ready to leave the neighborhood. But I keep wondering about Kevin. Is it drugs or disorder or both? And I worry what will happen with Elena.

I finally reach Kevin on his cell phone and he sounds strange. He's talking at an elevated pitch: his words form one long sentence. He tells me he's taking his final paycheck to go downtown, buy some merchandise, and then set up shop on the Venice Beach Boardwalk. Two weeks later I see him on the boardwalk and he doesn't recognize me. It takes him several minutes until he suddenly grins and says, "*Jooorjjjaaa* on my mind at Homeboy Industries."

We talk for a while, and he assures me he has not gone back to his neighborhood. I don't know what to think. Gang life provides a kind of malevolent but available structure for many homies. They know what to expect: violence, intimidation, threat—it's home. So many of them come from families of abuse, and the neighborhood mimics what is familiar. Without the gang, homies can be thrown into a kind of rudderless confusion. The most common response to this confusion is drug abuse. It's self-medication, pure and simple. Someone like Kevin—not working, not locked up, not banging—just doesn't know what to do. He takes drugs to soothe himself.

It seems like everyone is using drugs—it just depends which ones. The younger homies and homegirls rarely indulge in anything stronger than marijuana. They "just smoke bud" or get drunk. However, as time and violence take a toll, some veer into hard drug use. I meditate on this while I try to call Kevin, but his cell phone has been disconnected. This happens frequently with gang members—they use one cell phone number for a few months. Then they throw the cell away and start over again. I can't get used to this and I have to keep asking for numbers. It is not lost on me that I have had the same cell phone number since 1998.

Kevin Williams is not the only person I am having trouble contacting. I try calling my cousin Nick, but now his cell phone is disconnected. While I am at Homeboy, waiting to meet a homie who is being discharged from county jail, I start phoning family to find out what's happened to Nick.

"I don't know," my brother Chris tells me. "I haven't heard from him since he left rehab. And now he's in danger of losing his license. I think he's living in his car. If you hear from him, let me know."

I get off the phone and look at Hector and Fabian, who are sitting with me in Greg's office. They momentarily avert their eyes while I will myself not to cry. I try to explain.

"He's the most brilliant person I know, but he's not smart enough to stop doing drugs. He's lost everything—his wife, his children, his house in Hancock Park, his medical practice—but all he wants is meth."

"I was an addict, Jorja," Fabian says and comes over to put his arms around me. "I was just like him. I was blown every day for five straight years. No one could help me. You can't help him. He can only help himself. I know we say the same thing over and over again—he has got to want his own recovery."

"But it's meth . . ." I begin. Meth, or glass, creates a dual sensation of hyperalertness and exhilaration that lasts for several hours. It is much more addictive than heroin, and coming down from a hit of meth frequently causes depression and violence.

"I don't know if he's gonna make it," I tell Fabian, who understands self-destruction. I didn't know him at that time but I have seen a photograph of Fabian at the height of his meth addiction, and he looks like a cadaver in a Dodgers hat. The photograph is mesmerizing, but it bears no resemblance to the well-groomed artist who wears his long, shining black hair in a braid and insists, "I can't take any drugs or drink any liquor, I'm an addict." Fabian's recovery is his badge of honor. He also takes no prisoners—you are either in recovery or not. Period.

Fabian and Hector start talking about the toll meth takes, and I recognize Nick in their description. Fabian explains what happens to the mouth and teeth—the jaw locks, the teeth rot and fall out. "We all get meth mouth—one way or the other. For me it was the jaw," he tells me.

"Your cousin has resources; he'll make it," Fabian continues. "But what the fuck are we gonna do with Kevin? He reminds me of Milagro—he drives me crazy."

Fabian doesn't need to say more than this. Milagro Diaz is a painful topic for Fabian, for Greg, for Hector, for everyone who knows him. Along with Fabian, he belonged to an East LA gang, Primera Flats. Both left the neighborhood. But while Fabian had art, Milagro found a less positive replacement for gang life—heroin.

A month before, I had interviewed Milagro. He was clean and attending AA and working at Homeboy Industries. I invited him to speak at UCLA and encouraged him to stick to his recovery. Of course, I told Mark, "We have to help him."

Mark just listened patiently and then asked me what color paint I wanted to use in the kitchen remodel. He had heard all this before. And he was much more focused on the plans for renovating our cottage—his new, full-time job. After thirty-seven years, Mark had retired from the LAPD. This event had occurred without much public fanfare—a rarity in the Los Angeles Police Department. A long career of service, like his, was usually marked by a huge retirement celebration, complete with slide show, inappropriate jokes, and maudlin displays of emotion. I had sat through too many parties for Mark's colleagues—other deputy chiefs and commanders—who were clearly ambivalent about breaking the final tie with the department. *You can never leave the gang.*

Mark rejected all this, announcing he didn't want a party. While his colleagues tried, unsuccessfully, to change his mind, I braced myself for the tsunami of change I was about to encounter. Mark without the LAPD—what would that be like? And what would his emotional reaction be? I was frightened. Mark's attachment to the LAPD was the longest of his life—outdistancing his childhood and his marriages, including ours. I didn't know what was going to happen to our relationship. More than one LAPD wife had warned me—usually at a retirement party—"Wait until Mark retires—you're gonna go crazy. Your life is gonna be over. Your marriage will never be the same."

Only this last prediction turned out to be true. The day Mark and I moved his personal belongings out of Parker Center signified the beginning of a major change in our relationship. I knew this when Mark threw his uniforms into the dumpster behind LAPD headquarters.

"Don't you want to keep these? At least one of them?" I asked.

"Why?"

"I don't know . . . it's . . . it's been such a big part of your life. Something to remember it by?"

"I have memories—I don't need to hang on to things." Mark was remarkably matter-of-fact. "I've had a wonderful career and now it's over. In fact, I'm glad it's over. It's time to move on."

These were not just words. Over the next few months, it was clear Mark was finished with the LAPD. He rarely talked about the department and was only mildly interested when Bill Bratton announced he was stepping down as chief. While Greg, Celeste, and I madly handicapped who the next chief might be, Mark interviewed architects and contractors. He drove Shannon to school and experimented with different gourmet recipes. When I came home, he had a beautiful dinner prepared and was interested in the latest developments in the streets. Shannon was slowly adjusting to life with a full-time, stay-at-home parent. And I was learning to live without the black cloud of Mark's profession hovering over me. Mark had definite thoughts about most of the homies, including Milagro.

"Y'know, you need to see how Milagro does with his recovery before you start figuring out how to help him," Mark said quietly.

"What do you mean?"

"I remember with my own mom—she'd stop drinking, then start, stop, then start. Is Milagro really in recovery? Maybe he needs therapy too."

This was another retirement dividend—Mark was much more emotionally open. He talked a great deal about his mother's demons and his own. Still, I discounted what he said about Milagro. It took me almost two years and multiple relapses before I learned the extent of Milagro's demons, which included an absent father, a neglectful mother, and sexual abuse. I also learned that Milagro's story was not exceptional.

After interviewing gang members for ten years, I can safely say that the vast majority have been beaten, sexually abused, neglected, or some combination of all three. And they lie to themselves to compound the problem. Most men recall family memories that begin positively. Chino Sanchez, a gangbanger turned heroin addict, had assured me his father was "very loving. He was a good dad, he took care of me." But over the course of several interviews, the stories of abuse began to pile up. This loving father would hit him with a "two by four," burn him with cigarettes, and constantly tell him he was "trash, nothing, no good." Still Chino insisted, "He tried to be a good father." The women are less equivocal. They waste little time discussing the virtues of their mothers or fathers. Instead—when asked about their families—many of them, like Joanna, are off and running.

"My father was a motherfucker. He abused me. And I was his favorite! But he beat the crap out of me every chance he got." None of this is a rationalization as much as an explanation. These homies and homegirls have been abused, and their only cure is more anger, more rage, more banging. Greg Boyle keeps telling me, "People don't run to gangs; they are running away from something to the gang." And many run from the gang to drugs.

I sometimes wonder if being part of the neighborhood serves as an antidepressant, taken to avoid the pain of everyday life. Many of the homies and homegirls are self-medicating, using the thrill of gang life to avoid feeling depression, emptiness, loss—maladies they have experienced since childhood. Anyone who tries to leave the neighborhood has to replace the gang with something. They need the high and the excitement.

Milagro Diaz fit into all of those categories. His father had died when he was eight; he had been raised by the neighborhood from the time he was ten. He told me how an older homie—who was probably mentally ill—sexually abused him when he was very young. Perhaps this was what led Milagro to pursue women, with both great energy and success, from an early age. He always consulted me about his women, but his latest problem required extra help.

"I need to ask you something," Milagro began. "My girlfriend is the daughter of my cousin, so that would be—what, my niece? Can I marry her? I want to—I've never felt like this." Milagro proceeded to describe how they met at a bar where she is an exotic dancer. There were so many things wrong with this revelation, I didn't know how to respond. His presence in a bar doesn't bode well for his recovery. "Exotic dancer" is, of course, code for stripper. As for marrying his cousin, I call Joe Kibre, my former attorney and brother in arms. He is busily dodging tabloid reporters who have leaked the news that he is drafting the divorce settlement of an actress who has won the Academy Award and discovered her husband's infidelity all in the same month. Still, he takes a break from writing a forty-page brief to tell me that Joseph cannot marry his cousin. California case law is emphatic on that score.

"I don't think anyone in the state of California would investigate this." Joe pauses. "But what the fuck is going on with you? Who are these homies? Do you need a gun?"

I know Joe is half-joking, but I laugh, imagining what the homies would say if I walked around "strapped." I thank him for his concern. I am less amused when another one of Mark's former colleagues—a Gang Intervention Team (GIT) lieutenant—asks if I would consider working undercover for the LAPD. I consult Elie Miller, and she starts to giggle.

"How stupid are they?" she asks me. "Do you want to report this?"

I am not interested in reporting anything or anyone. I just don't want information about this offer on the street. I don't need this latest incident to convince me that the LAPD leaks like a sieve. I know which city officials and county supervisors are informants, who smoked marijuana in college, and who Daryl Gates used to jam up in the good old days. I am careful when I talk to people from the neighborhood. It is important for them to know that Mark is now retired, in therapy, and that we have a daughter.

I don't answer the phone when the GIT lieutenant calls again—blessing the gods for caller ID. I learned from what has happened to Mario Corona that the LAPD watches gangbangers carefully. Joanna has told me how vigilant the cops have grown, openly surveilling people in Florencia. Angel Duarte has been busted.

"I always knew Angel was big in the drug industry," Joanna tells me, and I feel like we are in Detroit discussing what the new line of Fords and Chevies will look like.

I ask Joanna what she thinks of Milagro.

"He's an addict, Mama," she announces. "Y'know you can't fucking trust an addict. I've been through it with Bullet. The first time they put a needle in his arm, he was fuckin' eleven years old—he's been an addict his whole life. That's why he can't fuckin' make it in the neighborhood. And he can't fuckin' make it on the outside."

Milagro's struggle with drugs was emblematic of so many struggles. I had seen this happen too many times. And when a homie replaces their attachment to a gang with an attachment to a drug, there is more trouble. It is a twisting road of negative attachments that invariably leads to the same destination—the criminal justice system.

The good news is that in 2000 voters in the state of California passed Proposition 36—the Substance Abuse and Crime Prevention Act. Prop 36 decreed that "a non-violent" individual arrested for "simple drug possession" (i.e., an addict, not a dealer) should be sentenced to substance-abuse treatment instead of incarceration. But before anyone can start celebrating a "Prop 36 sentence," he quickly learns there is an entire convoluted system of drug court and drug testing and sobriety groups and antidrug education he is required to undertake. No one skips out free. This approach has saved the already overcrowded California state prison system from housing even more inmates who were simply addicts caught with a controlled substance. Most people agree with the basic philosophy behind Prop 36. Virtually every active and retired police officer I know, including Mark, believes that drugs should be legalized so that addicts can get what they need, the state can tax the product, and cops can be freed up to do what they really want—fight crime.

At any give time, about 10 percent of the homies I connect with, including Milagro, are involved in some sort of Prop 36 arrangement—although their tendency to relapse is stunning. Right now, after another relapse, Milagro is on his way to rehab again. My cell phone rings. My brother Tony is calling to update me that Nick has resurfaced and once again gone into rehab—this time at the Salvation Army facility. It's a long way from Betty Ford. He's out of money and out of luck. The state of California is proceeding with action to take away his medical license, and rehab is a dodge to avoid any sort of punishment. My brilliant, be-loved cousin. Tony gives me the address of the rehab center, but I don't write it down. I'm not sure I can be around Nick right now.

People from the neighborhoods share this sentiment. They don't want to be around drug addicts. They are dangerous. This lesson is reinforced two days later when Joanna's cousin Carlos comes into Homeboy to talk with me.

He has moved out of Bell and relocated to a small shack in back of his sister's house in Pacoima. I don't know what this means in terms of his standing with Florencia. Is he moving away from them? While Carlos is safe in Pacoima, there are new problems. His cousin, Michael, has failed to pay his drug dealer.

"He burned his connect," Carlos tells me, "and they're looking for him." In the meantime, Michael has been arrested on narcotics charges, and his grandmother has used her house to secure bail.

"Everyone argued with my grandmother," Carlos explains. "We don't wanna give up our property. We've lived in Bell a long, long time." I never knew that Carlos and Joanna's sweet little drug dealer grand-mother lived in Bell. This all makes sense. The city of Bell, in southeast Los Angeles County, has swamped the news headlines in recent weeks, including reports of a city manager earning nearly $1 million a year in salary and benefits. Local talk shows were devoted to answering the question, "Is Bell governable?" I want to answer, "Of course it is. And the lunatics are running the asylum."

Carlos's family is part of something most people can't imagine. The American dream sometimes reaches into the gang, as midlevel drug dealers work at accumulating enough money to buy houses— usually in impoverished areas. The cash in the bureau drawer gradu-ates to the single-family residence—it's the offshore bank account of choice. No one trusts his or her local savings and loan, with good reason.

But there are problems with homie alternative-investment strate-gies. A few days later, Carlos is back at Homeboy, breathless with fury. When I ask what's happened, he starts by explaining that he puts his cash in a hiding place in his drawer and always pays his landlord two months in advance.

"But now my cousin—Michael—bailed out of jail, found my money, and took $600. Y'know, I remember, when I first got outta prison, he stole all my clothes. After he did that, I didn't say anything. I waited until one night when my grandmother went to play bingo and then I gave him a beatin'. I told him, ya better not steal anything else muthafucka, and now—fuck—he steals my $600. It doesn't matter that I beat the shit out of him before—he still stole my fuckin' money.

"He needs rehab," Carlos goes on, and then outlines an elaborate plan to get the "dog" team or the "cat" team—to go "get" his cousin.

I have to explain that the PET unit, the Psychiatric Emergency Team he has renamed, does not act like a vigilante force. "I'm not worried about his addiction right now," I tell Carlos. "You know your cousin is gonna get himself killed. He's burning his connects, he's upsetting you, he's selling out everyone." Carlos nods vigorously while I wonder, *Why on earth am I advising a member of Florencia?* He knows more about what's in store for his cousin than I can ever imagine.

"I *know!!!*" Carlos shouts in agreement. "I don't wanna kill him, but I would like the neighborhood to give him a whuppin'." But then Carlos openly admits that he's worried about something happening to his cousin because "it would kill my grandmother, she has a heart problem—she has a bad heart. And if she gets sick, I gotta take care of her."

There's something wrong with Carlos's story. Just exactly where is Michael? Right now, according to the latest FBI reports, Florencia is one of the biggest gangs in America. It's hard for me to believe that the neighborhood has not tracked down one small-time drug addict. And the grandmother owned one of three houses on one lot—why didn't they just take her into one of the other houses? Carlos has a single in Pacoima and she is living there? It doesn't make sense.

Meanwhile, Joanna walks by and motions that she wants to talk to me, ignoring Carlos.

"Joanna is pissed at me," Carlos admits.

I assume that this has something to do with Bullet, and I am right. Bullet is using again—for what feels like the millionth time. Joanna has told Bullet that if he doesn't go to rehab he is not a man. While I disapprove of her particular brand of therapy crossed with tough love, I am keeping my mouth shut. Carlos, who is not on a first-name basis with sensitivity, has intervened.

"I told Joanna—you're just gonna drive him into using more. Leave Bullet alone." Joanna overhears Carlos's explanation and turns around.

"Mind your own fuckin' business," she spits out. "You're still in the fuckin' neighborhood. I'm tryin' to get out, and I'm tryin' to get Little Marcos's father off of crystal meth. I don't need your drama."

Two weeks later, Carlos tests dirty for THC—the derivative of marijuana. He is fired from Homeboy, which practices zero tolerance for drug use and routinely tests its employees. Carlos goes walking with me and tells me the news. He is near tears.

"Can I come in and volunteer at Homeboy while I get my unemployment?" he asks. I look at him with a jaundiced eye. Between Nick and Milagro and Bullet, I've lost my virginity. I'm channeling Fabian: you have got to want your recovery. Meanwhile, Carlos is adamant that he will come in—with or without pay.

That afternoon, I meet a homie in Rampart who tells me he has just gotten out of rehab at the Salvation Army. I describe Nick, and he immediately says, "I know him—the doctor!!!" I am not sure I can take much more of this, when I get a text from Elena who wants to see me "right away."

I drive over to Homeboy and find Elena working in the café. I am overjoyed to see her. She looks healthy and happy.

"What's up?" I ask.

"I'm pregnant."

SEVENTEEN

The Ties That Bind

I don't know what it would be like to have love without pain.

—Dimples

The Homeboy case managers are meeting to discuss their clients. I half-listen, but my mind is on Elena, who has just purchased her new membership card for Dysfunctional Families, Inc. I signal to one of the therapists, Christina Dominguez, that I need to talk with her, and we walk outside.

"What are we gonna do about Elena?" I ask her.

"We can't do anything now—she needs to report him for abuse and she won't." What we both avoid saying is that we're pretty sure Elena got pregnant to resolve her problems with Kevin.

I can't find Kevin anywhere. I finally drive down to Leimert Park so I can talk to Maniac.

"Man, I knew you would ask me," he sighs. "I don't know much except he's doin' a lotta meth." While he's talking I notice something. As so many homies would put it, he looks "tame." His cornrows are shorn and his new appearance renders him photo-ready for *GQ*. "He's never gonna be able to get out of the neighborhood unless he stops doin' alla this shit."

"Do you think he's got a problem—should he go to rehab?" I think out loud about the extent of Kevin's addiction.

"I don't think so—I think it's worse than drugs. I think he's really fucked up."

We are reaching critical mass here—Maniac, Greg, Hector, me—all agreeing that Kevin Williams is mentally ill.

Maniac, however, wants to change the subject. His girlfriend has just given birth to a boy and he scrolls through photo after photo on his cell phone. He also shows me the new gold ring he has bought himself in honor of his son's birth.

"I got my baby mama some diamond earrings," he adds.

At this point I want to ask him his investment strategy. There's no way he can afford all this—the laptop, the bling—with no visible means of support. "So, what's going on?" I ask.

"Oh, this and that." Maniac is evasive.

"Are you dealing?"

He bursts out laughing. "Nah, but I got some stuff goin'. Some hardware."

I remain silent.

"I'm not really workin' anymore. I'm just helpin' the neighborhood."

I wince. "You're so smart—why are you doing this?"

But I already know the answer to the question. Maniac has not been caught. Maniac has never been caught. Maniac has been in the Rollin 60s for twelve years and has never gone to prison. Why fix it if it isn't broken? The threat is minimal, and the economic reward is way too great. So he's not committing crimes—he's just putting guns in the hands of his homies. I am shaken. I leave. I never find Kevin. The next day Elena texts me that she and Kevin are fine. He is looking for a new job. "No worries," her message ends.

It is the day after Easter, and Homeboy is filled to the rafters. Joanna texts me and asks me to come upstairs to the office she shares with three other staff members. She is alone.

"Bullet relapsed—again," she announces.

"I was afraid of that," I tell her.

"It's because of all the trouble."

"Have you heard from DCFS?"

"Those fuckers—they closed the case."

In the past two weeks Joanna's life has grown increasingly complicated. She has stopped her outside enterprises and is back working at Homeboy. With Bullet in rehab, she assumed responsibility for his twelve-year-old son, Joaquin. So now she was watching Joaquin along with her own kids, Sonia, Juan, Lupita, and Little Marcos. A few days later, the hood version of *Eight Is Enough* went off the rails. Lupita, who is six, told Joanna that Joaquin had tried to fondle her. Reluctantly, Joanna called the Department of Children and Family Services and reported what had occurred. This is probably the most dramatic sign yet that Joanna wants to change. It is no small thing that she contacted the same agency that had previously investigated her and temporarily removed Sonia, Juan, and Lupita from her. Everyone I knew who belonged to a neighborhood feared DCFS second only to law enforcement. So many of them had been "in the system" as children themselves. Now, they might be abusive, neglectful, indifferent parents—but no gang family wanted DCFS to take their babies away. Still, Joanna had logged a complaint and met with a social worker.

DCFS assigned a caseworker to further investigate. After one week, the worker reported that there was no evidence of sexual abuse. I understand why. On the continuum of what DCFS has to investigate—child pornography, fathers making their children engage in sex with animals, the parenting skills of Mel Gibson—this case was low on both risk and lethality. But for Joanna, the damage was done. She returned Joaquin to his drug-abusing mother and managed to reassure Lupita that she was safe.

This all unfolded just as Bullet was getting released from thirty days at rehab and instructed to attend 12-step meetings every day. Homeboy was in the midst of a hiring freeze and there was nowhere else he could find a job. Instead of working, he went back to meth.

"Where did he get the stuff? And how did he pay for it?" I ask Joanna.

"It was that fuckin' Angel Duarte. You know he's trouble. He got it for him." This was the same Angel who Joanna had described as "very high up in the drug industry." I had never liked Angel, and I already knew that he had bailed out from a previous charge. But he had been arrested two nights earlier for drug dealing. When federal agents broke into his apartment, they found a cache of weapons and meth. Angel had kidnapped someone from Saint's neighborhood and beaten his face and skull with a baseball bat. "Your problems are bad, but they're not that bad," I tell Joanna. She quickly agrees.

"What happened with Bullet?" I ask, not sure what to say at this point.

"We went to Walmart on Saturday and I see he's wearin' sunglasses inside there and a towel around his neck. I got suspicious. But I let him spend the night. I woke up at three in the morning and he's starin' at the TV. So I asked him, 'Are you usin'?' and he acted really mad, '*No!*' I asked if I could see his arms and he told me no. But the next day we're at the park. Bullet reached out to hug Marcos—he forgot and I saw his arm had track marks. I told him to get out. I told him I wasn't gonna ask him for any child support—but I wanted him to stay away from us."

The depth of her betrayal is evident. Although Joanna protests that she doesn't need anyone, she is still heartbroken that Bullet relapsed. She has no tolerance and openly admits it.

"I said bad things to him because I'm so fuckin' mad, but it's 'cuz I'm so hurt."

The situation with Bullet is a no-win. To further complicate matters, after throwing Joaquin and Bullet out of the house, Joanna took Sonia up to visit her father, Flaco, in prison. I am beginning to need an organizational chart for Joanna's offspring. Bullet was upset that Joanna took Sonia to see Flaco, insisting that Joanna was still in love with him. This whole notion is laughable—except for Bullet's jealous rage. Meanwhile, Joanna says that she was proud that Sonia confronted her father and told him that she can't trust him because he's never around. I refrain from pointing out that he's not around because he's in prison.

Instead, I go looking for Elena, who is peacefully chopping vegetables in the kitchen of the Homegirl Café. I hate to admit it, but she is glowing and looks even more beautiful.

"Oh, Jorja," she squeals in delight when she sees me. "I'm so happy and Kevin is doin' so good."

I feel like a complete phony, but I smile. "So tell me how you are feeling—what are you doing—how far along are you?"

Elena cradles her belly. "I'm about three months along—we go to see the doctor next week. Kevin's mom is so happy, and my mom is so happy. Kevin has really calmed down. And he has started a new business."

Now what? I think, then brace myself, asking what this might be.

"He's workin' on producin' his music. He says he is gonna make money. Y'know he could do this, Jorja. Kevin could be a rap star."

Of course. Kevin was always interested in the fast buck. I have already met too many homies planning their careers in rap music or hip-hop. This has replaced sports as the gang exit strategy. No one is interested in athletics—instead, everyone dreams of being Snoop Dog. Kevin is no exception.

"I don't mind that he goes out at night—I know that he's tryin' to get his music business goin' for us," she says. "We're living with his mother now—so the money pressure is off of him too. We just couldn't afford the rent."

"So let me know what happens after the doctor next week?"

"For sure!"

Who knows? Maybe something good will come out of this mess, I think. Joanna has seen me talking to Elena, and comes over to me afterward.

"You know Kevin has been beatin' her."

"I know."

"You know he is one crazy motherfucker."

"I know."

"Jorja, now that she's pregnant, he gonna beat her even more. That's what my man who beat me did. They beat you if you don't have a baby. They beat you if you're pregnant. They beat you if you wanna leave them."

"I know." I sound like an idiot. I can't think of a thing to say. At the end of our marriage my former husband got physical with me. He also took a knife and slashed the canvas top of my car. He pretended that he threw my keys into a dumpster and told me he thought of strangling me in the middle of the night. I want to tell Joanna that I had experienced domestic violence, but I was a middle-class woman with a therapist, a lawyer, and a credit card. All I can say is, "Joanna, you've been through it and I've been through it, but Elena won't get better until she's ready." Joanna listens carefully and then responds in a soft voice.

"Y'know, most of us—we don't know when we are victims of domestic violence—it goes so far back. I was fourteen years old the first time a guy beat me up. I hit him back, but I'm learning it didn't matter even if I did hit him. I'm still traumatized." She is serious in a way I have never seen her before.

"I'm so worried about everyone here. Look at Rosa—she's alone, her new baby is blind, she doesn't have any papers so she can't get any welfare. She's on relief and all she gets is a hundred dollars. And every time her baby daddy comes over, he beats her up."

"Why is she taking this?" I ask, and Joanna rolls her eyes and explains that the baby's father is a notorious shot caller.

"He'll kill her, Jorja. He's had three babies with three girls. He told Rosa, don't count on me. I don't belong to you, I belong to the neighborhood. He doesn't care about his woman, he doesn't care about his baby; he only cares about his fuckin' neighborhood." Joanna is disgusted. "Fuck him. I told Rosa, 'Come over, you can stay with me.'"

Rosa is the latest in the continuing line of women whom Joanna has mothered since Luisa. She is forever the tattooed earth mother of the neighborhood. I ask her why she takes care of people.

"I think I'm trying to give people what I never had," she says without hesitation. Her insight takes my breath away. "And I know I'm so guilty about my son dying—I wanna make up for that—that's what I'm always doing. And I wanna stop all the domestic violence."

This is the problem with no name. On the laundry list of issues including child neglect, poverty, lack of education, drugs, unemployment, jail, and mental illness, domestic violence is absent—it's almost as if the neighborhoods and social services conspire to make sure nothing more is added. And, for most of the homegirls I know, domestic violence is "normal."

Two days later, Joanna and I continue our discussion of relationships in the neighborhoods. I am also beginning to understand just how complicated Joanna's domestic arrangements are. Roberto lives downstairs from her and is her landlord. He is the "good boy," the husband who only joined Florencia to please Joanna.

"He used to sit in the car while I did things," Joanna said, making it sound like she was completing a few household errands rather than the armed robberies she would routinely commit. "He would wait there, with the motor running," she continued. "He never really knew what was going on—he said he didn't know. But we had two kids together and he was a good father."

Joanna knows I'm having trouble keeping track of her children. "I've had five kids," she tells me, and I try to count them up. She had two children with Flaco: Flaco junior, who is now dead, and Sonia. Then, with Roberto, she had Juan and Lupita. Finally, with Bullet, she has Little Marcos. I have never known Bullet's real name—but finally Joanna tells me it is Marcos. Joanna suspects she is pregnant again, but it turns out to be a false alarm.

"Now I want to be a mother, I can't get pregnant. In the old days, I didn't want to stay home. I used to batter Roberto when he wouldn't let me go out. I wanted to go out and bang, and he'd tell me to stay at home with the kids; he didn't want me to go out," Joanna confided. "He was a big, stocky guy with a good body, but he never hit me. I hit him."

I sit and digest the information that Joanna was a batterer as well as a battered spouse.

"Has he ever gotten married again?" I finally ask.

"No."

"Has he ever been in love with anyone else since you?"

"No."

"He's still in love with you," I tell Joanna.

"No, he says he can never get married again because he was traumatized by me." Joanna is laughing when she tells me this. "I felt kinda bad whenever Bullet stayed over—I would ask if Roberto heard us." Her meaning is clear.

"Roberto puts up with everything—including Luisa." I know that Luisa has surfaced again with a brand new tattoo: a mustache. She is living at Joanna's.

"I'm worried about Baby Girl." Joanna shifts gears abruptly. We both know what Luisa is doing. It is not enough that she wants to shed her skin as a woman and live as a man. Luisa has now decided to switch gangs—something no one does—leaving Florencia and reinventing herself as a Playboy Crip. She is playing an incredibly lethal game and lacing it with the cyanide of drug use. Luisa has admitted as much to me, explaining, "When I get high, it's a rush, I'm afraid my homies are gonna kill me." It is Russian roulette, neighborhood style. I ask Joanna why Baby Girl is doing this.

"I don't know—she wants to commit suicide I guess." Joanna has never heard of the *DSM*—the *Diagnostic and Statistical Manual of Mental Disorders*—but she diagnoses on a daily basis.

"I'm gonna have to kick Luisa out if she keeps this shit up," she says. "I don't understand."

Joanna goes into a long soliloquy about "the lesbian thing" and how "women in love with women are just as fucked up as women in love with men." But she also looks thoughtful, as if she's performing some sort of internal calculus.

"Y'know as women we really seem like we like pain. Like my mother—my father really abused her and she still loved him. He's dead and she says he's the only man she's ever loved. It's crazy. And I stayed with Juan, my boyfriend who battered me—I just thought I couldn't go. I didn't think I could make it on my own."

I nod while she talks, remembering my own experience. I had been afraid to leave my first marriage—unwilling to surrender either my status or my security. The memory of that marriage has faded, but what I vividly remember was that I was terrified that *I could not make it on my own*. Joanna struggles with the identical dilemma. She still required a man by her side.

"I wanna find an older guy," she is telling me. "I want someone who is responsible. But I am afraid they can't get it up." I reassure her on this point. She listens raptly when I tell her that Mark is as old as her father, then graphically explain that there has never been a problem in the physical aspect of our relationship. Ever.

Joanna is shaking her head. "These fools use glass and then they can't get it up. So they use more glass and then they really can't get it up."

"I know how you can find a new boyfriend," I say. Joanna is all ears. "*Don't look.*"

She is laughing and I ask her, "Did you ever wish you met Roberto now?"

She nods, but adds, "I can't go back there. But y'know he was the only man who didn't abuse me."

The problem of abuse seems to be dominating her thoughts. "Y'know, Jorja, things have changed in the neighborhoods. They used to say it was okay to hit a woman. Now it's not."

I have finally thought of a way to help Joanna financially without raiding my checking account. Several Los Angeles County agencies request training on domestic violence. I draft Joanna and a member of the Homeboy staff—Agustin Lizama—as instructors for the daylong session. It is organized for forty people. Ninety show up.

I open the session with a brief overview that includes the stages of domestic violence, but the real education begins with Agustin. His story is complicated. He was battered by his girlfriend and battered her in turn.

"I met her in January, she was my girlfriend in March, and by April she was pregnant. She had a good job, but then she got pregnant and she was on maternity leave. That's when the trouble between us started. Everybody is different—everyone goes through different experiences—but the one thing I will tell you, you don't know how to respect shit in a relationship. The neighborhood never teaches you that. I learned that the hard way."

Joanna then takes the stage and announces, "My boyfriend battered me. He told me he was afraid I was gonna leave him. No one batters because they feel strong—you batter because you are angry—and weak." The room is silent as Joanna continues.

"This is not an easy group to work with—gang members. You gotta go after layer after layer of stuff—they have fifteen to twenty years of learning to do things this one way. When I'm working with gang members who are batterers, I've gotta break it down to them in certain ways—in a street way. The challenge for me is learning how to humble myself and work with them. They are all batterers, but they don't know any other way. Maybe because they learned it from their fathers who were batterers."

Joanna talks about working with the women like herself, insisting that it's often difficult to tell who is the victim and who is the perpetrator.

"I knew these two people," she recalls. "The man told a woman to leave the house, she said no, and he went to get his keys to leave. She bit him, he called law enforcement—but they refused to make an arrest because the man claimed to be the victim."

After the training, Joanna can't stop talking.

"Y'know, there's a lot I couldn't say. There's a lot more that happens behind closed doors, but the neighborhoods teach us we can never call the police. This isolates women in the neighborhoods more."

It's obvious that no one with even the most distant connection to a neighborhood ever trusts the police. Never. When Mark comes in to volunteer at Homeboy, I watch while Joanna reacts to him with a mask of hauteur.

"Your husband intimidates me," she finally admits.

Mark is a little over two years out of the LAPD. He spends most of his time on community projects, sitting on advisory boards, doing a little consulting, and—unbelievably enough—helping out at Homeboy. He is still in therapy. I am still in therapy. But I know he is a different person. Two weeks earlier, Daryl Gates, the longtime chief of the LAPD, succumbed to cancer. The current chief, Charlie Beck, called to invite Mark to the funeral. Mark, pleasantly noncommittal, thanked him for the invitation. I was already picking out what I would wear when Mark told me, "I don't want to go."

I was stunned. This was heresy. Daryl Gates *was* the Los Angeles Police Department. Even the *New York Times* had noted his passing.

"Why not?"

"Daryl Gates was not a nice man. Let's just say that."

I want to tell Joanna how different Mark is. But I leave it alone. She'll discover this herself.

After the domestic-violence training, I arrange to meet with Elena. I am anxious and determined to make sure nothing happens to her.

"You didn't get yourself out of MS-13 to get into more trouble with Kevin," I tell her.

Elena has bruises along the side of her face and her arms. It is clear that the abuse is escalating. But she will not call the police. I urge her to go see the Homeboy attorney Elie Miller, who is smart and compassionate.

"I will," she promises, but I am not so sure.

I know that despite the abuse and the problems, Elena loves Kevin. She wants to believe he will be better, that he will leave the neighborhood. Like so many women, she holds out the unexpressed hope that her man will go straight.

And every once in a while, there is redemption. I witnessed this the day that I sat in a pew of Dolores Mission Church and watched while

Louis Perez married Judy Viramontes. Louis kept telling me this was going to be a "real homie wedding," although the homie had long ago left the neighborhood and his bride sold life insurance. Their wedding, with a reception at the home of the bride's mother, represented the triumph of love over the neighborhood. All Louis and Judy wanted was a home, children, and a normal life. It is something Louis has never experienced.

Gangster family relationships, just like everything else in the neighborhoods, are dysfunctional. *Is anything in gang life simple?* I want to scream. Still, there are certain constants. The father *rarely* figures in the family narrative. Fathers remain offstage and absent—dead, incarcerated, or with another woman. The mother is a major player, and she is universally revered—African American or Latino, whatever the ethnic mix. Sometimes the mother doesn't necessarily deserve this; she too might be missing in action. Most discussions surrounding "gang family structure" invariably focus on the "father wound." But I often found myself wondering about the mother wound. What about the absentee mother—whether it was drugs or partying or incarceration—who abandoned her children to raise themselves? What did she do to her family? And what about those mothers the homies cried over—single parents, well intentioned, who worked three jobs to care for their children but were never at home?

I tried to spend time with what researchers would call "the control group"—the individuals who grew up in the same geography as the gangbangers I knew but did not join gangs, barrios, neighborhoods. And again it all came down to their mothers. Every one of them talked about their mama or their *madre*, living at home, keeping an eye out, chasing them up and down the street to make sure they ate dinner and finished their homework. What was going on?

I had my own problem with mother wounds. When I was growing up, my mother and I clashed wildly over what was to be a familiar theme—my rebellion against conventional life and the Greek community. Along with my father, she consulted an elderly Greek priest, who counseled, "Jorja Jeane is a little bird who belongs to the world. You will have to let her fly." My parents came away unconvinced and insistent on order. They were not interested in freedom. What they wanted was control. In fact, my mother told me, sotto voce, that she and my father felt that I had some very serious problems. But as I listened to her speaking I thought about her own serious problems. The fact that she could not drive on the freeway—a severe disability in Southern California—and that she spent at least one day a week in bed with a migraine headache, the household brought to a standstill. I felt emotionally abandoned. And I rebelled against her, my father, and the whole Greek ethos. I vowed if I ever decided to have children, *I would never be like her.*

Now that I was raising my own daughter, I was determined not to repeat my parents' mistakes. I wanted to be there for Shannon, providing her with the experience of unconditional love that I had longed for. And yet, because I spent so much time in the streets or at Homeboy with people from the neighborhoods, there were times I ran the risk of emotionally abandoning Shannon. She doesn't rebel. Instead, she confronts me.

"You scare me, Mom," she begins. "You never think about how dangerous it is. Promise me you'll be careful. Promise me you won't go out at night." I am listening to my daughter and I am thinking about a line in a poem she wrote. "I am a child of cancer." She has lost one mother to a horrible disease but has the courage to trust me—the woman who became her second mother. I am amazed at Shannon, in awe at her ability to love. I promise her that I will be careful. But I am not sure it is a promise I will keep.

Just like my family relationships, the picture with the homies and the homegirls is complicated. A little over one year into the study at Homeboy Industries, I had collected a large sample of three hundred homies, and it seems like so many have been locked up, have relapsed, are on the run. In reality, only one-third of my sample goes back to gangbanging—but everyone who falters breaks my heart. I'm beginning to wonder how anyone leaves the neighborhood. I want to cry.

Instead, I wait.

EIGHTEEN

Fathers of the Community

I think it's funny, it's a funny, funny thing—no one is asking
us how to solve the problem. No one be asking us—everyone
else has the idea. You tell me how some skinny white guy
downtown knows how to fix what's wrong with us.

—Maniac

For several weeks in 2010, gang violence has spiked. Homies I see on a
regular basis suddenly drop off the radar. After asking around, I find out
that most of them have been locked up. But a few are carefully avoiding
their neighborhoods, barricading themselves at Homeboy Industries.
Carlos is there, front and center, shakily telling me how his cousin was
shot right in front of him, victim of a drive-by. Comforting Carlos, I
wonder why there was a hit. According to William Dunn, an LAPD
detective, in his book *The Gangs of Los Angeles*, "In 1993, Eme, as an
organization, hosted a very public picnic in Elysian Park. . . . At this
picnic, over 3,000 gang members from throughout Southern California
were in attendance. At its conclusion, it was announced to reporters in
the crowd that Eme had negotiated a number of truces between warring
gangs and, most important, declared a moratorium on drive-by shootings." Dunn claimed that later "Eme amended their edict: gang members could shoot from the car, but only as long as they opened the door
and put one foot on the ground." Khalid Washington had assured me
that representatives from both black and brown neighborhoods had met
and agreed there were to be no more drive-by shootings. But Carlos explained that the driver had actually stopped the car; the shooter opened
the passenger door and started firing. "That way it's not a drive-by."
Evidently the neighborhoods understood something about the nuance
between the letter of the law and the spirit of the law.

I don't want to press Carlos, who finally stops shaking long enough to tell me he has to go to his anger-management class. Later, Hector offers more information: Carlos told him his cousin had taken a bullet in the neck and died in his arms. This all took place in America's newest hot spot, Bell. A few hours after the shooting, three members of Florencia had shown up at Carlos's house asking, "What's up? Do you want to take care of business?" Carlos withdrew from their offer of revenge, saying he was going to sleep. "He handled that beautifully," Hector declares, "but now he needs therapy." When Hector approached him, Carlos initially resisted the idea but later went to see Christina, one of the mental health staff.

That night, Carlos does not want to go home. Instead he helps set up for Greg's book signing at the Homegirl Café. *Tattoos on the Heart*, Greg's beautiful book of stories and experiences he has shared with gang members, has just been published and there is a major celebration and launch. For one evening, homies and public figures celebrate together. But no sooner do things settle down with Carlos than there is trouble with Ronny, who calls to tell me that his cousin, who was shot two nights earlier, has just died. Ronny is still at the hospital. I ask him if I should drive out to see him, but he tells me it's not safe, the neighborhoods are shooting at everyone. For once I listen.

For the next week, Ronny doesn't want to leave the house, but his girlfriend, Destiny, finally convinces him to return to work. He stays planted in the lobby of Homeboy until closing time. I sit with him, sharing the Greek butter cookies Mark has packed in my lunch, which he makes for me every morning before I go out to interview homies.

"I just can't handle it," Ronny tells me. "I really can't."

I remember what Ronny had said back in Nickerson Gardens—that no matter what happened in his life, he would always be seen as a member of his hood, including in his own heart. While we eat cookies, I ask him, "Do you ever think you'll see yourself differently? What if you became a schoolteacher? How would your neighborhood see you?" He barely hesitates.

"It doesn't matter what I think I am. I'm still a member of my hood." It comes to me, while he's talking, that this is all he possesses.

"Where do you belong?" I ask him. He explains that Bounty Hunter Bloods is his hood. And his family is a set or a clique.

"But in your feelings—your heart—what's the difference between your set and your hood?"

"I don't know," he says.

The next day Ronny doesn't show up. I call Destiny, but she doesn't answer. I have learned that, for most people in the neighborhoods, telephones exist for texting, not talking. So I text Destiny and she quickly responds that she is not with Ronny. When I tell her we need to talk, she texts me that she can't; she is waitressing during lunch hours at the Homegirl Café. I tell her we can talk after lunch. All this avoidance isn't a good sign.

When the lunch rush dies down, we walk outside and Destiny tells me she's scared: first Ronny's cousin was killed and now two more of his homies have been killed.

"I don't wanna say any more," she says quietly. It's time to fill in the blank.

"Does Ronny wanna retaliate?" I'm not afraid the way I used to be. When violence is in the air, it's best to be blunt. Destiny starts energetically shaking her head.

"*Oh no.*" She is loudly emphatic, then looks around carefully. "You can't tell him I told you. Ronny's afraid to leave the house. He doesn't want revenge—he's afraid they're gonna come after him. I keep telling him he should come to work."

I don't tell Destiny what I really think Ronny should do—which is move out of Bloods territory. His family and associates in South LA are as extensive as their ability to get into trouble. There are too many people around to draw Ronny into violent activity, invoking family loyalty.

"Does Ronny have any strikes?"

"No, he doesn't," she says, and despite what I see as a good prognosis, she is anxious. "He doesn't have any strikes. But he's on parole. And his PO is dyin' to violate him." I soften and tell her that I know both she and Ronny are good people. I trust them. While there are good probation and parole officers, Ronny has drawn a bad hand. His parole officer is setting him up to fail—calling him all hours of the day and night, demanding drug testing, stopping by Homeboy to make certain he is working. "I'm worried his PO is gonna come by," I admit.

"Ronny's gonna be here tomorrow," she tells me. "I'm gonna get him to come to work. He has gotta come to work."

There is more violence, and it is claiming both brown and black gang members. Smiley, a nineteen-year-old trainee at Homeboy, is crying. His cousin, who, just like Smiley, was MS-13, has been shot and killed. Smiley carries around a coffee can, collecting money for the funeral. Carol Biondi quickly writes a check and stuffs it inside. She is Mother Teresa with a manicure—she just cannot help herself. If there is a birthday or a death or an upcoming trial, Carol finds a way to quietly help. She has stopped by Homeboy to pick me up so we can drive out to Scripps College to talk with Tom Hayden's students about gangs and juvenile justice. The three of us go out to dinner after class and focus on the plight of Alex Sanchez, who has finally been released on bail to await trial. He has no money and no way to earn a living. Out comes Carol's checkbook. Tom is worried that the judge, Manuel Real, is unpredictable and hopelessly biased in favor of the government. Carol and I wonder how Alex is going to feed his family. There is no doubt among the three of us that he is innocent and that the US attorney just doesn't understand the gang problem on the ground.

Two days later I go to see Hector, asking if he can talk to Ronny. Despite his management status, Hector relates well to homies, whether black or brown. Even the most hardened guys, with long prison records, relax around him. I listen while he talks to two men, both just released from Folsom two days earlier. They show all the signs of institutionalization, the usual dividend of long-term incarceration. It happens to almost everyone who has been locked up—their independence and sense of responsibility, often not strong to begin with, diminishes so much that once they are back "outside," they feel overwhelmed and unable to manage the simplest demands. Of course, this piles more psychological problems on top of the PTSD and depression they already suffer.

"You're kinda stiff," Hector begins. "But I understand, you're just out of prison, emotions and stuff. Y'know, it's hard to change. When you got into the gang—you had your reasons—you got hurt. If you're born and raised that way in a neighborhood, that's some deep shit in your brain. If someone comes to you and tells you, 'You can't think that way no more,' you can't do it. You gotta decide you want to do it. And you gotta leave. For good. And you gotta see, the youngsters are looking to you for guidance."

One of the guys listening to him says, "I wanna do this. I think I got it." The other guy remains stiff—he wants to believe, he is leaning his upper body forward, but he won't look directly at Hector. These guys look so young and yet so old.

Hector's words come back to me a week later while I sit in a small, hot room at Toberman Neighborhood Center. Everything Hector talked about fits in with the discussion at this gathering of OGs and prospective gang interventionists. Most of the men here expressing an interest in street intervention are just out of prison. This is one of the few jobs available to them, particularly with the economic downturn. At Homeboy Industries, the staff finds that living up to one of its core values, "Jobs, Not Jails," presents an ongoing challenge. Hard-core street intervention provides a positive employment option, but it also puts many of these former gang members right back in the neighborhoods they are trying to avoid.

Big Mike sits next to me at one end of the table. The meeting has been organized to teach these men street fundamentals: how to practice "violence interruption" and effectively talk gangbangers out of shooting one another. These OGs are expected to communicate with the younger gangbangers.

A former gangbanger turned pastor and intervention leader, Ben Owens, is running the meeting. He is neatly dressed in a pressed white shirt, tie, and vest. Ben—who is also known as Taco—usually wears a jacket as well, but it is 9:45 a.m. and the temperature has already soared to 81 degrees. I don't know how these guys are going to sit through the next five hours. I don't even know how I'm going to sit through the next five hours. All of the faces around the table—with two exceptions—are black.

One of the OGs points to me as if I am on exhibit and asks, "Who she?"

Taco patiently explains that I am a researcher, writing an evaluation to describe the impact of street intervention.

"She will spend time with you in the streets, you will talk to her. She writes what we do so we can apply for more funding and get more money to pay you."

I introduce myself and explain how confidentiality protects gang members, unless they start planning a crime in front of me.

"We're not gonna tell you stuff, we can't tell you stuff," one experienced interventionist, Eric, insists. He addresses the group. "We've been in the pen. We know we can't tell her everything."

I try not to smile. Every time a new group of men comes out of prison, wanting to become interventionists, we go through the same drill. Some of the men here—like Eric—will never talk to me; some—like Felipe Mendez—will become close confidants. Some hate women; some need a mother. But right now this is a show of force precisely for my benefit. More importantly, they are posturing in front of one another. They are like dry drunks—maybe they've left their neighborhood, but they still act like gangbangers.

Carl, an interventionist in training, kicks back. He reminds me of Khalid, with the same blend of arrogance and charisma. In a sign of disrespect to everyone in the room, he wears sunglasses. His mouth is pressed in a thin, tight line. If Carl has actually left his neighborhood, I will parade through the streets naked.

"What are people in the neighborhoods gonna do when we show up with her?" Carl begins. "It's not happenin'. People won't talk to me if I'm with someone like . . . her." I still don't have a name. It is "she," "her," or, in some extreme cases, "it." I am reminded of how the men in the LAPD refer to their spouses as "the wife." It doesn't matter what community I am operating in; for a female, nouns and pronouns appear in place of a name.

But Big Mike is vouching for me.

"No one questioned me when Jorja Leap was with me. When you've gotta license to operate, they will accept her."

"Well, what if shots get fired?" Suddenly they are acting as if they are worried about my ass. I doubt it.

"I took care of Jorja Leap. You will need to protect her," Big Mike adds. "Now pull yo' heads out of yo' asses. She's here to help us. And she's a good lady."

The discussion shifts. The interventionists are no longer interested in me. Instead, Kenny Green is reminding the homies that they are role models.

"People in the neighborhood know you. When a kid sees you—they learn," Kenny begins. "If you gotta beer in your hand, these little kids are watchin' you and they're gonna grow up one day and remember that. They see you as false, as frontin' if you say you're a good citizen but act another way. I thank God that I always remembered they were watchin'. Those kids grew up, they're major bangers but they remember what I'm like—what I represent—the positive side of things. If you fail, you can lose them faster than anything. You can lose it in a second. Look what happened to Mario Corona."

I wince when he brings up Mario's name. Mario is serving three to five years at Federal Corrections on Terminal Island—a few miles away. But no one wants to dwell on this. Instead Kenny starts talking about the importance of community-based organizations, including Homeboy Industries. One OG rolls his eyes and says, "Here we go again with hardcore and wraparound services." Eric joins in the ridicule.

"They keep talkin' about tattoo removal, like that's gonna solve the problem. What a bunch of bullshit. It's useless," he says, warming to his task. "First of all, every teenager in LA is gettin' a tattoo, gettin' a piercing—it's not street anymore. It's mainstream. Fuckin' Angelina what's her name has got more tattoos than one of my little homies. It doesn't mean a thing. Puttin' em on, takin' em off, it's all a bunch of bullshit."

"Quit fightin' you foo's," Big Mike shouts, again. "How many times am I gonna have to check you?" he asks in mock frustration.

Taco picks up from here, trying to get the group back on track. "Don't forget, different people see you in different ways. In the community you're called noble, the neighborhoods may call you the 'get along' guy. You get along with people. But just remember, law enforcement says 'Once a gangster, always a gangster'—a tiger doesn't change his stripes. You might be a hero to the community but law enforcement still says we are gonna get him."

Taco almost concludes this monologue but then adds, "If you think your phone is tapped, if you think someone is watchin' you—keep thinkin' that, because there's a good chance you are. Everyone is watchin' you." Paranoia abounds here, with good reason. The interventionists are not trusted on either side—the gangbangers believe they are snitches; the police believe they are gangbangers. They are the ultimate double agents. *Welcome to my world*, I think.

Carl breaks in and begins to talk about something I have noticed: The life on the street has changed.

"You guys know," Carl begins, "the injunctions have stopped any general congregatin'—there are no meetings. Now we gotta take the next step. We gotta teach these youngsters to stop warrin'. You know what I'm sayin'. These same dudes that you hate so much are the same ones who've got your back in the yard. You know what I'm sayin'. My name used to be a household name in the streets, but now—I just got outta the pen and there are these dudes who don't know who I am. You know what I'm sayin'."

You know what I'm sayin'; I stop counting at twenty. But despite Carl's speech tic, I listen closely.

"Things are changin'. Bangin' is over. The things that individuals in the streets are doin' have changed. The game is changin'. You know what I'm sayin'. I'm not sure anymore if we should deal with gangs. I'm wonderin' if we should wait until they're ready to embrace change." His words stop me in my tracks. This is Greg Boyle with tattoos, just out of prison, raw. But he is on to something. Big Boo chimes in.

"These individuals who got caught up in the early '90s need somewhere to go—rather than gettin' out there servin' the neighborhood. We need to find somethin' for people gettin' out of the pen to do. They need jobs. Otherwise they go back to bein' soldiers."

Andre speaks next. "I been shot thirteen times and I survived. And I deserve every bullet I got, y'know I was out there." He brings a valuable outlook. "I don't speak on the pen. I speak about life." He is one of the individuals leading today's training, along with Big Mike,

Taco, and Kenny. These are men who have been working in the community for more than a decade, trying to bring about change. Many did this informally and without pay for years. Now, funded by the Mayor's Office and by private foundations, they feel a sense of pride and status.

"Even though it shouldn't take money to make these youngsters listen—it works."

"Yeah, but we gotta do more than get them money. We gotta get them schools and jobs," Kenny adds.

These men—whether experienced or just out of prison—know better than anyone that the communities need more than street intervention. The old ways of banging are gone. The large meetings William Dunn wrote about, those called by Eme and monitored by law enforcement, no longer take place. As a result of the injunctions and the gang-suppression units, gangs have gone underground, and negotiate in new and different ways.

As 2010 passes, I grow even more aware that something is going on with the men in the neighborhoods. I'm not exactly sure what it is. The feeling of change is reinforced when Mark and I take on a project evaluating a community-based antigang initiative led by Aquil Basheer. We are the weirdest trio imaginable—a retired LAPD deputy chief, a former political activist turned fire fighter, and me, the godmother of every gang-banger who crosses her path.

Aquil has set out to do nothing less than return a community to itself by training OGs and veteran gangbangers to serve as interventionists. No one is required to declare their neighborhood status—whether active or retired. All Aquil asks is that everyone attend training offered by the PCITI. Along with a tendency to occasionally mangle the English language, Aquil is wed to acronyms. The PCITI is the Professional Community Intervention and Training Institute, and it is his baby. He intends this training program to instruct these "community interventionists" in everything from CPR and self-defense to program evaluation. Julio Marcial has stepped up with funding from the California Wellness Foundation, and the project is off and running.

Along with Celeste Fremon, Mark and I attend orientation for the

PCITI on an early-summer evening. The sky is still light, and the men who sit in carefully lined-up chairs are unaccustomed to being out before sundown. These are all OGs, and they look shy, withdrawn, uncertain of how to act. One man sits through the entire presentation wearing ear buds.

Aquil approaches the front of the room full of confidence and energy, his face shining brightly under the spotlights. He introduces himself and begins speaking about the institute and the training it will offer these individuals—the people Aquil refers to as "the fathers of the community." Aquil treats each of these tatted-up, vicious-looking OGs with dignity. And respect. And expectation. He tells them they must apply to be in the class. When one man expresses anxiety and moans, "I can't work a computer," Aquil quietly responds, "It'll be all right, brother."

I sit in the audience, speechless. Even after thirty years of teaching, I know I could never do this. Aquil commands total respect—and he comes by his street cred honestly, from many sources. Part of his strength is encoded in his DNA. His father was the first African American to integrate the ranks of the Los Angeles County Fire Department. Aquil works as an LA City firefighter and has now accumulated thirty years on the job. He shows no signs of stopping. At the end of his presentation, the OGs swarm Aquil. We all leave the orientation session inspired.

Mark observes every class session and is adopted by the OGs who clamor to include him in their graduation. At the ceremony, these former gangbangers all high-five Mark and embrace him while I watch. A week after graduation, we meet Aquil to discuss his outcomes—which are dazzling. He and Mark talk about their pensions and benefits, city employees swapping hints about retirement. But their easygoing banter belies Aquil's appearance, which is pretty menacing. His head is always carefully shaven and when his mood grows heated, his eyes turn into impenetrable slits.

"I can be an angry black man, Jorja. I can do some real harm," he tells me. But I have never seen any evidence of this. Instead, all I see is his passion for community organizing. I am also astonished at the depth of Aquil's emotional tolerance. It allows him to embrace both Mark and me—even though we embody the white devils that his Black Muslim faith preaches against.

I do not think Aquil has ever claimed any neighborhood. Instead, the violence he acted out in his youth came in a more political form—he was peripherally associated with the Black Panther Party, although I doubt he was ever a member. His icons are not Tookie Williams and Raymond Washington. Once the evaluation is complete, I invite him to speak at UCLA. In my class, he talks about Bobby Seale and Angela Davis, ignoring the puzzled looks on the faces of students who have no idea who the fuck Bobby Seale is.

"I know they don't know who the hell I'm talking about," he laughs, "but we gotta teach these youngsters." I think of how my students have no historical context—one undergraduate visited my UCLA office and recognized the photo of John Lennon and Yoko Ono, happily announcing, "I know who they are! Cheech and Chong, right?"

"I don't care what it takes to reach these youngsters—we are gonna do it. You and me, Jorja—we are there, at the barricades." But I have a different project for Aquil. I tell him about Kevin Williams and ask if he would be able to mentor this lost boy.

I make three separate appointments for Kevin to meet Aquil. I am convinced that Aquil can help—Kevin is, after all, the son of a Black Panther father. But he never shows up. I ask Elena what is going on, and she tells me she doesn't know.

"Y'know Kevin is worried about the baby. He wants to make money. He says he wants to make sure he can support his child."

"I think Aquil can help him."

"Kevin says he wants to start a boxing business—he'll train fighters and put them in the ring and then take part of their purse. He's really getting serious now—and he has stopped being so crazy with me. Stopped."

Elena's eyes dance with pride. I feel frightened.

Meanwhile, Maniac has disappeared.

I call Aquil to confide my fears to him. These are two young, strong African American men—both capable but troubled. They are both "in the wind."

"I don't know what to tell you, my sister. They're not ready to leave the neighborhood. We've gotta wait until they are."

Aquil does not know this, but he is putting forth the same argument as Greg Boyle. Is it any wonder that two weeks earlier, sitting on a committee to award the 2010 California Peace Prize, Greg and I both argued strongly that Aquil should be one of the honorees? Aquil believed you could not talk anyone into change—it had to come from within.

I want to know more about the change I am sensing. Aquil and I spend a great deal of time walking through different parts of South LA at night. The rumors fly. I get a call from a student intern in the Mayor's Office who tells me, "Everyone here is talking about what you're doing with Aquil at night in the projects. Are you planning a special program?" What I do with Aquil differs little from what I do with Big Mike. I am promiscuous. If someone wants to spend time with me in the streets, I am there.

One night we are out, and I share my suspicions with Aquil—that Kevin may be abusing Elena—and he immediately catches something.

"He's in a lotta conflict over who he is, sister."

"Why?"

"When a black man is with a Latino woman—there's trouble—I hate to say it, I don't want to say it, but it's not good—not for her, not for him, not for anyone."

A week earlier Carlos had talked with me about this identical issue after another homie reported that one of his Latina "sisters" had been seen getting into Kevin Williams's car.

"That's a wreck, Jorja," Carlos told me. "You can't have the Hispanic woman with the black man."

A week later Big Mike and I hold the opening session of Project Fatherhood at Jordan Downs. This is a special effort, in partnership with the Children's Institute, Inc., and the Housing Authority of the City of Los Angeles. With this project, Big Mike is finally getting some of his work funded, beyond the small stipend he receives from Jordan High. Every Wednesday night, for two hours, former gangbangers and fathers of all ages—from a seventeen-year-old expecting his first child to a forty-five-year-old with seven children, meet to talk about their dilemmas. Mike and I co-lead the group, but they are teaching one another. The older fathers attempt to mentor the youngsters. But the shadows in the room are the violence and poverty of the projects. After the first session, Big Mike walks me out to my car and tells me to lock the doors. It is dark in Jordan Downs.

"Be careful," he tells me. "Go straight to the freeway."

Ten minutes later, on Alameda, I count six LAPD cars speeding past me. Instead of turning onto the freeway on-ramp that will take me home to Santa Monica, I keep driving in the direction of the cop cars.

I call Mark to tell him what I am doing. "Be careful," is all he says.

When I get to the yellow tape, Khalid Washington is there. A sixteen-year-old Latino lies facedown in a pool of blood. The LAPD blocks the scene and tells us to move away. While we backtrack toward our cars, Khalid is on his cell phone, dialing Vicky Lindsay, who runs Project Cry No More. Vicky's nineteen-year-old son and her husband were both murdered in gang-related violence. To deal with her grief, she started a support group for mothers who lose their children to gang violence. "We are all trying to take back our community," she has told me. Tonight, she and Khalid work to find someone who speaks Spanish.

Somehow, in the midst of this death, color doesn't matter. Blacks and browns work together. "We gotta find someone to tell this boy's mother her son is dead," Khalid says. I give him Joanna's number. Khalid calls her and she says she will meet us. I get on the phone.

"Don't worry, Mama," she reassures me. "I got it. We all gotta help. No one else is gonna be there for us. We all gotta take care of each other."

NINETEEN

Answers

Nothing stops a bullet like a job.
　　　—Father Greg Boyle, SJ

Smiley has been shot in front of the Rampart MTA station at 7:30 a.m., getting ready to ride the bus into work at Homeboy. The LAPD possesses a security tape with film of the suspected shooter, and a gang detective has summoned Greg to see if he can identify the figure captured on tape. He can't. Meanwhile, Smiley is on life support at County/USC Medical Center, waiting to be declared brain dead. I am too sad to cry. This nineteen-year-old homie, abandoning MS-13 in order to survive, had talked to me the day before about how badly the cast on his broken arm itched. I drew a heart on the plaster, flanking it with the words "I" and "Smiley." And now he is gone.

It is summer. I am back from a Washington, DC, conference sponsored by the National Institute of Justice. Listening to the predictions of the FBI, NIJ, DOJ, and OJJDP (US Office of Juvenile Justice and Delinquency Prevention), I lived through three days of criminal-justice alphabet soup on steroids. Now I am trying to detox. During the conference, a few people managed to break out of their East Coast chauvinism long enough to ask, "How are things out there in the Wild West?" wanting to know what was going on in LA. But most of the conference's attention was riveted on David Kennedy, whose long hair and all-black attire had made it into the pages of *Newsweek*, the *New Yorker*, and the office of Attorney General Eric Holder. Accompanied by Jeremy Travis, president of John Jay College of Criminal Justice, Kennedy told Holder that their team could eradicate gangs in the United States of America. All they needed was $50 million. They have the answer.

Variations on their particular approach are being tried throughout the country. In Los Angeles, the Mayor's Office has devoted $20 million to a combination of community-based prevention and street intervention. The crime rate hovers at a thirty-year low and the mayor proclaims his success. He has the answer. The trouble is, too many people suspect him of political grandstanding. While his Summer Night Lights antigang program is a huge success, there are still problems in other city-funded efforts. Celeste Fremon and Matt Fleischer complete an investigative piece on these city programs, which reveals that some of the mayor's efforts are of dubious value. They report that it's nearly impossible to show the specific impact of street intervention. On top of this, their investigation exposes flaws in the city prevention program. Still, the mayor's office struggles with a problem confronting most antigang programs. Money.

Despite David Kennedy's showmanship, Eric Holder does not pony up the $50 million. In the end the government commits a whopping $12 million nationwide to fight gang violence. The message is clear: the gang problem is taking a backseat to other criminal justice issues.

"Law enforcement can't do it alone," Holder insists, and he invokes what is becoming a shopworn mantra. "We can't arrest our way out of this problem. We need to make demands that our enforcement efforts are complemented by strong prevention, education, and intervention initiatives. Putting gangs out of business will take . . . unprecedented, community-wide cooperation."

One week later, Homeboy Industries—the largest gang intervention and rehabilitation program in America—is faced with a lack of funding that will force Greg Boyle to lay off 330 workers. Mayor Antonio Villaraigosa declares that he will not "cut one single cop from the budget of the City of Los Angeles" despite the fact that there are estimates the city is facing a budget shortfall of half a billion dollars. No one wants to talk about gangs and no one wants to fund help for people attempting to exit them.

At Homeboy Industries, the staff gathers in the lobby. Greg is telling everyone that there is no money left, everyone is "laid off." He pauses to compose himself. "We should collect unemployment, all of us. I am going to apply and, y'know, that should be interesting." He then talks about Homeboy and what it means to "our community." It is clear who this community is: the homies who are present and those in prison—all who hope for redemption. Greg asks Ronny to pray, and he does so, eloquently, pleading, "We organized for our hoods, now we gotta organize for Homeboy—all the things we did for our neighborhoods we gotta do for Homeboy." The meeting is followed by a groundswell of activity. Homies keep coming in to tell Greg how much they love him. Within hours, the media descends; reporters and cameras take up their posts outside the building. Marcos, whose tattoos are in various stages of removal, comes in to tell G he will work without pay. The CNN reporter interviewing Greg, practically in tears herself, asks, "What will happen to Homeboy?"

Throughout its history, Homeboy has been dependent on private financial support—foundations and donations—because there is no substantial federal or state funding directed toward long-term gang intervention. Instead, the State of California chooses to spend roughly $50,000 a year to keep an individual incarcerated—at either the juvenile or adult level. Greg is telling the CNN reporter that it costs as much to send a kid to Harvard as it does to maintain a kid in juvenile detention. He continues to explain that it costs about $20,000 per client to provide services at Homeboy—less than half the annual cost of incarceration.

Once the news is out, donations flow into Homeboy. Within two weeks, the doors open again, but it is a temporary fix. The dilemma of securing long-term funding has not been solved. As the weeks pass, I alternate between two major projects: helping Shannon apply to college and evaluating Homeboy's efforts.

When Shannon shows me her list of extracurricular activities, I think about Smiley. His CV would have listed the probation camps and detention centers he had frequented. Instead, here was my daughter, talking about schools that emphasized social justice and how they might regard her work in South Los Angeles, tutoring at-risk children who couldn't read. Shannon is talking about pursuing a career in education and working on social policy. She looks forward to the future with great excitement. This hopeful anticipation is something few gang members will ever experience. I am thrilled for her, but my chest hurts. I try not to cry.

I think again about the lack of hope the following Saturday, while

I stand at Smiley's gravesite. His mother is weeping and repeating the words "Mijo, mijo"—*My son, my son*—over and over again. Carol Biondi places a linen handkerchief in the weeping woman's hands. Smiley's mother tries to give it back; it is beautiful—a family memento—but Carol insists, "Take it." Greg Boyle is praying. Smiley is the 174th gang member he has buried.

Two days later, I am back at Homeboy, interviewing new trainees.

Throughout all of this, I am being bombarded with questions from a variety of sources——the media, the County of Los Angeles, the Department of Justice—what *is* the best approach to "the gang problem?"

Is the law enforcement suppression working?

Are the peace treaties holding?

Are the younger gang members more jaded, more sophisticated—less likely to bang on the corner and more likely to use social networks?

Are gangs gone or are they just different?

I don't know.

What I do know is that there is less violence and more drug abuse. I know that injunctions are keeping gangbangers off the street. But I also know that gangs are still alive. Buddy Howell, the director of the National Gang Center, comes to talk at UCLA, where I have organized a yearlong series of public lectures on gangs. He offers plenty of statistics, all of which show that, locally and nationally, crime is down and gang membership is up.

At Homeboy Industries, Hector Verdugo concedes that what law enforcement is doing has helped—to a point. He makes a swirling motion with his hands.

"What the police have done is this—they have creamed off the top of the problem and taken the worst criminals and put them in prison. They clearly are locking up the leaders, the shooters, the strongest parts of the neighborhood. That's why we've got such a low crime rate. All-time low, that's what the paper says. The police have the numbers—we gotta believe them. But there are more youngsters coming up and joining the neighborhoods. They're gonna be the next gangsters. What needs to happen now is the community and the schools need to step in and deal with what's below, what may rise up."

I agree with Hector's prescription. But there are problems. The California prison system is now the largest in the Western world—housing more prisoners than France, Germany, Holland, and Singapore combined. One out of eight prisoners in the United States is incarcerated in California. And the system itself cost the state over $10 billion a year. This investment has bought California the highest rate of recidivism and reincarceration in the United States, along with the bonus of running institutions that foster drug dealing, substance abuse, and institutional gangbanging.

What's more, I had reason to doubt the numbers Hector invoked. My UCLA colleague who consults with DOJ has told me that many researchers share a firmly held conviction that statistics are not reported accurately, even now.

I suspect that this is true, and not because I know the algorithms. I have continued my practice of spending nights in South Los Angeles, driving around with Kenny Green and Mike Cummings, watching what was going on in the street and reading notifications on Kenny's city-issued BlackBerry. Weapons are everywhere, and shots are being fired rampantly. There are reports of multiple gunshot wounds and cars speeding away from varied crime scenes. The police never show up. If the LAPD fails to make an appearance, it is as if the event never occurred: it's never registered as part of the statistical record. The gossip at DOJ was reinforced by the reality of the street. And I had access to much better researchers than DOJ. One of them was Ronald Dawson.

"It was really bad a few months ago," Ronny insists.

"I heard it was quiet—things were better?"

"They are better now, but I don't know about what's gonna happen. It's gonna be bad this summer. Everyone is just lyin' low. Everyone is just waitin' to see, sooner or later somethin' will get started."

This doesn't make me feel any better. This doesn't make me feel secure for the people in the poorer neighborhoods impacted by violence. There is a small earthquake the next afternoon about an hour after I finish teaching my class. I am sitting in my UCLA office when I feel the tremor. As soon as the building stops shaking, my phone rings. It's Joanna.

"Did ya feel that?" she asks. I know her seismological curiosity is a front; she wants to talk and I let her.

"Yeah, I did. Are you okay?"

"They're watching us," she confides.

I don't know just who is watching. Is it Florencia? The police?

"They know my grandmother has been in the hospital and everyone is around. You know my grandmother is the one who started all of this. She's the worst one of anyone in the neighborhood. I hate her. She's the worst kind, Jorja, she would send her kids out on the street."

I have never heard Joanna talk like this. I can't believe she's saying this *on the phone*.

"What about Bullet?"

"I picked him up from Kaiser today. He got detoxed. I'm tryin' to stay positive. He's gonna go to rehab." I hear Little Marcos laughing and screaming in the background. I know Joanna is checking in before the weekend. She will be speaking at my summer school class at UCLA next week, after she returns from the domestic-violence training she is attending.

"My grandmother is part of that whole fuckin' mess. You get a certain type of love in the neighborhood. It is sick love. And I'm never gonna go back to that."

Something has changed in Joanna. She has thrown her mother out of the house and disowned her grandmother. She is talking about moving far away from Los Angeles.

"I am so done with the neighborhood," she tells me.

This time I believe her.

I know that neither policymakers nor researchers could have saved Joanna. For ten years I have been on this road, looking for the answers. It has all come down to a Jesuit priest who listens to Amy Winehouse and tells the homie who confessed that he had been arrested for breaking and entering, "You are my son, I love you, but what the fuck were you thinking?"

I have known Greg Boyle since 1990, long before Homeboy Industries ever existed. There was an out-of-control gang problem in East Los Angeles and all he had was a bicycle and hope. While I worked in South Los Angeles, I kept hearing about what he was doing a million miles away in Boyle Heights. There was a gang war and it was being fought on two fronts—the Germany and Japan of the county were East and South LA. Pico-Aliso Village and Nickerson Gardens may well have been located on different continents. The gangs were different, the violence was different, the projects were different. In fact, twenty years later, the landscape remains divided, unrelated. The projects of Pico-Aliso have been razed and rebuilt, while Nickerson Gardens, Jordan Downs, and Imperial Courts stand unchanged from the time I worked there in the 1980s.

Greg and I got to know each other as "training consultants" for the Los Angeles County Department of Children and Family Services' six-week "Child Welfare Academy." The program was designed to introduce newly hired workers to the "problems of Los Angeles," in hopes they would know what to do once they found themselves dealing with parents who abused their children while they gangbanged and fought and smoked PCP. The consultants were on a fool's errand—we all knew it—but we functioned with an "as if" sort of mentality. "As if" anything we were teaching these young social workers was going to help.

I spoke from nine to twelve about attachment, separation, and loss; Greg spoke from one to four about gangs. He came early, accompanied by several homies, and at the lunch break sold sweatshirts and T-shirts emblazoned with the logo JOBS NOT JAILS. I knew Greg had started a program and that he had recently been the subject of a magazine piece in the *LA Times* by Celeste Fremon. He was young, earnest, and rode around the projects on a beach cruiser, trying to convince gang members not to shoot each other. He negotiated peace treaties and organized the local mothers in peace marches. If all of this sounds familiar, it's because he was doing what LA gang interventionists would claim was innovative—a decade before they ever got started. Bo Taylor and Mike Cummings and Felipe Mendez were still shooting people when Greg was riding around on his bike, imploring homies to put their gauge away.

At the DCFS training, we would hang out during the lunch breaks while the homies sold T-shirts, gossiping about politics and the LAPD. The training eventually ended, but over the years, I kept up with what Greg was doing through friends and at trainings, and every once in a while we would be thrown together on the dais—with Greg talking about the homies, and I once again intoning about attachment. His story was changing. There was more talk of putting gang members to work, and in 1997 he opened a bakery and a graffiti-cleaning service and a drop-in center for homies in East LA. I don't know when I was made aware of Homeboy Industries, but it became part of my life in ways I could not have predicted.

Greg had opened his first storefront agency at 1848 First Street. While I was involved in my first, then second, serious love affair, both taking place in a rented loft on the other side of the Los Angeles River, I would sometimes walk down to Homeboy and stop in just to say hello to Greg. This was before the loft district in LA was fashionable and before First Street was safe. To say I didn't know what I was doing would be an understatement. Greg was always in the middle of a crisis—someone was arrested, someone had been shot and was in the hospital, some-one had died and a car wash was being planned to pay for funeral expenses. There was a kind of energy in the room that I loved, but I was too busy directing traffic in my own life to get involved.

In 2001 he moved into a larger space, still on First Street, where I would visit much more frequently. In 2002 my loft was long gone and I was negotiating the commute from Westlake Village, balancing life on the home front with interviewing homies on the streets. Greg and I began what felt like a never-ending conversation—I wanted to evaluate Homeboy, and he looked upon my idea with a strange combination of warmth and what he later called "a hairy eyeball." There were more panels, more questions, and more "gang conferences" discussing the benefits of street-violence interruption versus long-term intervention.

From my experience with prevention and street intervention and research on violence and family dynamics, I knew the community-based approach that Homeboy and places like it offer represents the best of all the "answers." Gang members need to experience something other than the neighborhood. They need a family, they need a community, and they need to understand the story of their lives. Homeboy, of course, provides that family, that community.

I had come to know the meaning of love and family and it had changed my life. Despite mistrust and my need to run wild, a cop and a child had finally provided me with the security I craved, even though I had tried very hard not to admit it. My life had changed forever because of Mark and Shannon. The young men and women I knew needed that same kind of family—with all the craziness and control and security it involved.

Change is never easy—as Homeboy Industries discovered. By 2007, after outgrowing its storefront, the organization moved into a new, beautiful building in Chinatown—reaching far beyond East LA. This somehow seemed appropriate—the gang members Greg Boyle had served were gone, relocated. Greg and I talk about this on a summer day in 2010, while he is seeing a constant stream of people.

"We need to have a central location, because the gang members are coming from everywhere. They're no longer coming just from the projects. And they never really did."

An older black man, Eddie, who has joined us in Greg's office, says, "I used to be from East Coast Crips, but now I'm in recovery. I live in a sober living facility."

Greg nods encouragingly.

"I am looking for work," the man bravely states.

Greg immediately responds. "I remember you." Eddie is relieved and starts laughing. "You were around when I first got here in '84," Greg says. "And '86 is when we first started having wars with the East Coast Crips. That's when Eddie here—his girlfriend was killed. That was Mike Garrett's niece." Mike Garrett was a USC football star, winner of the Heisman Trophy. "No one was immune in those days." Greg is in a mood to reminisce. "It's changed so much now."

Of course it has. Gang members no longer depend on knives; they wield AK-47s. The neighborhoods communicate on social networks. With hip-hop music and baggy pants, gangbanging has gone mainstream. Yet the problem remains the same: gangs continue to attract youngsters and ruin lives, and exiting feels impossible.

But if the problem remains the same, so does the answer. Long-term intervention: job training and comprehensive services including therapy, anger management, and education. Mike Cummings and Felipe Mendez have both told me, "We need to do it all." While street intervention is sexy and delivers immediate results, comprehensive programs offer the best hope for long-term change. It is the most effective counter to the idea that *you can never leave the gang.*

It's not a straight line to redemption. A few months later, on a fall afternoon, five gangbangers from 18th Street walk into the Homeboy lobby, very deep. A group is "deep" when it comes in a pack demonstrating strength in numbers, the gangbanger show of force. Greg immediately calls them into his office.

"I feel disrespected when people come in deep," he begins sternly. No one is being called "my son."

"I know so many guys from your neighborhood, from before you were born. They would never do what you did! When you come in deep, it's so disrespectful. It's disrespectful to me and disrespectful to Homeboy. People look up and think there is something going on." The group listens solemnly. They are all of a piece, shaved heads, enormous tattoos, T-shirts, and medallions. It's quite a sight. And yet Greg points out the reality.

"You come in deep from weakness, not strength." The menace begins to disintegrate. Something emanates from their eyes and it is not rage. They are serving depression here, straight up. One of them—Angel—keeps craning to see what I am writing on my laptop.

"Don't pay attention to him," another homie advises. "Angel's special-ed." The group laughs, but Angel says, shakily, "There's a lot of us who're special-ed."

The young men—they are all hovering around the age of eighteen—are fairly engaged, except one who tilts back in his chair, mad-dogging Greg. He looks angry. Greg bears down and stares at him. The homie blinks.

"Why are you here? Are you looking for work?" They all nod. "Let's go see a job developer then." They have temporarily morphed into a quiet and respectful group who follow Greg, obedient ducklings. Nevertheless, I decide not to plan any future meetings with them in the community.

When Greg returns he is greeted by a huge homie, Cisco, who enters the office holding his baby son.

"This is my pride and joy," he explains as he hands the infant over to Greg for a blessing. When Greg finishes, Cisco looks down at the floor in embarrassment.

"What else do you need, my son?" Greg smiles.

"I kinda need a job, G."

"Don't worry. Let me give you a date for drug testing—that's the first step."

"Thanks, G—but there's something else. . . ." The homie is hesitating, still embarrassed.

"What is it, my son-for-life?"

"In 2002, you loaned me twenty-five dollars. I would like to pay you back now. I am ready to pay you back today."

Greg refuses the offer and tells him, "You've just made my day."

It is not always this easy. Later that day Destiny calls to tell me that Ronny has been locked up. She doesn't know what's going on and asks if I can go with her to county jail to find out. In the next week, Maniac texts that he is going out of town. I get him on his cell phone and he is brief. "I need a change of scenery for a while, Jorja. I'll call you when I'm back."

Kevin Williams still has no job, but he and Elena have welcomed a baby daughter, Susana, into the world. Hector Verdugo, who has completed graduate-level leadership training at UCLA, has been named associate executive director at Homeboy and is focused on ensuring its financial security. "We can never lay off our staff again. Ever," he insists. Bullet continues to struggle with his meth addiction, while Joanna and her four children have moved to Arizona, where she works as a domestic-violence counselor. Agustin Lizama has bought his first home, while Louis and Judy Perez have had their first baby, a son. Carlos Sanchez, Joanna's cousin, was arrested once again, convicted of assault, and is now serving time in state prison. Milagro Diaz completed drug rehab, was clean for eleven months, then relapsed again. Mike Cummings continues to work in Jordan Downs and together we co-lead the Project Fatherhood men's group every Wednesday night. Kenny Green serves as the lead organizer for the annual violence-prevention conference of the California Wellness Foundation and a supervising gang interventionist. Felipe Mendez continues to work in East Los Angeles as a gang interventionist, recently acting as part of a team that provided community support for the City of Los Angeles Summer Night Lights Program. Carol Biondi has been named president of the board of Homeboy Industries and continues to advocate for youth and carefully monitor the

Los Angeles County Department of Probation. Alex Sanchez remains out on bail awaiting trial on RICO charges and working to ensure the stability of Homies Unidos; he and his wife are expecting a baby son. Mark helps Greg whenever a homie is locked up, running interference at the LAPD. My cousin Nick is using again and has dropped out of sight. And Shannon is in her first semester at Pitzer College.

At Homeboy Industries, a forty-nine-year-old lifetime gangbanger whose skin and tattoos have begun to sag walks into Greg's office and announces, "I don't have an identity, I don't even have an ID card. I need help." He is followed by a sixteen-year-old member of Tortilla Flats—David Escobar—who has been in four probation camps since he was eleven years old.

"Can you hang here, son?" Greg Boyle asks.

"Everyone in Compton is my enemy," David answers.

"Yeah, but here everyone is your friend, no one is your enemy, and that includes people from all the neighborhoods in Compton."

"You mean—I would work here with enemies?"

"No hanging, no banging, no slanging. And you get a job here and services—you get a life. Can you hang here, son?"

David looks at Greg—angry, frightened, defensive, alone.

We wait.

This book would not exist without my agent, Michael Murphy, who first found me, then convinced me to tell this story—his encouragement is a gift.

In turn, the care and sensitivity of Helene Atwan and the staff of Beacon Press truly helped turn these early writings into a reality. My editor, Alexis Rizzuto, guided me with insight, skill, and intelligence: working with her was a joy. Special thanks to Bob Kosturko for his persistence and work with the extremely talented Fabian Debora on the book cover!

I am grateful to my Papa, Joseph Rosner, who has given me my life.

Every day, I am deeply thankful for the love and support of my remarkable family—Tony and Margie, Chris and Kim, Stacey and Danni. And many thanks are due the chosen family that surrounds and supports me: Joe and Malinda Kibre, Shelly Brooks, Tina Christie and Michelle Parra, Todd Franke—AB, the amazing Celeste Fremon, Elie Miller, Nina Bende, Penny Fuller, Larry Pressman, and my GT Marcia Berris. I am indebted to my colleagues at UCLA, who provided both the encouragement and space that has made so much of this work possible. I am also grateful to Carol Biondi for sharing everything "of the walk," and Julio Marcial, who is, quite simply, the real deal. Kenny Green holds a special place in my heart for his grace and courage.

There is no one on this earth like Greg Boyle, and I am thankful for his loving friendship and his living example of all that is miraculous.

Finally, I am deeply indebted to the homeboys and homegirls who have shared their lives with me. I live with them and learn from them every day with a never-ending sense of wonder.

This book is merely a down payment on all that is owed to my husband, Mark, who is the love of my life, and our daughter, Shannon, who is the meaning of my life.